Liberalism: Its Achievements and Failures

Modernity and Identity in Asia Series

Modernity and Identity in Asia Series

Globalization, Culture and Inequality in Asia
Timothy S. Scrase, Todd Miles, Joseph Holden and Scott Baum

Looking for Money: Capitalism and Modernity in an Orang Asli Village
Alberto Gomes

Governance and Democracy in Asia
Takashi Inoguchi and Matthew Carlson

Liberalism: Its Achievements and Failures
Kazuo Seiyama

JAPANESE SOCIETY SERIES

General Editor: Yoshio Sugimoto

Lives of Young Koreans in Japan
Yasunori Fukuoka

Globalization and Social Change in Contemporary Japan
J.S. Eades, Tom Gill and Harumi Befu

Coming Out in Japan: The Story of Satoru and Ryuta
Satoru Ito and Ryuta Yanase

Japan and Its Others:
Globalization, Difference and the Critique of Modernity
John Clammer

Hegemony of Homogeneity:
An Anthropological Analysis of Nihonjinron
Harumi Befu

Foreign Migrants in Contemporary Japan
Hiroshi Komai

A Social History of Science and Technology in
Contemporary Japan, Volume 1
Shigeru Nakayama

Farewell to Nippon: Japanese Lifestyle Migrants in Australia
Machiko Sato

The Peripheral Centre:
Essays on Japanese History and Civilization
Johann P. Arnason

A Genealogy of 'Japanese' Self-images
Eiji Oguma

Class Structure in Contemporary Japan
Kenji Hashimoto

An Ecological View of History
Tadao Umesao

Nationalism and Gender
Chizuko Ueno

Native Anthropology: The Japanese Challenge
to Western Academic Hegemony
Takami Kuwayama

Youth Deviance in Japan: Class Reproduction of Non-Conformity
Robert Stuart Yoder

Japanese Companies: Theories and Realities
Masami Nomura and Yoshihiko Kamii

From Salvation to Spirituality:
Popular Religious Movements in Modern Japan
Susumu Shimazono

The 'Big Bang' in Japanese Higher Education:
The 2004 Reforms and the Dynamics of Change
J.S. Eades, Roger Goodman and Yumiko Hada

Japanese Politics: An Introduction
Takashi Inoguchi

A Social History of Science and Technology in
Contemporary Japan, Volume 2
Shigeru Nakayama

Gender and Japanese Management
Kimiko Kimoto

Philosophy of Agricultural Science: A Japanese Perspective
Osamu Soda

A Social History of Science and Technology in
Contemporary Japan, Volume 3
Shigeru Nakayama and Kunio Goto

Japan's Underclass: Day Laborers and the Homeless
Hideo Aoki

A Social History of Science and Technology
in Contemporary Japan, Volume 4
Shigeru Nakayama and Hitoshi Yoshioka

Scams and Sweeteners: A Sociology of Fraud
Masahiro Ogino

Toyota's Assembly Line: A View from the Factory Floor
Ryoji Ihara

Village Life in Modern Japan: An Environmental Perspective
Akira Furukawa

Social Welfare in Japan: Principles and Applications
Kojun Furukawa

Escape from Work: Freelancing Youth and the Challenge to Corporate Japan
Reiko Kosugi

Gender Gymnastics: Performing and Consuming Japan's Takarazuka Revue
Leonie R. Stickland

Poverty and Social Welfare in Japan
Masami Iwata and Akihiko Nishizawa

Japan's Whaling: The Politics of Culture in Historical Perspective
Hiroyuki Watanabe

Health and Social Disparity in Japan: Japan and Beyond
Norito Kawakami, Yasuki Kobayashi and Hideki Hashimoto

The Modern Family in Japan: Its Rise and Fall
Chizuko Ueno

Social Stratification and Inequality Series

Inequality amid Affluence: Social Stratification in Japan
Junsuke Hara and Kazuo Seiyama

Intentional Social Change: A Rational Choice Theory
Yoshimichi Sato

Constructing Civil Society in Japan:
Voices of Environmental Movements
Koichi Hasegawa

Deciphering Stratification and Inequality: Japan and Beyond
Yoshimichi Sato

Social Justice in Japan: Concepts, Theories and Paradigms
Ken-ichi Ohbuchi

Gender and Career in Japan
Atsuko Suzuki

Status and Stratification: Cultural Forms in East and Southeast Asia
Mutsuhiko Shima

Globalization, Minorities and Civil Society:
Perspectives from Asian and Western Cities
Koichi Hasegawa and Naoki Yoshihara

Advanced Social Research Series

A Sociology of Happiness
Kenji Kosaka

Frontiers of Social Research: Japan and beyond
Akira Furukawa

A Quest for Alternative Sociology
Kenji Kosaka and Masahiro Ogino

MODERNITY AND IDENTITY IN ASIA SERIES

Liberalism: Its Achievements and Failures

by

Kazuo Seiyama

translated by

Leonie R. Stickland

TRANS PACIFIC PRESS

First published in Japanese in 2006 by Keisō Shobō as *Riberarizumu to wa nanika*.

This English edition first published in 2010 by
Trans Pacific Press, PO Box 164, Balwyn North, Victoria 3104, Australia
Telephone: +61-3-9859-1112 Fax: +61-3-9859-4110
Email: tpp.mail@gmail.com
Web: http://www.transpacificpress.com

Designed and set by Digital Environs, Melbourne. www.digitalenvirons.com

Printed by BPA Print Group, Burwood, Victoria, Australia.

Cover photo: A beam shines out into the night sky from a lighthouse—the Wilsons Promontory Lighthouse in Victoria, Australia. Image courtesy of *The Age* newspaper.

Distributors

Australia and New Zealand
DA Information Services/Central Book Services
648 Whitehorse Road
Mitcham, Victoria 3132
Australia
Telephone: +61-3-9210-7777
Fax: + 61-3-9210-7788
Email: books@dadirect.com
Web: www.dadirect.com

USA and Canada
International Specialized Book Services (ISBS)
920 NE 58th Avenue, Suite 300
Portland, Oregon 97213-3786
USA
Telephone: 1-800-944-6190
Fax: 1-503-280-8832
Email: orders@isbs.com
Web: http://www.isbs.com

Asia and the Pacific
Kinokuniya Company Ltd.

Head office:
3-7-10 Shimomeguro
Meguro-ku
Tokyo 153-8504
Japan
Telephone: +81-3-6910-0531
Fax: +81-3-6420-1362
Email: bkimp@kinokuniya.co.jp
Web: www.kinokuniya.co.jp

Asia-Pacific office:
Kinokuniya Book Stores of Singapore Pte., Ltd.
391B Orchard Road #13-06/07/08
Ngee Ann City Tower B
Singapore 238874
Telephone: +65-6276-5558
Fax: +65-6276-5570
Email: SSO@kinokuniya.co.jp

ISBN 978-1-920901-65-3 (Hardback)
ISBN 978-1-920901-47-9 (Paperback)

National Library of Australia Cataloguing-in-Publication entry

Author:	Seiyama, Kazuo, 1948–
Title:	Liberalism: its achievements and failures / Kazuo Seiyama.
ISBN:	9781920901653 (hbk.) 9781920901479 (pbk.)
Notes:	Includes index. Bibliography.
Subjects:	Liberalism.
Dewey Number:	320.51

Contents

Figures

Tables

Preface

The Idea of Liberalism

Thought that typifies the age

Through the dismantling of the Soviet Union in 1991 after the Eastern European Revolution of 1989, the great pillar called 'Marxism' which had hitherto prided itself on its immense and extraordinary power in the world of words and ideas was lost, giving rise to an enormous spiritual vacuum. At about the same time, the irresistible wave called globalism surged over the world. The (supposedly) ubiquitous and transparent principle of 'the market' had come to forge a direct link between economic activity in every part of the globe and our own livelihoods. In circumstances such as these since the 1990s, it has been the way of thought called liberalism that has offered an influential framework for pondering the normativity of society and various social issues.

From around the 1990s to the present day, no thought or ideology has been as much the focus of discussion about society as liberalism. In one sense, it might aptly be described as having represented the 'spirit of the age' of those ten-something years. It is a somewhat vague expression, but it does reflect the idea that society should be borne along by 'autonomous individuals' who are no longer directed by the state or guided by ideology, let alone live solely for the sake of a restricted in-group: rather they take responsibility for themselves.

Japan, for example, used to have an education policy called *yutori kyōiku* (which Japan's Ministry of Education, Culture, Sports, Science and Technology (MEXT) translates as '"room to grow" education'). This *yutori kyōiku* tends to be considered simply as a kind of philosophy that 'it is better to raise children in a free and unconstrained manner,' but that is a misconception. Its original aim was to build 'autonomous and creative' individuals, not ones who could merely faithfully regurgitate what they had been taught. What lies at the foundation of this policy is a liberal view of education which could also be described as extremely orthodox, such as typified by the early twentieth-century American philosopher Dewey's *Democracy and Education* (1916). What the phrase 'autonomous individuals with abundant creativity' signifies is the 'hoped-for image of persons' who will shoulder responsibility for a liberal society, and the *yutori kyōiku* policy was a policy that aimed to educate children to become such persons. (Whether the methodology was appropriate is another matter, however.)

Alternatively, in order to overcome the economic stagnation Japan has suffered since the 1990s, a variety of measures have been taken by firms themselves and by the government, these including attempts at 'achievementism' which aspired to depart from traditional collectivist Japanese-style management, as well as the financial deregulation dubbed the 'Big Bang' and the adoption of International Accounting Standards, carried out in the name of global standardisation. In addition, privatisation or semi-privatisation of public institutions was also pursued, starting with national universities. These phenomena are generally termed 'neo-liberalism,' but while they are not necessarily the same as 'liberalism,' they are in large part based upon the ideology of liberalism in respect to 'emphasis on individual responsibility' and 'elimination or extreme reduction of paternalistic intervention from the government.'

Even apart from education and economics, it has been since the early 1990s that 'self-responsibility' and 'self-determination' have constantly emerged as key words in diverse areas of society. The logic of 'self-responsibility' and 'self-determination' has frequently been employed in debates concerning the 'bioethics' of brain death and organ transplantation, or cloning and genetic testing. As well, the logic of 'self-determination' has been mentioned on occasion in connection with girls' so-called 'compensated dating (*enjo kōsai*).' It can probably be said that liberalistic thinking lay at the basis there, too.

In a similar period, profuse attempts were made in the worlds of philosophy and thought to theorise liberalism in a modern way. As is well-known, this began with Rawls' *A Theory of Justice* in 1971. This *A Theory of Justice* steadily attracted attention; critiques and commentaries were accrued. Further, from the 1980s, the work of other liberal thinkers such as Dworkin and Sen, and critical or affirmative discussion of this, was extensively developed. It was from around 1990 that such trends began to be widely introduced in Japan, pioneering roles being played by Tatsuo Inoue's *Kyōsei no sahō* (The etiquette of coexistence) (1986) and Takashi Kawamoto's *Gendai rinrigaku no bōken* (The adventure of contemporary ethics) (1995).

In Japan's case, the past several years have seen a remarkable expansion in publications on the themes of *seigi* (justice) and *kōkyōsei* (meaning something like 'public-spiritedness,' 'public nature' or 'publicness'), in addition to those whose main topic is 'liberalism.' Among these, the word 'justice' has also been frequently incorporated into the titles of papers and publications in the English-language sphere, while *kōkyōsei* is unique to Japan. The concept of *kōkyōsei* does not have an exactly corresponding English equivalent. Terms which are somehow comparable in English are 'public philosophy (*kōkyō tetsugaku*),' 'public sphere (*kōkyō-ken*)' and 'public reason (*kōkyō risei*),' while there is no single term to express *kōkyōsei* itself.

The Japanese word *kōkyōsei* is an expression used in the quest to conceptualise from a slightly wider perspective what 'justice' means to liberalism. Accordingly, this upsurge in debate about *kōkyōsei* and justice can be seen as riding the same wave as the mounting of interest in liberalism.

As such, liberalism and similar ways of thinking have become prominent in the world, but this has also been accompanied by the proliferation of discussions critical of liberalism. These could be divided broadly into the two camps of left and right. From the standpoint of traditional Marxism, for example, the 'omnipotence of the market' aspect incorporated in liberalism is singled out for criticism. Seen from that perspective, liberalism is one of the main ideologies which, along with globalism and neo-liberalism, underpin present-day capitalist economies, and is nothing less than a theory that tries to conceal the evils of exploitation and poverty by emphasising self-responsibility in the market.

Conversely, criticism is hurled from theoreticians in the position regarded as rightist or conservative, vis-à-vis the point that liberalism is an ideology of cosmopolitanism which ignores the significance of states, communities or cultural traditions, and that it emphasises self-determination and autonomy, making light of the importance to the individual of social responsibility and public interest. So-called communitarianism, though not necessarily entirely conservative, has been critical to liberalism from the viewpoint it shares with conservatism.

Apart from the above, there is also negative comment such as the following. Even if liberalism is not the principal target, for example, there is severe criticism directed at 'justice'—liberalism's most important value—claiming that liberalism inflates a self-righteous sense of justice, or that American military action has been legitimised in the name of 'justice.'

Alternatively, from many feminists comes the criticism that, because it is not sufficiently individualistic, liberalism cannot constitute a worthy theory for liberating women from the oppression that they suffer. Furthermore, the welfare-prioritised reallocation emphasised by contemporary liberalism is the target of attack from theoreticians taking a libertarian position.

What is liberalism?

What, then, might liberalism be? In actual fact, no book can be found that gives us a precise answer to this fundamental question. When asked by someone wanting an overview of today's political theory or political thought to recommend a volume, first I would probably say Kymlicka's (1990) *Contemporary Political Philosophy*. Kymlicka is a Canadian political philosopher who has developed his own theory about the problem conditions of cultural pluralism, basically from the standpoint of liberalism. The intention of his book was 'to provide an introduction to, and critical appraisal of, the major schools of thought which dominate contemporary debates in political philosophy' (Kymlicka 1990, p.1), and it discusses utilitarianism, liberal equality, libertarianism, Marxism, communitarianism, citizenship theory, multiculturalism and feminism. Yet a chapter on liberalism, which is crucial, is nowhere to be found. Though there is an introduction to and consideration of the principle of liberal equality, it does not deal with liberalism itself. For Kymlicka, liberalism was probably excluded from being a 'subject' for analysis because it is situated not as a 'subject' but as its own practice.

If one seeks to gain a general knowledge of liberalism, one must look for a different publication, and one candidate would probably be the 1986 explanatory volume, *Liberalism*, by the British political philosopher John Gray. In his book, Gray reduces liberalism to four characteristics: 'individualism,' 'universality,' 'egalitarianism,' and 'reformism.' A liberalism characterised solely by these four criteria, however, is actually quite different from the contemporary liberalism which developed after Rawls' *A Theory of Justice*. In fact, for example, there is no mention here of the two core theses which are generally regarded as constituting modern liberalism, as I will later explain—the 'priority of the right (=justice) over the good' proposed by Rawls, and the 'neutrality towards different conceptions of the good' presented by Dworkin.

In his book, Gray makes a distinction between 'classical liberalism' and 'modern liberalism' or 'revisionary liberalism.' 'Classical liberalism' belongs to the lineage of Hume and Adam Smith, and represents non-constructivism and gradualist liberalism. By contrast, 'revisionist liberalism' belongs to the lineage of Jeremy Bentham and J.S. Mill, and seeks to investigate the principles for the rational ordering of society.

Liberalism today can be said to be an extension of this 'revisionary liberalism.' That being said, it would still be a great misapprehension if these were thought to be the same thing. This is because contemporary liberalism, starting with Rawls' *A Theory of Justice*, aims to establish a normative principle to supplant the 'utilitarianism' championed by Bentham and Mill, which it criticises.

As such, Gray's *Liberalism* is about an extremely general 'liberalism,' rather than being an explication focusing upon contemporary liberalism. The term 'liberalism' is not unambiguous. The Japanese translation of Gray's book is entitled *Jiyū-shugi* (Liberalism), but in contemporary Japanese, the terms *'riberarizumu'*—a Japanese rendering of the English word's pronunciation—and *'jiyū-shugi'* are used differently, the word *'riberarizumu'* basically being employed to indicate contemporary liberalism. It does not incorporate such ideas as those of Hayek or Popper. By contrast, the term *'jiyū-shugi'* encompasses both Hayek and Popper, and is used to indicate a very wide range of thought which attaches importance to 'liberty' in general. It also includes social theories such as utilitarianism and libertarianism, which are often seen as conflicting with *'riberarizumu.'* Moreover, when people say *'jiyū-shugi,'* they are more likely not to have the ideology of contemporary liberalism such as that of Rawls or Dworkin in mind. In English, on the other hand, there is only one word: 'liberalism.' Of course, in professional discussions it is common for each writer to clarify to a certain extent what the term 'liberalism' signifies in the discussant's own explanation and context, but if the word 'liberalism' alone is used out of context, it is impossible to know whether it means the classical liberalism of the past, or contemporary liberalism.

Whichever the case, it is a pity that, regardless of the importance of liberalism to contemporary society, there are no books to be seen which explain whatever kind of theory it is, or which debate head-on its theoretical structure and the premises upon which it is based.

Circumstances surrounding *riberarizumu* in Japan

In Japan, for whatever reason, the majority of critical discussion in publications concerning liberalism tends to be developed not in the form of academic books, but as paperbacks for a general audience, or something similar.

Conversely, among publications and argument at an academic level, one seldom sees any discourse which directly criticises liberalism. It goes without saying that in the case of the United States, the home of liberalism, there is vigorous production of critiques of liberalism on a scholarly level from such standpoints as communitarianism, feminism and libertarianism. Many such discussions have, of course, been introduced into Japan in translation, and are very familiar to researchers. As an academic line of research specific to Japan, however, the current situation is that there are no theoretical attempts of the kind which criticises liberalism face-on.

At the same time, the standard of academic research in Japan on liberalism is certainly not low. Venturing to name some individuals, I would say that the work of Tatsuo Inoue and Mikio Watanabe, among others, is exceedingly rich in originality and creativity. Apart from these two, there is also prolific investigation that transcends mere commentary, concerning the main theories of contemporary liberalism which have been developed by such thinkers as Rawls, Dworkin and Sen. Still, as discussion that is critical of liberalism tends to be restricted to outside the realms of academism in Japan, fundamental debate about liberalism has not been enabled to happen. This is regrettable.

Further, the following point also needs to be made, namely, that common interpretations of Rawls' *A Theory of Justice* and later works—which are supposed to lie at the core of present-day liberalism—contain numerous misconceptions. Naturally, it is not only in Japan that misconceptions are circulating, but in the West, also, and quite mistaken understandings of Rawls are generally widespread.

One of the aims of this book, it goes without saying, is to dispel such misapprehensions about Rawlsian theory. That, however, is not all—I believe that gaining a correct understanding of the theoretical structure of contemporary liberalism is one of the most vital challenges in thinking about the various issues which contemporary society is facing, or in the practical concerns of investigating ways to solve them.

Even for sociologists who are engaging in the discipline of sociology, which mainly deals with empirical rather than normative investigations of society, there is an unavoidable necessity to confront normative questions as to 'what kind of systems and policies are desirable' in a variety of problem areas such as the family, gender, education, labour, class/social strata, welfare, minorities, minority culture, and so on. Each time, in one's investigation, one has to endeavour to answer the question of 'what form should the normative principles that constitute society take,' by assuming it as a personal responsibility. At that time, one can find the theory of liberalism to have already amassed a definite, well-contemplated body of thought concerning that question. Regardless of whether we ultimately accept it or not, we cannot adequately think about contemporary society without conscientiously grappling with the social ideology known as liberalism.

So, what kind of thought is liberalism, and what was it, in the first place? Why did it come to be in the limelight and be so frequently discussed or invoked? What has it achieved, and where has it failed? What manner of issues really lurk within liberalism?

This book aims to address such questions as these. I personally think that it is difficult ultimately to defend liberalism, and in this volume, I intend to offer a careful explanation of the reason for my opinion. I do, however, wish to stress the following point: though I might be critical of liberalism, it certainly does not mean that I think that it is something lacking in significance. In the present day, liberalism is not only the most powerful of theories for talking about the visions of society, but the wealth of intellectual creativity that has been demonstrated in its development also deserves enormous respect. We can learn a great deal from the project of liberalism, and, through examining it analytically, we may gain food for envisioning an idea of our own.

Part One

What does Rawls' *A Theory of Justice* signify?

Chapter 1

Normative Principles for Pluralistic Societies

In this chapter and the next, I first wish to explain the social situation as well as the social and theoretical issues which constitute a backdrop to present-day liberalism. In order to understand liberalism, it is vital to know what kind of questions the liberalism project seeks to address. Accordingly, contemporary liberalism should be grasped in a historical context and in light of changes in intellectual and theoretical concerns.

Questions posed in the brain-death issue

The brain-death controversy

In June 1997, after nearly a decade of discussion, the 'Organ Transplantation Law' permitting the transplantation of organs from brain-dead persons was passed by the Japanese Diet. A further year and eight months had to elapse before the first organ transplant from a brain-dead person was conducted under that law. Moreover, in that first case, thanks to the mass media, the entire process became the focus of nationwide attention from the populace, reflecting the fierceness of the debate leading up to the legislation.[1]

The series of disputes over brain death and the political process involved constituted a landmark achievement in the issue of the pluralistic condition of beliefs in Japanese society. The enactment of that law could be considered to be one relatively reasonable solution—albeit not a perfect one by any means—to the question of how people with different, opposing values and convictions could run a collaborative society together. Of course, it does not mean that the values and beliefs of the respective camps have converged and been consolidated into one. Opposition is still continuing even now. However, the majority of people from each of the divergent positions reached agreement as to the enactment of the Organ Transplantation Law. Unmistakeably, this was a radical change from the pre-enactment state of antipathy.[2]

The conflict over brain death can be split into two levels. The first is the question of whether it is 'permissible' to remove organs from the body of a person who has fallen into a state called 'brain death' and transplant them into somebody else. If it is not permissible, then one must forbid the act of 'organ transplantation from the brain-dead,' and, in certain cases, impose criminal punishment upon transgressors. On the other hand, if it is permissible, then to forbid it or impose criminal punishment would itself be incorrect. On this point, there was sharp polarity between the 'anti-transplant faction' which said that organ transplantation from the brain-dead should be forbidden, and the 'pro-transplant faction' which derided the idea of banning it.

The second level of conflict has been over the issue of whether one can consider brain death to be 'death of the person.' People who advocated transplantation stressed that 'brain death,' defined as 'irreversible cessation of function of the whole brain, including the brain-stem,' is death as a person when it has been medically validated that cardiac death would be inevitable, even if that person's heart were still alive; moreover, this is already widely acknowledged internationally as being death of the person. In counter to that, people opposed to transplantation argued that the three signs of death (cessation of heartbeat, cessation of spontaneous respiration, and fixed and dilated pupils) signalled death of the person; that it was hard to acknowledge that someone whose heart was still beating and whose body was warm was dead; and that the notion of death was cultural, and so it was unnecessary to follow other countries' lead.

People who thought that 'brain death, also, is death of the person' generally had a tendency to accept 'organ transplantation from the brain-dead.' This does not mean, however, that an unambiguous relationship was formed which equated transplant advocates with 'people who recognise brain-death as death of the person.' (The critic Takashi Tachibana, one of the most famous social critics in Japan, for example, who has energetically developed the anti-transplant doctrine, did not oppose the recognition of brain death as death, but made the pivotal argument that, given the current technology to do with judgement criteria for brain death, it was not possible to make a precise judgement of 'irreversible cessation of function.')

Other points of contention and questions have also been just as important as these. From the advocates' standpoint, for instance, the 'principle of self-determination' was often emphasised. This is the argument that, if the individual involved and her/his family members acknowledge 'brain death as death of the person,' then basically there should be no problem. If this applies, then the feelings of family members who do not want to allow the insertion of a scalpel into the person's warm body and the removal of its still-beating heart are respected. In rebuttal, the anti-transplant faction made the counter-claim that if 'brain death as death of the person' were recognised, then social pressure would be brought to bear upon people who insisted on the principle of 'cardiac death' to the bitter end.

The strongest point of argument for the pro-transplantation side is the fact that, by means of organ transplants, it is obviously possible to save a large number of patients. From the opposite standpoint, however, it has been asserted that the expansion of organ transplantation carries the risk of triggering organ-trading or moral hazards by doctors driven by greed for money or fame.

In debates such as these, the greatest point in the 'Organ Transplantation Law' which finally saw its establishment is in Article Six:

> In the case where the deceased has expressed in writing prior to death his/her intent to donate his/her organs to be used for transplant surgery, and his/her family members in receipt of notice to that effect do not object to the removal of said organs, or where there are no family members, a doctor can remove organs to be used for transplant surgery from his/her cadaver (including the body of a brain-dead person; the same shall apply hereinafter), in accordance with this law.

By means of this article, when stipulated conditions were met, the removal of organs from a body deemed brain-dead was legally authorised for the first time. As can be imagined from the wording of the article, the very heart of this law was in the fact that it left open the verdict as to whether 'brain death' constitutes 'death.' It obtained consensus by avoiding conclusions on an issue about which agreement was unlikely to be reached, and by focusing most simply and directly upon on the matter of legalising the harvesting of organs from 'the body of a brain-dead person.'

Some people might think that the brain-death issue is a scientific one, so that the question of whether death should be defined by the three signs of death or by brain death should be scientifically decided. They therefore think it is unjustifiable for the law thus to have avoided any scientific judgement. However, the brain-death issue was not seen as such a simple academic matter, and in actual fact it is not, either.

Problems in the legal system

As we have already seen, the brain-death question in Japan was fought out basically on two levels. The second, 'whether brain death is death of the person,' is ultimately an issue of belief. This is a similar situation to the abortion issue, with its questions about whether a foetus is a person, or whether an embryo is a person: in relation to which side they would take, people came to loggerheads on the level of belief. It is not easy to find a reasonable way of completely resolving conflict on the belief level. Of course, if one somehow forcibly converts holders of other beliefs to one's own faith, or exterminates them, then a 'final solution' such as that which the Nazis imagined could be achieved. But obviously such a 'solution' is something monstrous, which is the major premise of the debate, and unworthy of consideration.

Some proponents assert that whether brain death is death of the person is not a question of belief, but a scientific issue, and that an organ transplant law which keeps that ambiguous is committing a grave injustice. (One example is Yoshihiko Komatsu's 2004 publication, *Nōshi*: *zōki ishoku no hontō no hanashi* (Brain death: the real story of organ transplantation), from PHP Shinsho.) However, the fact is, there is still fierce controversy among scientists as to what criteria should determine 'death,' and it is obvious that this issue will basically boil down to the philosophical and religious question: 'What is death?' Hence, the issue should not be considered as scientific, but as an issue of 'belief' which ultimately cannot be decided by science (at least, not in its present state). It is a tricky matter, but we live by conflicting beliefs such as cannot simply be resolved by discussion.

The other level to the issue of brain death was the question of whether to '*mitomeru*' organ transplantation following brain death. Here, the Japanese verb '*mitomeru*' has a variety of meanings, including 'recognise,' 'allow,' and 'acknowledge.' First, obviously, someone who does not regard brain death as death of the person cannot, as an individual, allow organ transplantation from the brain-dead. Still, just because a certain person does not recognise it, this will not be sufficient reason for preventing other people from carrying out organ transplantation. In order to make it 'not recognised' in a form that constrained the actions of all people, it would probably be necessary to have it morally and legally 'not recognised.' Morality and law, as a general rule, are binding upon all people. There is, however, a big difference between morality and law. Law (here, primarily thinking of statutory law) is enacted by parliament in a form clearly visible to the eyes of all, and people's understanding of 'what law has ordained' is uniform, at least on the level of text—though there can be different interpretations of it. In morality, however, there is no such uniform text. In consequence, though someone might say 'morals do not permit it,' that just might be merely the personal understanding of the individual who thinks so.

In the case of the brain-death controversy, the focus of the argument for and against recognition gradually came to converge upon a particular point. The final point of contention was whether there should be a law allowing organ transplants from the brain-dead within clearly-defined conditions, or that such a law was not to be established. In the latter case, this meant that the question of whether organ transplantation from the brain-dead was legally recognised remained ambiguous. Accordingly, in the sense that it might constitute 'organ-harvesting from the body of a live person,' resulting in that person's death (in a meaning that anyone would agree upon), this would probably be categorised in terms of criminal law as 'bodily harm resulting in death' or 'homicide.' It was completely ambiguous as to whether such a charge would be applicable. But if organ transplant surgery were to be performed in Japan on a brain-dead person, it was almost certain that there would be someone who would file a criminal complaint against it. For that reason, for doctors in Japan, in material terms this meant the same as if organ transplants from the brain-dead were prohibited, if they considered the costs of litigation (including not only monetary costs, but also the time taken up by a lawsuit, and the loss of honour and trust that would accompany a criminal accusation), in addition to the possibility of receiving a guilty verdict.

As such, the brain-death problem was basically a matter for the legal system, even while incorporating religious and ethical issues, as well. In other words, it was a question of how to prescribe in a legal system what kind of acts relating to the phenomenon known as 'brain death' were to be tolerated by society under what procedures, and, conversely, what kind of acts were to be forbidden, as the object of sanctions by judicial authority.

Accordingly, from the perspective of how the system should be, questions such as the following were posed. Is it right to leave the act of organ transplantation up to the free choice of the respective individuals involved? If some sort of social rule is to be created, what kind of rule is preferable? In it, what should be forbidden by law, and what should be permitted? In relation to these matters, what kind of role should the state play, or not play? In implementing the rule, what kind of organisations should be set up, or existing organisations and groups utilised? And, under what manner of basic ways of thinking and ideals should these systems be configured, as a whole?

In today's society, such questions are being asked in every single domain of social life, not only about organ transplantation and bioethics or environmental ethics, but also about sexual and racial inequality, socioeconomic inequity, the welfare system, the roles of the government and the market, the education system, the nature of the family, individual morality, the relationship between the state and the family or the state and religion, and so on. It is not simply that a concrete solution is being sought for individual issues, however—rather, it can be said that something akin to 'normative principles to underpin society' is the goal.

The quest for normative social principles

Normative principles relating to society

The quest for normative principles to underpin society can be traced back to Ancient China and Ancient Greece—in China, it was an age of prolific activity, with Confucius as the leader, followed by the people called the 'Hundred Schools of Thought' of the Warring States Period. In Greece, it was the age when the so-called Sophists flourished, and which simultaneously saw the genesis of Western philosophy, centring on Socrates, Plato and Aristotle. These were quests which arose in the East and the West, probably completely independently, in approximately the same period. Both had a common social backdrop, in that there were numerous independent states existing in parallel within one linguistic and cultural sphere, and which repeatedly waged war against each other. More importantly, one can also point out a background in which a degree of book-publishing culture had developed in each of them, and a type of public sphere of speech had been established. In other words, these were social arenas for sparring with discourse and text, where any persons, in principle, regardless of social status, could present ideas to each other and mutually discuss them. In such a milieu, Confucius, for example, held as his ideal the kind of society where, following the model of the 'Rites and Music' system of China's Duke of Zhou (Zhou Gong, also spelt Chou Kung), the ruler would govern with virtue, and, under those circumstances, his subjects would widely practise mutual benevolence, pivoting around respect and affection towards their parents. Plato, for his part, regarded the ideal regime as one with a given class system, where philosopher-kings full of wisdom would rule according to reason.

Incidentally, in a speech delivered in Japan on the occasion of his award of the Kyoto Prize, Karl Popper (1902–1992), a leading authority on contemporary philosophy of science and social philosophy, spoke passionately as follows on the importance of a culture of publishing, referring to the 'Athenian miracle' in which spectacular advancements in thought were seen in fields ranging widely from natural sciences to social and political philosophy:

> But one day I read again Plato's *Apology of Socrates Before His Judges*—the most beautiful philosophical work I know. And re-reading a much discussed passage, I had a new idea. The passage [26 D–E] implies that there was a flourishing book market [*biblionia*] in Athens in the year 399 BC, a market, at any rate, where old books (like Anaxagoras' book *On Nature*) were regularly sold, and where they could be bought very cheaply (Popper 1994, p. 110).

And further:

> Our civilisation is, indeed, a bookish one: its traditionality and its originality, its seriousness and sense of intellectual responsibility, its unprecedented power of imagination and its creativity, its understanding of freedom and its watchfulness for it—all these rest on our love of books (Popper 1994, p. 113).

Popper emphasises that social and political philosophy, which are quests for normative principles that underpin society, require the kind of society where intellectual activity involving imagination and creativity can be developed freely and responsibly through the medium of open book markets. The open pursuit of normative principles to support society could be said to have begun in Western civilisation in the 'Athenian miracle,' which allowed the growth of the 'book market,' as Popper mentions, while in the East Asian region, it could be traced back to the age of the 'Hundred Schools of Thought.'

Since then, in many human societies, there has been an accumulation of pursuits which, though called by such diverse names as social thought, philosophy, ethics, and so on, have sought to supply answers to certain shared questions. Simply speaking, these have been nothing other than an activity to seek 'a desirable basic way for society to be' that anyone would be likely to find reasonable. This constitutes a quest not for a society in which the seekers are actually living empirically, but for one which does not exist in reality at present.

This is a line of inquiry called normative social theory, which is distinguished from empirical social theory. Empirical social theory, on the one hand, is a system of ideas which attempts to respond to the question of how actual society is constituted, and why it came to be so: for example, it tries to explain the present state of inequality in society, and what kind of mechanism gave rise to such inequality. By contrast, normative social theory is that which endeavours to debate what sort of social inequalities should or should not exist.

In recent times, the class system—which was accepted in Ancient China and Ancient Greece as a natural element in the composition of an ideal society—came to be viewed as most contrary to the notion of a desirable society. Instead, as is well-known, liberty and equality came to be emphasised as essential elements of a desirable society. Liberty and equality are often mutually incompatible values, but, as we will see later, the social theory called liberalism attaches importance to both of these contemporary values, and can be seen as an ideology which seeks normative principles such as would strike a balance between the two. In that sense, it could be said, liberalism most faithfully carries on the problem-consciousness of modern normative social theory.

Relativism

Here, what naturally is of concern is the fact that there are multiple, mutually-conflicting theories regarding what kind of society is a desirable society. The history of normative social theory has taken on a variety of aspects, it being a veritable museum full of disparate theories. We know this well from school classes in ethics and philosophy. It is a very different situation from the history of natural science and mathematics. In the latter, even if disparate theories happen to be posed simultaneously, they will eventually converge into some kind of 'correct' theory—at least, a tendency towards convergence can be recognised. In contrast to this, in normative social theory, such a convergence will not necessarily be acknowledged—at least, that is how it seems.

Then, the question: 'What kind of society is a desirable society?' could perhaps be regarded as being the same as the question: 'What kind of society would you prefer?' This is because there could be as many answers expressing different preferences as the number of respondents. Indeed, if the question were, for instance: 'What will you have to drink?' then it would be sufficient to reply by stating one's personal preference, such as: 'Coffee for me,' or 'No, I'll have tea.' Even if opinions were divided at this point, there would be no trouble, since this question is one relating simply to individuals' personal choice, and replies to it can simply be divided according to individual choice. Questions relating to the desirability of society, however, are not ones that can be answered thus by each person separately. To give an example, it is similar to a situation in which, given the precondition that only one kind of beverage can be provided, multiple people are asked what they want to drink.

This example might not be particularly apt, as it might be possible to obtain a consensus of opinion easily, seeing that individual preference ought to be afforded maximum respect. Instead, an example such as the following would probably be better.

Let us suppose that, at a certain meeting venue, there was the issue of whether to allow the consumption of food and drink during the meeting. Some might think: 'For the short duration of the meeting, people should curb their urge to eat and drink, and concentrate on the agenda,' while others might think: 'If there were drinks, at least, the meeting would run even more smoothly,' or: 'If it is not going to bother others, then participants should be free to eat or drink as they please.' 'Giving each person the liberty to decide' is one possibility, and it is a way to resolve the issue by dividing it along the lines of individual choice. But the important thing here is that the actual question of whether to select this method of settling the issue is something that has to be a unique decision in the context of the meeting, not something which can be split according to personal choice.

One must take note of the fact that obtaining a unique decision does not equate to that decision being normatively correct. Politics is a process for obtaining a unique decision among people, while governments are organs for that purpose, but the things that governments do are not always normatively correct. The goal of normative social theory is to address the issue of what kind of decision constitutes a correct one. Can there ever be such a thing as an unambiguously correct answer to that, however?

Value relativism and moral scepticism, which hold that such a thing cannot exist in principle, were also put forward by numerous proponents who were contemporaries of Confucius and Plato. In the Daoist philosophy of Laozi and Zhuangzi, the famed allegory in

Zhuangzi about 'dreaming of a butterfly' poses the question of what aspect of something as trivial as human success in life—publicly deemed to be valuable—is of greater worth than the cheerfulness of a butterfly fluttering around spontaneously. Again, in Plato's works, though ultimately to be argued down by Socrates, various sceptical Sophists make their appearance.

The spontaneous order and normativity

Even without consideration of what a correct determination is, the virtual establishment of some sort of unique decision sometimes occurs. One instance of this would be the case in which no actual consumption of food or beverages takes place because nobody wants to eat or drink anything. Conversely, in the case where everyone tacitly regarded eating and drinking in a meeting to be something as natural as breathing, and a matter of free choice, a spontaneous order—namely, consuming food and drink at one's discretion—would also arise.

The argument that most of the norms and systems existing in actual society constitute such a spontaneously-occurring order was expounded by the eighteenth-century Scottish philosopher, Hume, and research in the direction of this theory has been carried out actively even in recent times, examples being academic fields such as 'evolutionary game theory' and 'evolutionary economics.' These investigate what kind of behavioural principles become established within groups during repeated interaction by large numbers of individuals or subjects who have differing principles of behaviour and preferences. Certainly, there are also numerous ordered phenomena which can be thought to have arisen from such a mechanism. Language, fashion and the like probably have such a dimension.

A theory of spontaneous order like this, however, has parts which are fundamentally incompatible with investigation into the question of 'how a social institution should be.' These involve the difference between empirical and normative questions. In principle, it is possible to differentiate between the empirical question of how a particular order came into being, and the question of whether that order is a normatively desirable thing; and such a distinction ought to be made.[3] The belief that 'a spontaneous order is a good order for the very reason that it is spontaneous' is often observed among spontaneous order proponents, typified by Friedrich Hayek, famous for his *Road to Serfdom* and *The Constitution of Liberty*. In reality, though, there are both good and bad examples among things that can be identified as spontaneous orders. If good-quality commodities came to be supplied through market competition, then that would be a good spontaneous order, but, on the contrary, competition could also trigger the spread of oligopolisation, leading to the supply of nothing but inferior commodities at high prices.

A normative judgement as to whether a certain condition or system is 'good' or 'bad' is a judgement which arises when a phenomenon is viewed through a reflective mind. By contrast, a spontaneous order is an order that comes into being when it can be assumed that such a reflective opportunity either does not exist, or has no influence whatever. Accordingly, a spontaneous order is not 'good' in itself, but rather lacks the reflective cycle of 'good or bad?'

In that sense, normatively investigating the desirability of society means to consider reflectively, as a theoretical activity, the variously differing ideas of 'desirability.' And this transcends our personal notion of the 'desirability' that arises spontaneously within us.

Liberalism, representative of contemporary normative social theory

Liberalism then and now

The theory of contemporary liberalism, which began along with the 1971 publication of John Rawls' *A Theory of Justice*, is the central actor in contemporary investigations around the normative principles of society.

The word 'liberalism' is one which has been in existence since long ago, and in Japan, also, it has been translated from around the Taishō era (1912–1926) as *jiyū-shugi*. The erstwhile 'liberalism' and '*jiyū-shugi*' occupied a contrasting ideological position to conservatism and nationalism, and in Japan, its representative thinkers included Yukichi Fukuzawa, Chōmin Nakae, Sakuzō Yoshino, Eijirō Kawai and Tanzan Ishibashi. Though they have their respective differences, they share the idea that a better society will be formed by respecting individuals' freedom of thought, speech and economic activity, rather than depending upon state control and traditional custom. In Britain, from the mid-nineteenth to the early twentieth century, this was the standpoint represented by the Liberal Party, which stood in opposition to the Conservative Party. As can be appreciated from the above, old-time liberalism was developed mainly in nineteenth-century Britain, and was closely connected with economic liberalism. This more or less corresponds to what Gray calls 'classical liberalism.'

In contrast to this, contemporary liberalism is fairly new, and its origins can be found in the age of the New Deal in 1930s America. From this time on, the word 'liberal' became established as a term which stood for the New Dealers—in other words, a political position that advocated positive government intervention in economic activity, a policy of equality, integrationist doctrine, anti-racism, priority of welfare policy, and so on. Even now, in the United States, if one simply says 'liberal,' it indicates a person who holds such views. Unlike classical liberalism, in America it has taken on a very strong, 'social democratic' hue, with its emphasis on such things as welfare policy and equality. 'Liberal' in this sense has nothing to do with economic liberalism. It represents the 'American Left' in a situation where, unlike in European countries, no strong socialist camp has existed.

Yet contemporary liberalism is slightly different from the New Deal 'Liberal.' The most important difference is that, while the New Deal Liberal is directly concerned with concrete policies and political issues, contemporary liberalism has been developed rather as a theoretical movement. In a certain sense, it is not without an aspect of endeavouring to build a philosophical and theoretical foundation for the post-New Deal liberal political movement and political standpoint. However, one probably should not say that the various contemporary theories of liberalism are consciously aiming to give a foundation to the New-Deal-type liberal: rather, they are assuming a logical framework that is independent from it. In fact, in comparison to the social-democratic and interventionist egalitarianism of the New-Deal-type liberal, contemporary liberalism installs 'justice' as a superior value which can normatively consolidate equality and freedom, while also attaching greater importance to 'individual autonomy.'

Individualism

Irrespective of whether old or new, classical or contemporary, the greatest characteristic common to all of the various liberalisms definitely lies in their '*individualism.*' Liberalism regards 'the individual' as the sole ultimate entity. This, however, is not unique to liberalism, but is also shared by the majority of social theory since Hobbes. Especially nowadays, it is a thesis which forms a common foundation with both utilitarianism and libertarianism, though these are seen as conflicting with liberalism in other aspects.

The meaning of the statement 'the individual is the sole ultimate entity' is easily understood by looking at what kinds of propositions it opposes. What this statement seeks to refute is the frequent integration into theory of two 'super-individual entities' which are presumed to be things which are greater than all individuals. One, it goes without saying, is 'God,' who has for a long time reigned supreme over the European world. The other is 'the community.'

In Judeo-Christian tradition, a variety of moral norms, such as Moses' Ten Commandments and Jesus' Sermon on the Mount, are recorded in the Bible as being God's orders, or promises made with God. Accordingly, if the existence of God is presupposed, then these moral norms must apply *a priori*, as a matter of course. Naturally, God must be the supreme authority in relation not only to moral norms, but also to the shape of political organisations and the values that politics serves.

Nevertheless, modern secular social theory has had at its basic theme *how to build a society without the help of God.* This could be said to form the core of the 'modern age' that has emerged from Europe. One aspect of the overall progress of modern Europe has been the process of dismantling the medieval authoritarian order, which had the Roman Catholic Church as its zenith. It is well known that religious reformations and absolute monarchies have such a dimension. As for modern social theories, these have been manifested in secularistic rationalism such as is typically seen in Hobbes and French Enlightenment thought. Of course, it is not true to say that all theorists displayed naked animosity towards the authority of the Church. On a theoretical level, though, a common, tacit understanding that the authority of the Church and of God could no longer be depended upon came to be broadly established.

The idea which exists at the core of individualism is that 'it is possible to shape society based solely upon the various secular capabilities of all individuals, and to do so is the desirable way for a society to be.' This idea is most clearly expressed in the following words from *An Introduction to the Principles of Morals and Legislation* by the late eighteenth-century British philosopher, Jeremy Bentham, the founder of utilitarian philosophy:

> By the principle...of utility is meant that principle which approves or disapproves of every action whatsoever, according to the tendency it appears to have to augment or diminish the happiness of the party whose interest is in question; or, what is the same thing in other words to promote or to oppose that happiness.

> ...The interest of the community is one of the most general expressions that can occur in the phraseology of morals: no wonder that the meaning of it is often lost. When it has a meaning, it is this. The community is a fictitious *body*, composed of the individual persons who are considered as constituting as it were its *members*. The interest of the community, then, what is it?—the sum of the interests of the several members who compose it (Bentham 1789).

Society (the community) is a fictitious body, and it is only individual people that truly exist. Accordingly, the interests which should be protected or enhanced are nothing other than people's benefit and happiness. This is the fundamental principle of individualism.

As is distinctly apparent in Bentham's text, what individualistic theory is up against is not merely God, but also 'society (the community).' It is misleading, however, to say that individualism as a normative principle is against society, or that it negates it, because individualism, in spite of its name, not only does not repudiate society, but has had the precise intention to construct society by means of individualism itself. Even more strictly speaking, therefore, what individualism denies is 'society as something that comes before individuals, and stands in a superior position to individuals.' The term 'community' is frequently employed to refer to society in such a sense.

Theories that hypostasise society: the opponents of individualism

Here, in order to gain a clear understanding of the standpoint known as individualism, let us take a look at the characteristics of social theories which stand in direct opposition to it. Theories which recognise the kind of society that stands in a superior position to the individual are often called '*collectivist* social theories.' Generally, these are made up of ideas such as: (1) the existence of the 'interests of society' which cannot be reduced to a combination of all individuals' interests, and which should be given priority over any kind of aggregate of all individuals' interests; (2) society has its own will and objectives as a society; and, (3) all individuals exist as things formed by society and dependent upon society, rather than the other way round. Such a society is frequently also called a 'hypostasised society.'

The viewing of society in such terms is actually a more familiar practice than one might expect, and when people talk about 'nations' and 'ethnic groups' on the level of everyday life, they often see these as almost substantive societies. The expression 'national interest,' for example, is a mundane term used by politicians when talking about diplomacy and military matters. In today's Japan, there is an air of avoidance of the word *kokueki* (national interest), but it is also said: 'There is no *kokueki*, only *shōeki* (Ministries' interests).' Above all, not a day goes by without the words 'national interest' being heard in the United States, the very homeland of contemporary liberalism. As is clear from the expression 'United Nations,' the word 'nation' means a state as an independent actor-subject in international politics, and the concept of 'national interest' presupposes the view that there exists something which constitutes interest for that nation.

Yet another typical example of a hypostasised society (community) is the '*kaisha* (company)' in post-war Japan. The existence of the Japanese expression '*kaisha ningen* (company-oriented person)' reflects the fact that, for people who had lived their lives (in selfless service) by identifying themselves with their company and thinking primarily of its interests, based on the idea that the company would continue to endure and grow forever, the company was an entity which was greater than those people themselves, as well as other employees and managers. Such Japanese 'company-ism (*kaisha-shugi*)'—a term coined in the thick of Japan's period of high economic growth by the economist Jirō Sakamoto, by analogy with *shakai-shugi* (socialism)—has been taken by numerous social scientists to be the logic of 'the village (*mura*)' and 'the household (*ie*),' but it would be better to regard it instead as being modelled on the '*han* (clan)' of the Edo Period (1603–1868), or the '*ryōgoku daimyō* (fiefdom ruled by a feudal lord)' of the late Sengoku (Warring States) Period, which ended in the late sixteenth century. As proof of this, many of the themes of historical novels favoured by male white-collar workers were taken from these.

In this way, on the level of everyday life, the view of society as something substantive is certainly not unusual. On the level of scholastic social theory, however, it is extremely difficult to assert that society is something which has intrinsic interests and objectives; or rather, it is better to consider it to be impossible, in principle. That is discussed in my 1995 work, *Seidoron no kōzu* (The theoretical structure of institution), but I would like to give a simple explanation here.

The early nineteenth-century German philosopher Hegel is one of the representative theorists to have actively discussed society as something substantive on the level of social theory. Hegel's ideology is often viewed as being 'statism' or 'totalitarianism,' but what he is actually debating is not totalitarianistic at all, and even as statism, it is exceptionally mild. (The ideologies of totalitarianism and extreme statism flourished in the first half of the twentieth century, motivated by and under the influence of the Russian Revolution led by Lenin.)

For Hegel, 'freedom' was the highest value, and people and human society were conceived to be ethical when freedom was realised or aimed to be so. This point is of the pedigree of eighteenth-century Enlightenment thought. This freedom, though, by no means signifies freedom in the sense of living according to one's desires, but, as in the mind of the German philosopher Kant, who slightly predated Hegel, is freedom in the sense of conforming to moral necessity. In his *Philosophy of Right*, Hegel posits the notion of 'civil society' before the 'state,' but he writes of civil society as being:

> an association of members as self-subsistent individuals in a universality which, because of their self-subsistence, is only abstract. Their association is brought about by their needs, by the legal system—the means to security of person and property—and by an external organisation for attaining their particular and common interests (Hegel 1821, § 157).

The image projected here is of a society consisting of civil liberty where, with the presupposition of ownership rights and personal rights, people mutually pursue their various individual interests under certain rules. Here, however, 'in civil society each member is his own end, and everything else is nothing to him' (Hegel 1821, § 182), and this contains the potential for the myriad desires of each individual to conflict with each other. At that point, something called the 'the state' must materialise over civil society, as the 'actuality of the ethical idea.'

As is suggested in Hegel's statement: 'Since the state is mind objectified, it is only as one of its members that the individual himself has objectivity, genuine individuality, and an ethical life' (§ 258), for Hegel, the 'state' meant a particular ideal institution, such as one in which the freedom of each individual would blossom to its fullest extent; the particular and individual would correspond to the universal; and freedom and obligation would coincide. This is not to say that actual states are like this: one needs to understand that this is the concept of a state, as an idea. This state ultimately is something which, in one sense, unites with all individuals, but which, analytically speaking, is considered to be a collective entity that transcends each individual.

Tomoo Odaka, who taught legal philosophy at Tokyo University from before World War Two until the post-war, is a Japanese theorist who developed his own theories, based on Hegel, but also incorporating hermeneutics, phenomenology and sociology. In his principal work, *Kokka kōzō ron* (Theory of state structure), he bluntly asserts the following:

> A state is an organisation in the form of a supra-individual, single entity. And that organisation does not exist in the natural world, but has the realm of spirit as its domain of existence (Odaka 1968, p. 102).

According to Odaka, any organisation—not restricted to the state—exhibits uniformity, integrity and identity. What is meant by 'uniformity' and 'integrity' here is nothing more than its being consolidated into a unity; while 'identity' means the quality of being the same—as in the case of a company called A, founded long ago, but which still remains Company A even though times and its constituent members have changed. Such a property of organisations shows that they are not natural or empirical things, and differ from a mishmash of social relationships among people. This is because an organisation's identity as an organisation is not impacted even if there should be a turnover in its membership, and that identity cannot be sought on an empirical or natural level. Accordingly, Odaka claims, a state, which is one kind of organisation, does not have an existence in the sphere of factual phenomena, but as a 'form of objective spirit (*kyakkan-teki seishin seitai*).' Terminology such as this is extremely difficult to comprehend, but, in essence, it is a phrase which Odaka coined in order to express the fact that the thing in question exists as something not physical but spiritual, and, moreover, does so in an objective manner.

In opposition to individualistic social theory which asserts that the collective thing called 'society' is nothing but a fiction, Odaka considers that a collective thing exists not as something empirical, but in a spiritual realm, objectively.

Such theories of Hegel and Odaka contain important points of argument which cannot categorically be ignored, but they have huge drawbacks. In both theories, the state as an entity is assumed to exist on an ideal or spiritual level, not on an empirical one. Even supposing that a 'state' were such a thing, however, the problem arises of how to educe a normative answer to the question: 'What kind of state is desirable?'

Here, if we know the content of the thing called 'objective spirit,' then, based on this, it might be possible to conceive of constructing a state in ideological (= ideal) form. That probably means constructing a normative theory. What is important here, though, is the issue of who, with what sort of qualifications, would be able to know the content of such an 'objective spirit.' Theorists would be unlikely to have such a privilege, let alone politicians or bureaucrats. Accordingly, even if the view of the state as an 'objective spirit' were correct, a situation would occur in which there could be variously disparate opinions among people as to what it constituted. In that case, this would mean that people's 'subjective interpretation' about the content of 'objective spirit' would be piecemeal, and ultimately there would be no alternative but to return to a horizon in which 'all that really exists is each individual.'

As such, whenever one thinks of something which transcends the individual—as does a state—as a tangible presence existing independently from people, one must face the problem of who, in what way, could gain knowledge of such a tangible presence. Nevertheless, such a collectivist philosophy has not necessarily been rare among modern social theories, as can be appreciated from the example of Marxism, which hypostasised 'class.' Most social theory cannot escape 'hypostasising' something or other.

In this context, individualistic social theories, typified by liberalism, are ones that endeavour to base their thinking solely upon the indubitable existence of 'the individual.' It goes without saying that this was the theory that faithfully carried on the legacy of a problem-consciousness first born in the modern age, which tried to build a society without depending upon God.

Addressing pluralism

Conflict of interest on an individual level

If one eschews taking such a view of society as a substantial presence, then there is no alternative but to consider those things which are desirable and valuable in society on the basis of things which are desired or valued by each individual, personally. Yet while it may be easy enough to suggest making a basis of the values espoused by all individuals, this can involve countless variations. At one extreme, as in one form of utilitarianism, for instance, there is a view based on each individual thinking subjectively that 'it is pleasant for it to be so,' or simply that it is 'pleasant' for each individual (which is not the same as 'thinking that it is pleasant'). On the opposite extreme, there is also a theory based on what should be 'desirable for each person' for some reason, regardless of whether people are subjectively aware of it, or are thinking about it.

One of the major themes for contemporary liberalism is the issue of interpersonal conflict and disparity when the focus is upon the freedom, assets, resources and opportunities that people can enjoy as desirable conditions on an individual level such as this. Individual freedom and equality become problematic because people have differing interests and positions on those interests. When a cake is to be divided up, a conflict of interest can arise, and one person's freedom may rob others of their freedom. When one considers the desirability of society based on conditions at an individual level, such pluralistic circumstances become the focus of the issue. In other words, it is a question of how best to surmount a situation where each person involved has different interests, and to conceptualise the desirability of that society in an *impartial* form. This problem situation may be called 'interest pluralism.'

It is not only liberalism that has attempted to address the problem situation of interest- pluralism: the utilitarianism of Bentham and Mill, Marxism and socialism, too, or the concept of a welfare society and its opponent, libertarianism, also, each endeavour to answer the question of what method for reconciliation of differing interests among people is to be conformed to a normative requirement for society. Marxism, for example, held the view that if private ownership of the means of production, such as capital and land, were eliminated, then grave conflicts of interest among people would disappear by themselves. Present-day libertarianism, on the other hand, is based on the idea that, by establishing individual domains for each person in which they could make decisions freely on the basis on their own interest, and by covering the social realm as widely as possible with such demarcated free domains, the broad-scale pre-empting of conflicts of interest would become feasible. Alternatively—though it is not necessarily a normative theory, but with rather a strong tinge of empirical political theory—there is the theory of pluralist democracy, centred around political scientist Robert Dahl in the United States from the 1950s to the 1960s (such as in his 1956 work, *A Preface to Democratic Theory*), which was oriented towards theorisation of the concept of a political system for preventing autocracy through mutual checks and balances in a society made up of different group interests.

Issues of cultural pluralism and toleration

Among the questions that liberalism seeks to address are also issues of 'toleration' and 'cultural pluralism,' in addition to interest pluralism.

The issue of toleration is the question of how different religions, cultures and lifestyles can coexist within the same political community. Historically, the value of toleration towards different religions within a state was politically established along with the resolution of the turmoil of the seventeenth-century religious wars, in the form of the concept of a European order comprising nation-states, through the Treaty of Westphalia. This is an issue arising in a situation of 'cultural pluralism,' where people living according to different cultures must constitute a shared political space. Generally, Locke's *A Letter Concerning Toleration* (1689) is taken as being the point of origin of liberal toleration theory.

The question of cultural pluralism and toleration may be the greatest touchstone for today's normative social theory. This is because, as everyone knows, contemporary society is exposed to a plethora of culturally pluralistic conditions. Firstly, there has been a proliferation of movements aiming to maintain or strengthen cultural uniqueness by groups of people who, living within a single state, originate from traditional cultural communities with different languages and ethnicities. There are movements to maintain cultural traditions which arose as a result of the post-World War Two international mobility of labour: Turkish immigrants in Germany; Muslim immigrants in France; and Spanish-speaking immigrants in the United States, for example. On the other hand, even in places that for a long time had been regarded as part of a single modern nation-state, including Canada's Quebec Province, Spain's Basque Country, and Scotland and Wales in Britain, a heightening of nationalistic movements has come to be seen. Moreover, as is common knowledge, there has been serious ethnic conflict in the Balkan Peninsula and former Soviet regions since the dismantling of the Soviet Union.

Secondly, in domains controlled thus far by standardised cultural norms, there has been an expansion of movements seeking the diversification of lifestyles and equal recognition of these. This is especially marked in the domains of sexuality and the family, in which life hitherto had been ordered according to traditional cultural norms.

Movements championing equality and rights for homosexuals have not stopped merely at seeking the abolition of legal discrimination, but have extended even to the demand for institutional recognition of marriage between same-sex partners. Alternatively, there are also calls for the granting of rights equal to those of married couples to heterosexual couples who do not undertake the procedure of legal marriage. Many issues in bioethics, also, when seen from a different angle, involve sexual and familial norms. It goes without saying that abortion and assisted conception belong to this category, but brain death and euthanasia also are laden with questions of how family members should be involved in affairs such as 'illness' and 'death.' As we saw at the beginning of this chapter, the issue of organ transplantation is especially connected with a conflict that is closely related to belief and culture in terms of what 'death' means to people. As for matters involving sexuality, there are also such issues as pornography, prostitution and so-called 'compensated dating (*enjo kōsai*).'

Naturally, in regard to such pluralistic situations, it is all too simple to give voice to the doctrine of absolute toleration, which says: 'Why not acknowledge the diversity of culture and lifestyles as they are?' If other people and states were to cease interfering in the various ways that individuals follow their own chosen lifestyles, then the majority of conflict and antagonism in society would probably disappear. In actual fact, there are many people who express tolerance to certain limited domains. However, people who are tolerant in relation to religion might not be tolerant in matters of organ transplantation, nor does it necessarily follow that people who are tolerant about sexuality and pornography will also be tolerant of scandals in politicians' private lives. Furthermore, dealing equally with all kinds of diverse cultures on a legal and institutional level actually generates many problems. For example, giving equal rights to all languages implies having to teach all languages on an equal footing in school education, but that would be impossible. Beyond that, it would also be almost impossible to inscribe all statutes and official documents into all languages. Then again, it would also probably be problematic to ban unfavourable treatment in employment due to trouble with proficiency in official languages. There are few people who would go so far as to argue that prostitution and going naked in public are matters of free choice, even if they would say that love and clothing are people's own business.

The issue of pluralism on a cultural level normally harbours difficulties that far surpass simple toleration. The so-called 'headscarf incident' that occurred in France in 1989 is symbolic of that. As is well-known, this incident was contested over the pros and cons of schools banning the wearing of Islamic headscarves to school. There has also been a series of similar incidents since then in France, culminating in the enactment in 2004 of a law banning from public schools all items which express religion, such as the Islamic headscarf. What lies at the root of the issue is the fact that, as part of the institutionalisation of religious toleration in modern society, the intrinsically liberal view that public education should be purged of religiosity stood in direct opposition to the practice of religious freedom, as in the wearing of a headscarf. Here, the form of dress demanding 'freedom' is one rooted in a traditional cultural community, while what has gone over to the side oppressing that freedom is the separation of state and religion, which ties in with the lineage of liberalism.[4]

When we investigate 'normative principles of society' in the present day, interest pluralism on the level of the individual and cultural pluralism on the level of culture constitute the focus of the issue. How might we be able to overcome this problem, and go on to construct the kind of 'normative principles of society' that could universally apply for all people or all cultures? What sort of conceptual scheme or theoretical system should be put together for that purpose?

This is the basic structure of the problem situation that contemporary liberalism is endeavouring to address. Then, in response to the question of what kind of theory liberalism is trying to establish, has it been successful in presenting 'normative principles of society'? And can it be seen as appropriate in the midst of this problem situation? How far has it succeeded, and from what point has it failed? From the next chapter onwards, those are the issues that this volume will attempt to make clear.

Chapter 2

The Impact of Rawls' *A Theory of Justice*

A giant earthquake that shattered the slumbers

The epicentre of contemporary normative social theory

As already stated, the representative theorist who pursued the normative principles of today's society is John Rawls, the American philosopher. His *A Theory of Justice* (1971) has indeed been the greatest epicentre of contemporary normative social theory diversely developed in the present day by various theorists.

Here, in passing, is something of deep interest from the perspective of the sociology of knowledge. Most scholarly pursuits are carried on in some kind of academic community. If one regards an academic community as a collection of people, then it will be composed of those who have a certain common (and mutually-understood) concern for investigation, but it would be better to think of it as made up of theories, debates and interests, rather than of people. What makes this community a community is its commonality of investigative concern. (The same goes for other communities, such as a family, a society or a church: it is not the people themselves that constitute a community, but rather an understanding among the people who gather there that they are 'bound together by a shared interest.') Contemporary normative social theory, too, has formed such an academic community. This community, in one sense, was newly created on the impetus of Rawls' *A Theory of Justice*.

One way of understanding the process in which a science is developed is through the lens of Kuhn's 'paradigm revolution' in his *The Structure of Scientific Revolutions* (1962). It presents a view that the scientific world is not so much a market with pure, perfect competition among various theories, but rather a community. This is, in fact, an effective framework for understanding science. However, it is misguided to consider an academic community as an insular space bound together by common paradigms, where nothing but internal communication is repeated in language that is valid solely within that space.

Science should be regarded rather as following a process similar to the respective spreading of large and small aftershocks (of which some can be greater in magnitude than the original) that are triggered by the sudden occurrence of a certain gigantic earthquake. Typical examples of such giant temblors are Descartes and Kant in philosophy, Adam Smith and Keynes in economics, Marx in social theory, Newton and Einstein in physics, and Darwin and Mendel in biology. At such a time, rather than a closed scientific world being consolidated, new horizons are opened up. New questions, new conceptual schemes, and new ways of thinking are startlingly presented, and most people are receptive to that impact, going on to participate in a shared quest aiming for a new intellectual order on those new horizons.

Rawls' *A Theory of Justice* was a mighty jolt in normative social theory. It went on to trigger various large and small 'aftershocks' comprising many famous and up-and-coming scholars, not only in specialised political philosophy and legal philosophy, but even in general philosophy and ethics, and also extending to economics, politics and sociology. So, what elements in Rawls' *A Theory of Justice* were the sources of such a shock?

There seem to be two keys for understanding this question in sociological terms: the dawn of the late modern period, which had 1968 as its point of origin, and the stagnant condition of moral philosophy and ethics which centred on the collapse of utilitarianism.

1968, it goes without saying, was the year when student insurrection flared up around the world. America was embroiled in the morass of the Vietnam War, but it suffered a serious blow, both militarily and politically, in the Viet Cong's Tet Offensive in February; and though it had been announced in March that the then President, Lyndon Johnson, had withdrawn from seeking re-election, the storms of the anti-war movement raged on university campuses all over the United States. In May, the so-called May Revolution erupted, and Paris' student district (the Latin Quarter) overflowed with hot-blooded students with dreams of restaging the numerous 'revolutions' that had been played out in Paris from the end of the eighteenth to the mid nineteenth century. In Japan, occupation of campus buildings by students at various universities began: in June, at Tokyo University, prefaced by the latter's handling of students in the Faculty of Medicine; and in July, at Nihon University, where the issue came to light of the disappearance of a huge sum from the university budget. These marked the beginning of the Zenkyōtō (Joint Struggle Committee, a nationwide student union) movement that reached its climax with the Asama-Sansō Incident in which members of Japan's United Red Army held a woman hostage at a mountain lodge for some ten days.

As some of these movements became wildly extremist and lost their political effectiveness, they are regarded as having been nothing more than simple rebellion by youth that lacked any direct significance whatsoever on the level of the political and economic institutions. In fact, in one sense they were merely spectacular revelry. However, if one looks back from today's standpoint, those revels were the harbinger of a long-term change of times (though the parties concerned might have been unconscious of it). Those movements challenged two mighty structures of intellectual authority that hitherto had reigned in the West and Japan, and dismantled them both. One was the social theory of industrialism or modernism, and the other was Marxism. In Japan, there was the further dissolution of post-war intellectuals who had constituted a specifically Japanese type of intellectual authority, and the stratum of educated intelligentsia itself. Following the model of Kuhn just mentioned, one could say that the knowledge paradigms which hitherto had been dominant as social theories started to disintegrate. That was not something confined solely to the realm of academism, either. It was also connected with a broad-ranging seismic change among ordinary people on the level of ways of regarding and thinking about the things that underpin society itself. It was in this period that the ecological movement and feminism began to gain citizenship as a 'new social movement' (a term coined by French sociologist Alain Touraine), in place of the labour movement and the class question. While new issues were found as problems to address, old schemes lost their credibility. That was the historical significance of the student insurrection.

Put simply, the early 1970s were an age when orthodox intellectual authorities were losing reliability, but from the opposite perspective, it can also be said to have been a time of aspiration for new intellectual authorities. Especially in the case of the United States, confidence in the American socio-political system plummeted to an extreme low due to the Vietnam War and the Watergate Incident. The question was how to redefine American justice, which had reached its zenith with victory in World War Two, and during the Cold War.

The situation in moral philosophy and ethics

As a background independent of the above, an inherent problem situation existed in moral philosophy and ethics. The monograph

Rinrigaku nōto (Notes on Ethics) by Ikutarō Shimizu, who was the leading intellectual in the AMPO riots of 1960, makes excellent reference material. In this period, Shimizu was in the process of transforming from his former standpoint as a progressive intellectual into a conservative controversialist, and his papers with the same title were serialised in the journal *Shisō* (Thought) from 1968. When these were published as a book in 1972, Shimizu writes as follows in an afterword entitled *Yohaku* (the margin):

> Nowadays, morality neither receives as much respect as science or the arts, nor has its *raison d'être* recognised to the same extent as that of economics or politics. From the start, it is perceived to be something old-fashioned, something unpleasant...If moral theory were to endeavour to have some kind of down-to-earth function instead of consisting from beginning to end of commentaries on various theories, ancient and modern, then it would first have to prove the necessity for morality in an age freed from starvation; and next, it would have to create its own morality as an object [of study] (Shimizu 1972, pp. 322–323).

In Shimizu's mind, a new foundation for morality is needed in the present age. But can moral theory respond to the task? Such problem-consciousness prompted Shimizu, as a sociologist, to pen his *Rinrigaku nōto*. His hand, however, is anything but cheerful. What explicitly is the focus here is individual morality, but, naturally, the field of vision in which Shimizu problematises moral theory also encompasses what this volume calls normative social theory. Ethics and moral philosophy do not address the academic challenges specific to the contemporary age, nor can they be expected to have the ability to do so, can they? Shimizu could not help but hold such a view, and it seems that such feelings were not necessarily those of Shimizu alone.

Here, there is stagnation in moral theory, or more precisely a sense that there is a lack of moral-theoretical backing to support normative thinking. This probably could be regarded as a feeling that arose when the two giant theories of Marxism and modernism lost their credibility, and it was realised that there was no hope to be found, even if hope were sought from moral theory. (Historicist social ways of thinking such as Marxism and modernism had an aspect of moral philosophy that supplied ethical values. Shimizu, incidentally, having been disappointed with moral philosophy, gradually leaned in the direction of the 'ethics of nationalism,' but that digresses from the main theme of this book.)

For Shimizu, the ethics and moral philosophy of that time had been in a long slumber after the dawn of the twentieth century. (Rawls was as yet unknown to Shimizu.) In fact, an aspect of the time can be illustrated as follows:

The first half of the twentieth century was an age of severe conflict among diverse social theories or ideologies—some with a Marxist bent, others grounded in nationalism or fascism, or various religions and cultures. They all had ethical implications. In the case of Marxism, for example, many intellectuals considered that it was personally ethical to dedicate themselves to a movement for historical change. Ethno-centric nationalism, on the other hand, reasoned that there was an intrinsic meaning in living 'for the sake of the community.' Each of these, in its respective way, also made vehement assertions about 'what constituted a desirable society.' In a sense, such various ideologies could be considered as normative theories which were pursuing a theoretical objective equivalent with what nowadays are discussed in terms of justice and publicness. After World War Two, however, and particularly in the 1960s, most of those ended up being discredited. It was only traditional moral philosophy and ethics, with their focus on utilitarianism, that continued to survive in the realm of academism without being caught up in wars or the frenzy of revolutionary turmoil. It was that kind of moral theory that disappointed Shimizu.

The collapse of utilitarianism

As stated in Chapter One, the utilitarian theory which began with Bentham was truly an individualistic example of modern normative social thought. It was not premised on any collective entities like class and nation, as were Marxism and nationalism, but attempted to conceptualise the desirability of society as a whole, strictly adhering to the perspective of the thoroughly mundane individual. These days, the word 'utilitarianism' tends to be regarded as meaning something that only values the enhancement of people's selfish satisfaction, but it originally was nothing of the kind. It has been an extremely moral doctrine.

John Stuart Mill's famous observation that 'it is better to be a human being dissatisfied than a pig satisfied; better to be Socrates dissatisfied than a fool satisfied' (1973, p. 410), is one which asserts that individuals ought to aspire to interests of high moral value to themselves. Furthermore, in his 1869 work, *The Subjection of Women*, Mill advocates an epoch-making doctrine of equality between the sexes.

As a normative social principle that preceded liberalism, utilitarianism primarily was the most compelling, as can be inferred from the fact that Rawls later constructed his own theory of justice in a form that countered utilitarianism; and in the following sense, it was an egalitarian, universal and individualistic ethical theory. In other words, as is well known, it establishes the principle of 'social desirability' through its slogan, 'the greatest happiness of the greatest number,' but this slogan is firstly egalitarian in that it 'counts the amount of all individuals' happiness equally,' and is an impartial (unbiased) principle in that it 'never attaches more importance to the happiness of a specific individual than to that of others.' Utilitarianism represented nineteenth-century British social ideology not because it existed for the sake of self-serving individuals, by any means, but because it was a powerful idea that provided the principle of social desirability.

From about the turn of the twentieth century, however, the word 'utilitarianism'—rather than signifying the moral theory of Bentham and Mill—gained currency as a label that, in one sense, nebulously expressed the spirit of bygone ages. More specifically, it became a generic name for the social theory of Victorian Britain, and was regarded as an object to be overcome.

It also incorporates nuances of what perhaps ought to be called 'economism,' the reason being that in the neoclassical economics which originated with Alfred Marshall, an empirical proposition, namely that 'people rationally maximise their subjective utility,' was laid down as a fundamental hypothesis for understanding economic phenomena; and it also came to be asserted normatively that 'it is a good thing to maximise people's utility.' Utilitarianism came to be understood as something that was intimately connected with economics. It was economics that translated utilitarianism from an ethical theory into empirical science and policy science, and, conversely, the normative foundation of economics was regarded as lying in utilitarianism.

This, on the other hand, was the point from which sprang a general tendency among people who disliked economic-supremacist ways of thinking to avoid or disparage 'utilitarianism' as an attitude of judging things solely from the perspective of personal interest, and being indifferent towards their morality or public nature. This is evident, for example, in the fact that in his 1937 publication, *The Structure of Social Action*, Talcott Parsons, a renowned American sociologist, criticised the social evolution theory of Spencer (which does not have much to do with utilitarianism) and micro-economic, atomistic social theory (which cannot precisely be called utilitarianism), calling them both 'utilitarianism.' Moreover, even when Parsons' book was prolifically reviewed, this slippage in the meaning of utilitarianism was not problematised (though in the 1980s, after Parsons' death, this slippage gradually began to be pointed out.)

After World War Two, and especially the 1960s, was the heyday for economics. In the developed countries of the West and in Japan, economic growth continued long-term, giving rise to a high-consumption society. Proud of that achievement, economics enjoyed a strong position, and it was in this period that economics came to occupy an almost regal status in the social sciences, large volumes of new research having been generated that made full use of quantitative and mathematical models.

On the other hand, as already stated, ethical theory itself was at a standstill. Deserving special mention is the fact that, not long into the post-war, even though a cataclysmic event had occurred, shaking the very foundations of utilitarianism's existence, there were hardly any new efforts in response to it from the side of moral theory.[1]

This 'cataclysmic event' was Kenneth J. Arrow's 'impossibility theorem' which was presented in his 1951 work, *Social Choice and Individual Values*. In addition to this volume, Arrow had made exceptional contribution to the elaboration of the 'general equilibrium theory' situated at the absolute core of economics, and for that achievement he was later awarded the Nobel Prize for Economics, but his 'impossibility theorem' had an aspect that would undermine the basic premise of economics. (On this point, the artisan-like professionalism of Arrow, the leading authority in mathematical economics, is interesting.) Yet what is important here is the particular kind of destructive impact that the impossibility theorem had vis-à-vis utilitarianism and individualistic normative social theory in general. Let me explain:

Firstly, it is important for the theme of this book to start with a certain degree of accurate understanding of the substance of the theorem, though it has been introduced in many texts because of its fame. Formally, this is expressed as follows:

Arrow's impossibility theorem

1. Assume that each individual ranks various feasible social states in order of preference, from the perspective of utility to her/himself.

2. Suppose there is a response mechanism which relates any given set of people's rankings to a single ranking of society as a whole. This is called the 'social choice function.'
3. However, there is no social choice function which can satisfy all of the following conditions simultaneously:
   a. for any pair of social states *x* and *y*, if all individuals' rankings are identical, then the ranking of society as a whole with respect to that pair should follow suit (Pareto principle);
   b. for any pair of social states *x* and *y*, the ranking of society as a whole with respect to *x* and *y* should be the same for two sets of individuals' rankings, if each individual's ranking in both sets with respect to *x* and *y* are the same (independence of irrelevant alternatives); and
   c. there should be no individual such that the ranking of society as a whole consistently mirrors her/his ranking order, regardless of other people's rankings (non-dictatorship).

Here, the 'ranking of society as a whole' is what stipulates a 'desirable social state from a collective perspective,' and 'individuals' ranking' expresses all individuals' subjective utility. Accordingly, what this theorem means is that, if conditions a. to c. are presupposed, then 'it is impossible to deduce a desirable social state from a collective viewpoint, solely based on the amount of people's utility (or its order).'

'Utility' is used in economics comprehensively to express the various concepts which have been discussed in utilitarian theory by means of such terms as happiness, pleasure, good, and so on, but it may be regarded fundamentally as meaning 'an individual's subjective interest.' So, this impossibility theorem is something that pronounces the project of utilitarianism—which has endeavoured to envision the notion of social desirability based solely upon each individual's subjective interest—to be 'impossible.' One cannot help but call this an extremely serious affair.

The instant it was published, Arrow's impossibility theorem triggered enormous responses. Many scholars tried various schemes in an attempt somehow to find a theory such as would make the social choice function possible, but in the end all of these merely confirmed that the social choice function was indeed impossible, no matter how the conditions were relaxed within reasonable parameters.[2]

Strangely, it was mainly scholars specialising in economics who reacted actively to this issue aroused by Arrow, and one could even say that experts in ethics and moral philosophy were entirely out of the loop. (I am not sure of the reason for this. Their degree of mathematical training was not a significant hurdle. The level of mathematics that social choice theory employed in that period was one that even humanities students could easily acquire. So, it would have been possible for anyone—provided they had the inclination—to understand the various studies.) In any case, this time-honoured area of scholarship just watched on in silence for twenty years while specialists in the economics field developed diverse approaches to the issue of 'social desirability,' using such conceptual instruments as game theory, Pareto optimality and the maximisation of utility.

Rawls' *A Theory of Justice* made its appearance in such a context.

Principles for a system of cooperation

Rawls' *A Theory of Justice* was a work that heralded the resurgence of moral philosophy (Rawls being a professor of philosophy, not an economist.) *A Theory of Justice* was received as a decisive new response from the side of moral philosophy towards the problem situation provoked by the moral collapse of American society from the 1960s onwards, and its pre-existing theoretical defeat.

Justice as the first virtue of institutions

Now, in concrete terms, what was it about Rawls' *A Theory of Justice* that so drew people's notice? Rawls himself gives a comprehensive outline of the theory in his book's first chapter, entitled 'Justice as Fairness,' and even a reading of that alone conveys where the impact and attraction of Rawlsian theory lie. The first section, entitled 'The Role of Justice,' begins with the following words: 'Justice is the first virtue of social institutions, as truth is of systems of thought' (Rawls 1971, p. 3).

Rawls was probably the first to employ wording such as 'the... virtue of social institutions.' Originally, 'virtue' meant something relating to the individual: a moral characteristic that individuals ought to have. Courage, honesty, diligence, compassion and so on are likewise. Rawls uses the word 'virtue' not in reference to individuals, but to 'social institutions.' This distinctly proclaims that what subsequently is to be discussed is not the virtue of individuals, but the virtuousness of society.

Moreover, the phrase 'of social institutions' is used. A particular theoretical standpoint is incorporated in the choice of the expression 'of social institutions' over 'of society.' This is a position that considers society not as a given, but as something which is constructed by us. Until then, there had been a tendency in the thinking of Marxist and social-evolutionary theory to regard society in a deterministic manner, as illustrated by the words, 'the inevitability of history.' This means that the question of what form society will take is already decided beforehand, surmounting people's will. Here, the 'vision of a desirable society' is not something that we 'think up,' but something already fixed which we merely 'discover.' Rawls' theory stands in direct opposition to such a view of 'society as something given.' It pushed the perspective of 'society as something we progressively create ourselves' to the forefront.

At the same time, Rawls establishes 'institutions' as being those aspects that should take on a moral nature in society. Here, society is considered as a single moral entity. And the aspects for which society should take moral responsibility are set up as 'institutions.'

So, why is 'justice' the first virtue? Rawls' words continue as follows:

> A theory however elegant and economical must be rejected or revised if it is untrue; likewise laws and institutions no matter how efficient and well-arranged must be reformed or abolished if they are unjust. Each person possesses an inviolability founded on justice that even the welfare of society as a whole cannot override. For this reason justice denies that the loss of freedom for some is made right by a greater good shared by others (Rawls 1971, pp. 3–4).

This short passage well expresses the groundbreaking newness of Rawlsian theory. Firstly, 'justice' is positioned as a value on a different level from 'good' and 'welfare,' and the assertion is made that the value called 'justice' takes priority over 'the good.' What is meant by the term 'the good' here is a notion that inclusively expresses the favourable quality that all things have vis-à-vis people, and is what constitutes the 'goodness of life' for individuals, ranging from qualities that bring about pleasure and happiness, to matters related to self-expression and meaning for life. Accordingly, basically it is first of all a value connected to the individual. Things that are commonly good for multiple individuals are called 'the common good,' and those which have such a quality are termed 'common goods.' What economics routinely calls 'public goods' equates to 'common goods' in this sense.

From the 1950s into the 1960s, prior to Rawls, this notion of public goods was the typical way of conceptualising 'social desirability.' Set at the base of this concept is what is 'good' or 'goods' for the individual. By contrast, the novelty of Rawls' theory lies in its having set up a value called 'justice' at a point above what is good for each individual and for individuals collectively. It goes without saying that this strategy has a significance that overcomes the theoretical difficulties raised by the aforementioned impossibility theorem of Arrow's. In other words, it was a strategy meant to establish the notion of 'social desirability' at a point basically separated from the level of the question of what sort of utility (good) all individuals will receive from society. It is assumed that there is a value called 'justice' which differs from such an individual level, and which takes priority over it. This thesis, namely 'the priority of the just over the good' which was lucidly hammered out by Rawls, later became one of the radical theses of liberalism's ideology.

Secondly, the reason for 'justice' taking priority over the good in this way, as well as the reason for 'justice' being a more vital virtue than efficiency or orderliness, is that institutions which are not just are simply unjust, and 'must be either rectified or abolished.' In other words, 'justice' is the primary virtue that provides the raison d'être for institutions. Institutions which have no reason for existence must not exist. Institutions are things which we ourselves create. We ought to make institutions that have a reason for being. The concept of 'justice' primarily means the quality of having such a reason.

Thirdly, what constitutes the substance of the reason thus known as 'justice' is a certain 'inviolability' in each person's case. Here, it is not yet explained in detail what that is, but it is suggested that a certain kind of 'freedom' is one of its aspects. It is thought that establishing something inviolable, with the institution meeting the criterion for justice, means that such an inviolable thing is set up to be inviolable. Here, too, yet another characteristic of contemporary liberalism makes its appearance. There are things, material or non-material, possessed by each individual and which should not be violated even for reasons of 'social welfare' (roughly corresponding to what is termed 'public welfare (*kōkyō no fukushi*)' in the Japanese Constitution). These are things which are fundamentally independent again of individual 'good,' because good is, in one sense, subjective. If a certain person thought that she or he could dispense with a certain kind of freedom, then guaranteeing that freedom might not mean an increase in 'good' for that person. What Rawls regards as 'the inviolable,' however, is not such a thing. In Rawls' mind, the inviolability of the inviolable is something effected on a higher plane than that of each concrete individual's opinions.

Principles of justice

From a slightly different angle, Rawls further explains that justice is the first virtue of institutions, as follows:

> Let us assume, to fix ideas, that a society is a more or less self-sufficient association of persons who in their relations to one another recognise certain rules of conduct as binding and who for the most part act in accordance with them. Suppose further that these rules specify a system of cooperation designed to advance the good of those taking part in it (Rawls 1971, p. 4).

Here, he employs the expressions 'let us assume,' and 'suppose,' but Rawls in essence regards 'society' as such an 'association that has a system of cooperation.' What is called an 'association' here is almost equivalent to what was differentiated from a 'community' and conceptualised by the sociologist Robert M. MacIver as being 'an organisation of social life, definitely established for the pursuit of one or more common interests' (MacIver 1917, p. 24). Rawls clearly employs MacIver's concept.

In a society as an association, people basically have free entry and exit, and people participate in it because the 'social cooperation' that is effected in the association can provide a better life for all people than if they were to live alone. However, it does not necessarily follow that arbitrary social cooperation will 'provide a better life' to all people. There must be appropriate agreement as to how the increased benefits generated through cooperative labour will be distributed. In other words:

> A set of principles is required for division of advantages and for underwriting an agreement on the proper distributive shares. These principles are the principles of social justice: they provide a way of assigning rights and duties in the basic institutions of society and they define the appropriate distribution of the benefits and burdens of social cooperation (Rawls 1971, p. 4).

If one combines this with the previous quote, here will be shown the two fundamental characteristics relating to the 'principles of justice.' Firstly, these constitute the conditions that enable people to participate spontaneously in an association. The 'principles of justice' are the conditions which, when the idea of an association with fixed constitutive principles is presented, must be met by those constitutive principles in order for all people to think that they may participate in it. In that instance, there is the premise that people are already equal and free. What is meant by the word 'fairness' when Rawls mentions 'justice as fairness' is the sort of arrangement to which free and equal people would agree under conditions of perfect 'voluntary will.'

Secondly, the substance of principles of justice is taken to be the 'way of assigning rights and duties in the basic institutions of society,' and, by that means, to 'define the appropriate distribution of the benefits and burdens of social cooperation.' People participate in an association for the very reason that the benefits of cooperation are generated within one. Hence, the main role of justice principles is to respond to the question of how to distribute the benefits and burdens of social cooperation. Rawls specifies that method of deciding as 'a way of assigning rights and duties.'

Rawls calls the kind of society that is effectively regulated by principles of justice with these two characteristics a 'well-ordered society.' He has not simply dubbed it as such. Rawls says that in a society led by justice principles with the above two characteristics, people are likely to have the mutual understanding that they themselves live under fair public justice, and have a common appreciation that though there might be small conflicts of interest, they accept the current basic institution and also accept each other, sharing the 'bonds of civic friendship' (solidarity). In other words, the kind of serious conflicts that would lead society into division or that could only be resolved by violence will not arise, nor will the motivation as such to overturn that society's basic structure in a revolutionary manner. A well-ordered society comes into being as the result of 'justice of fairness' holding sway.

The above is a recapitulative commentary on what is stated in the first few pages of *A Theory of Justice*, but, in one sense, the vital essence of Rawlsian theory is encapsulated in this part, because this is where Rawls' basic ideas about the role played for society by what he calls 'justice principles' or simply 'justice' and its significance are set out.

The anatomy of *A Theory of Justice*

The argument developed in *A Theory of Justice* does not, by any means, stop at the general meaning of justice. The two characteristics stated above ('fair conditions for participation' and 'the assignment of rights and duties') have merely set up the theoretical significance (one could say *function*) of 'justice,' with substance yet to be added to it. Substantive principles of justice must actually be derived, and reasons relating to the method of derivation have to be presented. This is fulfilled (at least seemingly) by the theoretical mechanisms which are generally seen as characterising Rawls' *A Theory of Justice*, such as the original position, the veil of ignorance and the maximin rule. These come together into a single entity, to comprise a system of reasons for deriving substantive principles of justice or for justifying them. This can be said to form a 'logic of justice derivation' (which I will explain and discuss in the next chapter).

What is more, the 'substantive principles of justice' are formulated and described as two principles. (These two principles are presented repeatedly in *A Theory of Justice*, with slight variations in the wording each time, but there is no great difference among them.)

As such, Rawls' *A Theory of Justice* is made up of the following three pillars. (These do not, however, necessarily follow the order in that volume.)

1. The theoretical significance of principles of justice

Here, the meaning to society of the value called 'justice' is theoretically confirmed: that is, justice—as the thing which enables people's social cooperation in an ordered, fair society—constitutes the fair basic rule relating to the way in which the benefits of social cooperation are allocated; and justice as fairness occupies supreme position among the virtues (desirable qualities) of social institutions. As such, justice takes priority over 'good.' The substance of this kind of justice is illustrated by the 'principles of justice.'

2. The derivation logic for principles of justice

Here, the method in which substantive 'principles of justice' are derived is described in the following terms: namely, that a certain hypothetical situation called the original position is established; and there, hypothetical citizens' representatives, called 'parties' by Rawls, take on the role of deciding principles of justice. Under established conditions of impartiality in which information pertaining to individual interest and resources is hidden by a veil of ignorance, these representatives rationally choose desirable justice principles on the basis of the maximin rule. By means of a conceptual scheme such as this, known as a social contract in the original position, the fairness and impartiality of the content of the principles is guaranteed.

3. The substantive principles of justice
Here, the content of the derived justice principles is described as being two principles, and a commentary on their meaning is developed.

i. (The first principle) 'Each person is to have an equal right to the most extensive total system of equal basic liberties compatible with a similar system of liberty for all'.
ii. (The second principle) 'Social and economic inequalities are to be arranged so that they are both:
   a. (the difference principle) to the greatest benefit of the least advantaged, consistent with the just savings principle, and
   b. attached to offices and positions open to all under conditions of fair equality of opportunity' (Rawls 1971, p. 302).

Of these, as we will see later, as a matter of fact, the derivation logic in the form shown in (2) only has a somewhat secondary role for Rawlsian theory. In *A Theory of Justice*, however, it is described in a way that suggests it occupies a central role, and here I present it in line with conventional interpretations.

Moreover, though I will later examine in detail the content of the concrete principles of justice in (3), especially in relation to the 'difference principle,' I wish to provide a word of preliminary explanation here. Rawls frequently emphasises that the 'difference principle' transcends utilitarian theory. Utilitarianism asserts a normative principle that considers a condition in which there is maximisation of the total amount of people's benefit in society as a whole to be 'desirable in terms of the community,' but there are two main problems to this. The first, as already seen, is that if one tries to consider people's benefit as subjective 'utility,' then the issue of comparison of utility between individuals and the issue of Arrow's impossibility theorem will arise. The other problem is that if one focuses solely upon the total amount, then one completely fails to consider inequalities in distribution of benefits to individuals. In other words, no matter how unequal people's benefits might be, if their aggregate is large, then utilitarianism judges that society to be a good one.

Rawls considers that the 'difference principle' overcomes these two problems in the following manner. Firstly, in order to avoid making the same mistake as utilitarianism in the issue of utility calculation, it sees the concept of 'benefit' not through 'utility,' but through the notion of 'primary goods.' Primary goods are assumed to include 'rights, liberty, opportunity, income and wealth,' and 'self-respect'—the things that 'all rational people desire.' Such primary goods, for Rawls, are things whose quantity enjoyed by each person can be objectively measured to a certain extent, and thus it will be possible objectively to make an issue of the conditions of their allocation.

Next, in answer to the second problem, the 'difference principle' considers an equitable distribution of benefits through the imposition of a prescribed egalitarianism vis-à-vis the distribution method to be desirable, not merely the 'total amount' of benefits.

In like manner, Rawls' *A Theory of Justice* is a far more egalitarian theory than utilitarianism, and what lies at its core is nothing other than the 'difference principle' of ii(a).

Social morality

The meaning of 'justice'

Since Rawls, there is one thing that has clearly changed greatly from pre-existing ethics and moral philosophy: the fact that 'justice' has become the major theme for these areas of inquiry. Until then, there had been hardly any scholarly works that made 'justice' their topic. Instead, themes such as morals, ethics, rights, liberty and democracy used to be raised. Since Rawls' *A Theory of Justice*, however, a series of books and papers relating to normative theory established 'justice' across the board, even if they were not works whose aim was to comment on Rawls. Books which hitherto might have simply been entitled something like *A History of Moral Philosophy* have now been launched into the world as being 'of the justice-principle lineage'—just as if Aristotle, Hume, Kant and the like had all been discussing 'justice' all along.

Why has 'justice' become the major theme? In one sense, the reason is clear-cut: it is because the traditional nomenclature of academic disciplines such as moral philosophy and ethics was clearly not appropriate for the theme of pursuing normative principles for society rather than individual ethics; and, at the same time, though rights and liberty were elements of normative principles, they could not be all-embracing.

It has been rarely articulated in discussions in 'ethics' and 'moral philosophy' that there are two different questions; one is the question of 'what kind of personal morality individuals should follow' or 'what way of living is a desirable one,' and the other is that of 'how social institutions should be.' Those two questions have been debated without a sharp distinction having been made between them. The former, though, is an issue of 'personal morality,' a theme which Confucius' 'do not do unto others what you would not want done to you,' Christianity's 'love thy neighbour,' and Kant's moral philosophy have severally expounded. In contrast to these, the latter question examines 'the morality of society.' A judgement such as that a 'good society' is a society without poverty or oppression, or is one where people are at peace and can live happily, demonstrates one way of answering this question. The two issues are basically different things, though they may be connected in a form such as the agreement, for instance, that 'it is a good thing for society as a whole for each individual to be moral.' In some ways of thinking, it also could be asserted that 'even if each individual person is not moral, society of itself should be moral.'

However, traditional concepts in ethics and moral philosophy cannot unambiguously reflect the pursuit of 'the morality of society.' On this point, the notion of 'justice' has been extremely effective for giving a clear identity to the activity known as the quest for societal morality, which is differentiated from individual morality. By this means, the theme of interrogation has been distinctly presented. And one can see that the once-gloomy concerns of inquiry were liberated from then on, and a torrent of debate of various kinds came to be seen, as if floodgates had subsequently been opened. (Apart from that, there is also a temporal background in which 'justice' came to be loudly discussed within cultural pluralism.)

Actually, however, a particular modification arose in the concept of justice when Rawls established it as the first—the supreme—virtue of social institutions. The notion of justice in moral philosophy originally conformed to Aristotle's *Nichomachean Ethics*. There justice is classified into several kinds. The idea at its basis, however, is, 'to treat equal things/persons equally, and unequal things/persons unequally.' To cite a familiar example, it was justice that decided whether to pass or fail two people with identical test marks in the same way, or to impose the same penalty on people who committed the same offence. This is generally called 'justice as balance.' In other words, the achievement of a certain balance is justice, and on those occasions, the normative decision as to what constitutes a balance is given in advance.[3]

Rawls' concept of 'justice' differs from this. First, we should not mistakenly interpret it as merely being 'distributive justice,' though there are many who think thus. Distributive justice is a normative idea relating to how resources, opportunities and assets should be shared by people. It is true that, out of Rawls' two principles of justice, the difference principle in particular focuses on this question, but it is only one element of a normative principle that qualifies as justice. For Rawls, 'justice' means the morality that society (institutions) should possess, namely, the fundamental quality that a normative principle of society should fulfil. Distributive justice is one element within that.

Why establish the priority of the right over the good?

Rawls frequently emphasises that 'the right takes priority over the good,' but 'the right' is neither justice as balance, nor distributive justice. 'Rightness'—or 'justice'—is a quality that basic normative principles should have. That is the very reason why it takes priority over 'the good,' because 'justice' is the fundamental condition for a society to be a society.

Often, the assertion that 'the right takes priority over the good' tends to be understood in the sense of 'what we think of as being "right" must be prioritised over what we think of as being "good."' Even as a term in everyday use, the word 'right' of itself emits a powerful significance from the start, and it is no mystery that there is a general feeling that 'justice' has the greatest authority among the various normative values. The assertion that something is 'just' perhaps cannot help but make all other normative assertions bow down, just as the Tokugawa Shōgun's hollyhock crest inscribed on an *inrō*—a set of nested boxes hung from the bearer's waist in Edo-period Japan—once inspired absolute obedience and awe among the populace. Accordingly, the priority of the right over the good appears to be something natural. In actual fact, however, this differs considerably from what Rawls has in mind.

For Rawls, the right takes priority over the good not because justice in its general sense is the supreme value. If that were his opinion, then he probably would have discussed the question of *why* the right takes priority over the good. However, he has not done so. What Rawls was pondering was the necessity for the setting-up of some sort of normative principle on a level superior to that of 'good,' so as to establish a society with a consistent order applicable to all individuals whose different conceptions of goodness harboured latent potential for conflict. Yet God or various equivalent transcendental beings, as well as hypostasised collective things like states or ethnic groups, can also become a basis of normative principles that order society, as things that transcend values on an individual level. Of course, Rawls' theory never depends upon such culture-specific or orthodox transcendental beings. A quest for a normative principle transcending cultural or traditional limitations, and tying people together into a joint society, as well—that is what Rawls conducted in the name of a 'theory of justice,' and 'justice' is what he called the value at the forefront of the aspirations of such a quest.

Since Rawls, the notion of 'justice' has gone on to be widely established, especially for theorists of liberalism, as the thing that indicates the core value when investigating 'a desirable society.' Not only have numerous books and papers with 'justice' as their main theme appeared, but 'justice theory' has come to mean the name of an academic discipline in place of conventional moral philosophy and ethics. This is only because 'justice' was set up by Rawls as the word indicating a common value in society, and the foremost one among all common values. At the same time, it meant that the 'morality of society' had been expressly topicalised.

So, how might Rawls have derived the substance of his concrete principles of justice? And by what logic could we present a specific normative proposition to the general public as something valid? Let us consider this issue in the next chapter.

Chapter 3

The Contractarian Model and Reflective Equilibrium

The logic of the original position

The impartial perspective through the veil of ignorance

It is well-known that Rawls used a hypothetical social situation called the 'original position' when substantively formulating his principle of justice. The 'original position' is an imaginary social setting in which people could reach a consensus as to 'what constitutes a normative principle of fairness.' Its most salient feature is the fact that people are under a 'veil of ignorance.' To make the consensus impartial for everyone, this 'veil of ignorance' sets aside some kinds of knowledge that people have, particularly of their own social origin, talents, and the resources they have. People know that various differences in such properties exist, but due to that veil they do not know what kind of properties are ascribed to themselves, and so they never speculate as to what kind of normative principle would be beneficial to themselves. The theoretical device which excludes particular interests from deducing a normative principal, instead guaranteeing its choice from an *impartial* (not belonging to any specific person) and *symmetrical* (belonging to everyone) standpoint, is the 'veil of ignorance.'

A consensus reached through this kind of procedure, Rawls maintains, is guaranteed to be 'fair.' 'Fairness,' in the Rawlsian formulation as examined above, is a feature of normative principles which enables free and equal citizens to participate spontaneously in social cooperation. Why does Rawls reaffirm the feature of 'fairness' here in formulating normative principles? This is because his image of 'free and equal citizens' is represented as persons in this hypothetical original position, under the veil of ignorance.

This idea of a veil of ignorance in the original position was a revolutionary development for normative social theory. To specify a good society, or public goods, what line of reasoning we should employ is the most fundamental and most controversial question. If one presupposes the existence of some kind of transcendent being, then that itself will establish a way of reasoning. For example, if one assumes the existence of God, then one can depend upon the perspective of divine commandments; and if one presupposes the notion of the inevitability of history, then it will not be impossible also to argue that the inevitable is desirable. However, modern social theory cannot afford to rely upon baseless transcendent beings and mega-theory that are deemed to be mistaken.

As noted in chapter 1, utilitarianism is an attempt to conceptualise the good society by referring not to such mysterious things, but to (supposedly) detectable utilities of people. The utilitarian way of setting up an impartial position is that of 'counting all people as equal.' This leads to the concept of 'aggregate happiness,' as formulated in the well-known slogan: 'the greatest happiness for the greatest number.'

The most cogent feature of the Rawlsian theory of the 'veil of ignorance' is that by means of this artifice, we can find an impartial position in a different manner from that of utilitarianism. The defect in the utilitarian way of reasoning is that weighing individual amounts of utility in an indifferent manner misses the question of unequal distribution of utilities. Rawls, by contrast, attempts to be impartial, not by giving the same weight to all benefits, but by excluding particular interests in the choice of normative principles. What is important for Rawlsian formulation is this kind of impartial standpoint, from which we can find a desirable option for everyone, not for a particular individual. This impartiality, he argues, enables a choice to be considered a 'fair' one. From this reasoning, he deduces two principles of egalitarian justice.

It is important to note, however, that it is not actual people that make choices in the original position. The original position remains a strictly fictitious world. The subjects who make a choice in this fictive setting are hypothetical 'parties' as representatives of citizens like us. This hypothetical structure is as follows (see Figure 3.1). In Rawlsian theory, what we as citizens have to do is to accept the principles of justice chosen by the hypothetical parties in the original position as being justice principles for us, ourselves.

The maximin rule

Parties in the original position, Rawls explains, collectively choose one set of normative principles under the veil of ignorance. The next

Figure 3.1: The original position and principles of justice

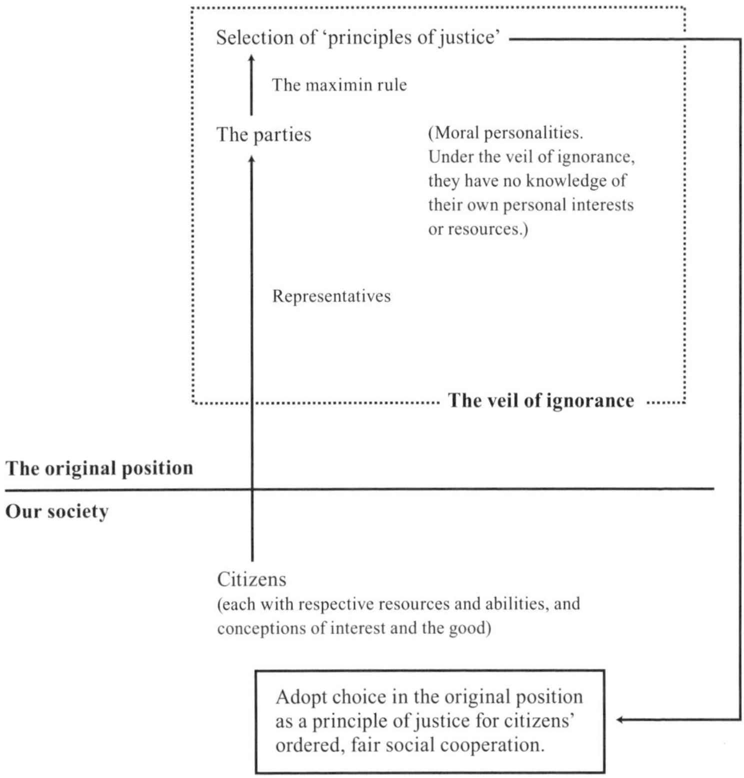

question is: how do people in such an original position find substantive principles of justice? To reply to this problem, Rawls employs the idea of rational choice based on the maximin rule.

The maximin rule in game theory was thought up as one of the rational solutions in a strategic situation. Suppose, for example, that when you are about to take the end-of-term examination for a certain class, you think that if possible, you would like to idle away your time and sit the test without having studied for it, or anything. The teacher might set difficult questions in the examination, but again, might set easy ones. If hard questions are set when you have been lazy, then you will fail, and the worst possible situation will arise. The teacher, on the other hand, wants the students to study, but does not want to make the questions unnecessarily difficult, if possible. However, the

Table 3.1 The examination game

Student	Questions set by teacher	
	Easy	**Difficult**
To have fun	10, 3	0, 5
To study	3, 10	7, 7

Values in each cell in the left-hand column represent a payoff for students, and those in the right-hand column represent a payoff for the teacher

teacher also wishes primarily to avoid letting even students who have been having fun pass due to the questions having been too easy.

In such a case, the payoff structure of the game is expressed in the manner seen in table 3.1.

For you, the student, which will be the rational behavioural choice: to have fun, or to study? If you know that the teacher will set easy questions, then of course it will be better to enjoy yourself. But you cannot know that kind of thing in advance. If, on the off-chance, hard questions were set, then your game would be up.

On the other hand, conditions are thorny for the teacher, too. She or he does not want to be disliked by the students for setting difficult problems, either, and compiling the questions and marking them are a chore, in the first place. If the students are going to study anyway, then the teacher will want to get away with easy questions. But if the teacher passes students who have done nothing but fool around, then next year's students will have even less inclination to study.

A combination of rational choices in a game situation is called a 'solution.' There are several different conceptions of solution in game theory. The most prominent one is the 'Nash equilibrium,' conceived by the game theorist, John Forbes Nash, winner of the Nobel Prize for Economics and model for the film, *A Beautiful Mind*. Nash equilibrium is a set of strategies such that if players unilaterally change their respective way of choosing, they cannot increase their own payoff. Regrettably, Nash equilibrium does not exist in the payoff structure in Table 3.1. In the case of a combination such as at the top left (to have fun/easy), for example, the teacher can raise her or his payoff from 3 to 5 by independently changing to (have fun/difficult). (Though even if the student independently changes his or her choice, switching to (to study/easy), the payoff will drop from 10 to 3.) In the case of other combinations, also, it will always be possible for one of the players to increase the payoff by independently changing his or her selection.

'Dominant strategy' is another famous solution concept. When a particular choice of one's own always yields an equivalent or greater payoff than any other choices, regardless of one's opponent's selection, then this choice is called the dominant strategy. If a dominant strategy exists, then it will be rational to choose that one, whatever choice one's opponent makes. Again, though, no dominant strategy is present in Table 3.1.

So, you can resort to the *maximin strategy*. Under the maximin strategy, you assess, for each of your choices, the worst payoffs arising from your opponent's moves, and choose the alternative that will yield the most favourable payoff among such least-favourable payoffs. In Table 3.1, if you choose 'to have fun,' the worst payoff is 0, but 'to study' is 3, so the latter is larger. According to maximin strategy, the student's choice will be 'to study.' On the other hand, the maximin strategy for the teacher is 'to set difficult questions.' Accordingly, if each party adopts the maximin strategy, the student will study, the teacher will set hard problems, and a payoff distribution of (7,7) will occur.

The name 'maximin strategy' was applied because one chooses the best out of the worst (the maximum among minimums). It is the maximin rule that determines choice by means of the maximin strategy. At one stage, the maximin strategy was regarded as the most prevalent solution concept in a strategic situation. This widespread acceptance was partly due to a theorem presented by von Neumann and Morgenstern, the original founders of game theory, proposing that, in any zero-sum mixed-strategy game, a maximin solution will always exist as a saddle point. A zero-sum game is a game in which the sum of the payoffs of both players is 0 for any combination of strategies. And, if you do not fix a particular move, but assign a probability to each choice, your strategy is called mixed-strategy. The existence theorem for the maximin solution is simple and beautiful, and is compared to the general equilibrium theorem in economics. But because its premise of a zero-sum situation is too specific, however, interest in it later gradually waned.

In game theory, the ordinary assumption is that each player will try to maximise her or his respective payoff as much as possible. But in some cases it is also assumed that strategies for some players are determined by whim or coincidence rather than rationality. In a game such as in Table 3.1, if one makes the new assumption that payoff for the teacher either does not exist, or can be ignored, then the teacher becomes that kind of player. In this circumstance, the teacher will determine whether to make the problems easy or hard without considering whether the student studies or not (by mere whim, or for some other reason). So, the teacher's payoff will be removed from Table 3.1, and the student's payoff structure alone will remain. Even in this situation, there is still the issue of choice for the student: whether the teacher will set easy or difficult questions is absolutely unknown in advance. Accordingly, the maximin strategy remains meaningful. Regardless of whichever type of problems the teacher may set, the rational choice from maximin strategy will still be 'to study.'

In game theory, this kind of player, who chooses a strategy—by coincidence or some other mechanism the other player does not select—and affects his or her opponent's payoff, is called 'nature.' If a person vacillates as to whether to take an umbrella to work or not during a rainy season, the subject of the choice whether 'to rain' or 'not to rain' is 'nature' itself. The choice mechanism of the player called 'nature' cannot be known. It is also meaningless to consider 'nature's' payoff. But because one's own payoff is affected by the other player's (nature's) choice, also constitutes a game situation.

A game in the original position

In Rawls' original position, the parties face a game situation played against 'nature,' such as the following. The respective parties will select one set of justice principles from among various conceivable ones. On the other hand, 'nature' will ascribe different kind of traits to each party, such as social status, talents, resources and conception of the good, which will come to light when the veil of ignorance is stripped away. Under the veil of ignorance, the parties cannot know what kind of traits they each have, though in actual society people live by utilising their respective characteristics. Furthermore, their choice of justice principles will affect payoff structure differently depending upon what particular kind of traits they have. They might choose a principle such as would enable especially-gifted people to obtain much higher payoffs, or a principle that gave less-privileged people the same payoffs as others.

Now, to simplify matters, let us assume that there are three types of principle and three types of trait. If we express the payoff obtained by persons with Trait j under the condition of Principle i by r_{ij}, then a payoff structure such as table 3.2 can be sketched:

Table 3.2 A game in the original position

Choices by the parties	Unknown traits of the parties (nature)		
	Trait 1	Trait 2	Trait 3
Principle 1	r_{11}	r_{12}	r_{13}
Principle 2	r_{21}	r_{22}	r_{23}
Principle 3	r_{31}	r_{32}	r_{33}

This is the situation in which a party is placed when she or he chooses a principle of justice in the original position. Here, the substantive player is only that party, and the payoff will belong solely to that party.

In Rawlsian formulation, *rational* strategy for the party under such circumstances is to comply with the maximin rule. As the party is under the veil of ignorance, which trait she or he possesses is unknown and is only decided at random. In that case, it would be rational, in Rawls' view, to assume the worst possible situation. So, the rational strategy is to choose the principle whose least-desirable outcome would be the best among various alternative principles for her or him. It is just the same as taking an umbrella, when one does not know whether it will rain or not, but thinking that it would still be better to carry an umbrella around for nothing than to get wet in the rain. By this reasoning, Rawls claims that it would be rational, following the maximin strategy, for a party to choose the two principles of justice such as have been shown in Chapter Two in this volume.

In this way, 'justice principles' can primarily be derived as the rational choice of parties under the veil of ignorance in the original position. Moreover, Rawls asserts that these justice principles constitute justice principles for us ourselves. However, the so-called 'rational choice of parties' does not exist in reality. Its existence is only imaginary in Rawls' theory. In other words, it is Rawls himself, and nobody else, who establishes 'what rational choice in the original position is.' This fact, however, though not being hidden, is not emphasised, either. Normative principles are presented to his readers as something that are decided by an outer world, transcending readers and speakers (=theorists).

Utilitarianism, unlike this, is not contractarian. The basic procedure for determining what is socially desirable is to aggregate what is desired by people who actually exist. The ultimate foundation of desirable society lies in happiness for empirically-existing people. So, in principle, that can be decided by us ourselves directly.

By contrast, in Rawls' *A Theory of Justice*, what is desirable for society is primarily determined in the fictional original position. It is not we ourselves, but hypothetical parties, who choose justice principles. The salient feature here is that the decision in such an imaginary world bind us ourselves.

Such a contractarian construct, namely *A Theory of Justice*'s choice in the original position, was very cordially accepted by many scholars. It is no exaggeration to suggest that the greatest reason for the enormous impact which *A Theory of Justice* had as the epicentre of contemporary liberalism lies in its contractarian characteristics.

But, why did its contractarian formulation have such appeal? How, in the first place, does this kind of hypothetical contract have a binding force for us? Why should we accept hypothetical parties' fictitious choices as being our own?

The normative power of the fictive social contract

Original contract theory and mundane contract theory

Social contract theory is a major aspect shared by many social theories of the early modern period, from Hobbes, Locke and Rousseau to Kant. *A Theory of Justice* has fitted into the traditions of such normative investigation, and this is a factor in the spotlighting of Rawls' volume. But the logic of social contract theory is not obviously persuasive to us. Let us consider it in more detail.

The basis of social contract theory is that we have to obey a rule because we have promised to do so. We have to keep our promises, and the provisions of the promises normatively constrain the parties who have made them. Appeal to this general rule for validity is the basic feature of social contract theory.

In religious social contract theory, namely in Judaism, Christianity and Islam, it is precisely the contract which human beings made with God that ultimately forms the foundation for the various normative restrictions imposed upon people. Naturally, doubts may arise as to why the hypothetical 'original contract' (even if firmly believed to be true) can have the power to bind us even in the present day.(I am afraid, though, that only those who do not share the Judeo-Christian tradition might dare to harbour such doubts.) If we presuppose individualism as a way of normative reasoning, then it will be odd for an ancestral contract to have a binding force to its descendents. In the case of Judaism, however, this problem is solved by assuming that the contract was one made between God and all Jews. In other words, the contract is not something between a certain individual and God, but something between a certain community in its entirety and God, and through a particular individual being a member of that community, he or she automatically becomes one of the subjects on one side of the contract in question. In Christianity's case, the whole human race becomes a party, instead of the Jews.

It is not so simple, though, for modern social contract theories. The contract they contain is not one between God and a community. Civil and mundane versions of contract theory can not presuppose the existence of God, while under a religious background the contract with God is entirely real and valid, as long as God's existence is regarded as real. For mundane social theory, however, such a fictive character as God may not be presupposed.

The 'contract' in mundane social contract theory is one between people. Yet if the question is raised whether this kind of contract has ever existed in reality, the answer is definitely 'no.' Each social contract theory from Hobbes to Locke and Rousseau assumes a 'state of nature,' and from this theoretical supposition it deduces social institutions and norms, which are somehow distinct from natural rights and natural law. A 'state of nature' here means not an 'savage, primitive condition,' but an imaginary, conceived state, just as in the case of the absolutely straight line and the point that is solely a location, with no area, in geometry. The early social contract theorists initially assumed a state of nature as a perspective, like Archimedes' Point, that enabled them to relativise existing social phenomena.

Here, if one views the state of nature itself as exemplifying social desirability, and regards actual society as a degenerate form of this perfect condition, then it becomes a narrative like Rousseau's 1755 *Discourse on the Origin and Basis of Inequality among Men* (which does not contain social contract theory, unlike the same author's *Social Contract Theory*), or Marx and Engels' *Communist Manifesto*. In other words, return to this state of nature is considered *the* right solution.

Mainstream social contract theories, on the contrary, consider the state of nature rather as a still-incomplete, undesirable condition. The social contract is a consensus in which people in an undesirable natural condition promise to accept—as commonly binding—institutions or norms, in order to overcome their own situation and generate a more desirable state. Clearly, a double fiction is in existence here. The state of nature is a fiction, and so is the contract concluded under it. Why was a theory consisting of such made-up ideas to have such persuasive power over us?

The contract as a narrative

If one reads Rousseau's *Social Contract Theory*, which developed social contract theory in its purest form, it will be understood that the keys to this question lie in two 'constraints.' The first constraint, it goes without saying, is one which the people who make the original agreement impose upon themselves by means of that agreement. In Rousseau's formulation, first a political entity as a public persona manifests itself through the social compact, and second the three types of promises—mutual promises between people, the people's promises to the polity, and the polity's promises to the people—establish their various obligations. This reasoning, however, is not a historical observation in an empirical sense, but simply a hypothetical narrative told by Rousseau. It is true that he himself does not assert that the story is true, by any means. For Rousseau and for us, too, this is nothing more than a fable.

One more constraint manifests itself from the fable, however: the constraint binding the reader who reads this narrative. What is narrated in social contract theory is the composition of an imaginary political community, but the clarity and symmetry in its construction, and the public-mindedness and fairness of the people featured with it, clearly have the power in themselves to appeal to readers. Like Don Quixote reading tales of chivalry, readers become able to understand reality through stories, and to interpret the latter by comparing them with reality. Anyone who reads the following words of Rousseau's, for example, will have a tendency to end up thinking that actual human beings indeed 'are all equalised by convention and legal right.'

> Instead of destroying the natural equality of mankind, the [social contract] substitutes...a moral and legal equality for that physical inequality which nature placed among men, and that, let men be ever so unequal in strength or in genius, they are all equalized by convention and legal right (Rousseau 1762, Book 1, Chap. 9).

It goes without saying that, logically, this conclusion remains confined within his narrative of social contract theory. But for readers who take idealistic strength from the world within this narrative, the real world will appear to be intrinsically homologous to that in social contract theory, and all of the various constituents of the narrative will be perceived as if they illustrated the intrinsic, should-be-true form of actual society. In other words, it is precisely the world of stories—which are fictional—that was intrinsically real, while the actual, empirical world starts to seem like its warped, temporary guise. Its composition may be expressed as in Figure 3.2.

Methodically speaking, the original form of social contract theory is that, based on the fact that we or our peers have actually made a contract, the terms of that contract bind us. This format has its roots in Judaism, but it is not only religion, but also the institution of the written constitution that is often given a contractarian interpretation. This understanding is based on the normative principle that says one is constrained by what one has promised. This format is tacitly employed in the thinking of Hobbes and Locke, as well.

The social contract theory of Rousseau differs from this in some points. In Rousseau, while the social contract narrative is a fiction, it constrains us by means of the normative appeal of the fair and impartial composition of that storybook world. Here, strictly speaking, it is not by the fact that 'there was a promise' that we are bound. But through our reading about the world in that narrative, the notion of normative values already latent within us is explicitly evoked, and by the inference that 'under conditions of fairness, one would expect to enter into such and such an agreement,' the agreement in question comes to be conceived as 'desirable.'

Social contract theory in Rawls

This scheme can be found in Rawlsian social contract theory, as well. Both the parties in the original position who determine the principles of justice under the veil of ignorance, and the citizens that those parties represent, are all nothing more than the characters that appear in Rawls' theory—in other words, they are a fiction. The selection of principles there and the consequent claim crystallised as two principles of justice exist only within a narrative realm in Rawls' theory. If the principles that the parties chose were accepted as just for them, this choice would still be confined to within that narrative. If so, then how could the fictional choice come to be accepted as being just, for Rawls himself and for us, too?

Figure 3.2: The mechanism by which the contractarian narrative constrains us

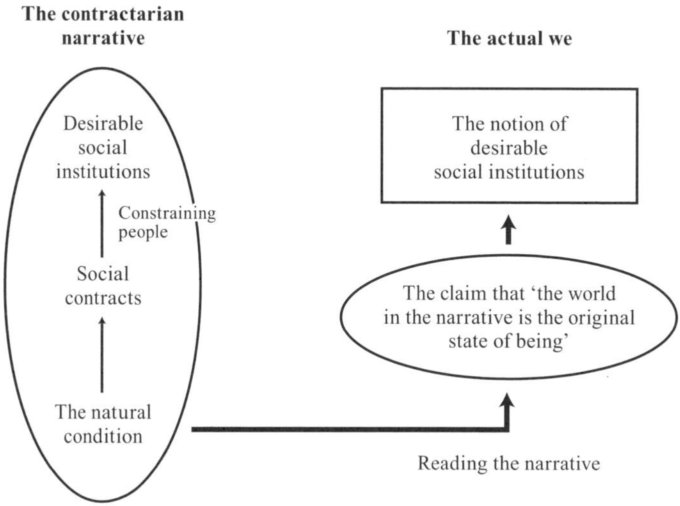

After having once explained that choice in the original position means principles of justice, Rawls notes as follows:

> A final comment. We shall want to say that certain principles of justice are justified because they would be agreed to in an initial situation of equality. I have emphasized that this original position is purely *hypothetical*. It is natural to ask why, if this agreement is *never actually entered into*, we should take any interest in these principles, moral or otherwise. The answer is that the conditions embodied in the description of the original position are *ones that we do in fact accept*. Or if we do not, then perhaps we *can be persuaded* to do so by philosophical reflection. Each aspect of the contractual situation can be given supporting grounds...These constraints express *what we are prepared to regard as limits on fair terms of social cooperation* (Rawls 1971, p. 21; emphasis added).

Here, Rawls reasserts that (1) the hypothetical consensus in the original position is in fact something which we ourselves would actually agree to; (2) the reason for this is that the conditions set up as the original position are ones which we actually would be likely to accept as 'fair' through rational reflection; and (3) therefore, the justice principles which are fair terms of social cooperation for those parties are simultaneously fair terms when we ourselves enter into social cooperation. In short, because 'each aspect of the contractual situation' in the world in Rawls' theory is also accepted by us as being fair, the principles of justice thus agreed upon there should also apply to us.

The contractarian fiction of Rawls' original position appealed to many readers, but the strength of its appeal depends on the lasting credibility of the idea that this narrated world, fictive though it is, appeared to be intrinsic for us. It is the idealistic strength of the normative value of the original position itself that supports the normative validity of the two principles of justice deemed to be derived from it.

However, because such mundane social contract theory does not rely upon the religious conviction of 'a promise previously made,' it has the following kinds of inherent weakness. Firstly, the appeal of social contract theory depends upon its attractiveness as a story, however fictional it may be. In the case of Rawls, it depends upon whether we actually think that his construct, 'choosing principles by means of rational choice, namely, the maximin rule under the veil of ignorance in the original position,' even as a fiction, still represents 'a reasonable way of deciding under conditions of fairness.' If the narrative of the original position is not sufficiently convincing, then the social contractarian theoretical significance will lose its validity.

Secondly, social contract theory is *a priori* and deductive, and so the concrete institutional proposals derived from it will not necessarily be really desirable in our eyes. This is a grave issue that has haunted the social contract theory of Hobbes and Rousseau. Severe criticism from Hayek towards these deductive social theories pointed out its 'constructivist' character, and condemned the idea that normative principles derived from fictive stories have only 'illusory relevance,' and that there is an extremely high danger of them bringing about 'unintended injustices.' In Rawls' case, also, one cannot say that the two justice principles are without such risks.

In actual fact, though Rawls' *A Theory of Justice* received extremely high evaluations from many advocates, at the same time (as I will examine in the latter part of this chapter and in the next) it also came to attract a number of sharp criticisms. These were attacks on the two fragile aspects of social contract theory.

Yet Rawls, with his keen insight, seems to have well apprehended the issues generally attaching to contractarian construction, if not the various points that drew criticism. In Rawlsian theory, the role fulfilled by 'reflective equilibrium' is related to this. Let me explain this next.

Reflective equilibrium

What does 'reflective equilibrium' mean?

No small number of scholars interprets Rawlsian theory as being constructed exclusively of the kind of contractarian logic as discussed above. In actual fact, though, Rawls' *A Theory of Justice* is not constructed in a purely contractarian manner. It is actually more elaborate. Without considering another theoretical logic lying at a more profound level, his theory of justice cannot be well understood. In his theory, the logic of the social contract is nothing more than its outward face. The crucial logic constituting *A Theory of Justice* is 'reflective equilibrium.'

The concept of reflective equilibrium is extremely difficult to comprehend, partly because Rawls himself has not explained it very thoroughly. There are people who understand this simplistically to mean that 'we should derive what is right for society by means of our reflective deliberation.' But if Rawls himself considered that it were possible to derive normative principles through our reflective deliberation, why did he have to set up something as fanciful as the original position? If we can formulate principles of justice only with 'our own reflective deliberation,' such a chimerical story will simply unworthy of examination.

Other theorists regard the role of reflective equilibrium as checking whether the various justice principles derived in the original position match our intuitive moral judgements relating to justice. If that were the case, though, then there would be no necessity to go so far as to use such a term as 'equilibrium.' It would probably have been better to call it something like 'verification by intuitive judgement.'

Another misunderstanding of reflective equilibrium is that it constitutes deliberative and reflective consideration about the appropriateness of the establishment of the original position. But this is not correct, either. The setup of the original position was hypothetical from the very start, and however much one might deliberate reflectively upon it, there would still be a quality of 'supposing, for argument's sake' about it.

What I would like to remind you here is that the contractarian fiction of choice in the original position will forever remain a made-up story. But whoever could fashion this story, and with what qualifications?

Moreover, in case you accept the framework of this story, regarding the ideas of the veil of ignorance and rational choice under that veil as being fundamental in securing the impartiality of the establishment of conditions for the parties, there would still remain broad scope for questions, these being: what is hidden by the veil of ignorance? What kind of choice constitutes rational choice? And, is it appropriate in the first place to appeal to a standard of rationality in the parties' choice? Rawls himself replies to these questions as he explains the original position in detail. But, regardless of the answers to these questions, it cannot be automatically deduced from some postulated presuppositions. Detailed descriptions and explanations of the hypothetical original position had to be supplied, not through an objective, logical deduction, but through various multifaceted considerations, both empirical and theoretical, on the appropriateness of the setting. It is obvious that the people who are envisioning the conditions under which the parties are placed are Rawls himself, and we ourselves who read his work. Nowhere outside of us ('us' including Rawls) does there exist a subject that constructs the original position.

In the scheme in Figure 3.1, Rawls poses the question of whether justice principles chosen in the original position suit 'our considered convictions relating to justice,' stating as follows:

> By going back and forth, sometimes altering the conditions of the contractual circumstances, at others withdrawing our judgements and conforming them to principle, I assume that eventually we shall find a description of the initial situation that both expresses reasonable conditions and yields principles which match our considered judgements duly pruned and adjusted. This state of affairs I refer to as reflective equilibrium (Rawls 1971, p. 20).

Here, Rawls indicates a hidden variable, 'our considered convictions (judgements),' which is not included in Figure 3.1. (The word 'convictions' is also used alternately with 'judgement.')

What, then, do 'considered convictions' and 'considered judgements' signify? Rawls only says that religious intolerance and racial discrimination go against justice. In other words, he simply raises the example of normative judgements that have been established as common sense, but there is no general explanation as to what constitutes considered convictions. This might appear odd at first glance, because it is impossible for us to follow the process leading to reflective equilibrium unless we understand what considered convictions are.

In actual fact, though, the key to apprehending Rawls' 'reflective equilibrium' is shown here. Firstly, the reason why the substance of considered convictions is hardly discussed at all can be understood as there having been no alternative. That is, if one were to cite considered convictions concretely, then that would become a kind of premise. It would contradict what Rawls has in mind, because the substance of 'considered convictions' is by no means what has been specified in advance. A 'considered conviction' is not a 'ready-made conviction.' Surely, it belongs on our side, not to any other transcendental existence. But our considered convictions are expected to change within the process of reflective equilibrium. If they were something fixed, then that would probably be destructive to Rawlsian theory. If so, then there would be absolutely no necessity to take the trouble to conjure up such a fanciful narrative as the original position. In that case, we would need simply to derive justice principles based on the fixed convictions. Rawlsian strategy, though, is not like that.

A little prior to the text cited above, we read that if there are 'discrepancies' between our judgements and the various principles of justice, then '[w]e can either modify the account of the initial situation [(= the original position)] or we can revise our existing judgements' (Rawls 1971, p. 20). In other words, in the process of reflective equilibrium, we may amend our configuration of the original position on the one hand, or change 'our existing judgements,' on the other. Thus Rawls does not see 'our considered judgements' as being fixed. They can be altered in the process leading to reflective equilibrium.

On the other hand, in this process towards reflective equilibrium, it is also possible to revise the configuration of the original position. Because substantive justice principles could be varied according to how the original position is hypothetically set up, then the justice principles thus derived could be incompatible with our existing normative judgements. So, certain adjustments are needed between the configuration of the original position and our normative judgements, until equilibrium is reached. As such, in cases where the derived justice principles do not conform with our normative judgements when we try to match them up, three ways of alteration are possible: improving 'our considered judgements'; amending the 'conditions in the contractual environment'; or changing both. By checking and revising, we seek to make our 'considered judgements' suit our 'principles of justice.' The end-point of such a process is, namely, 'reflective equilibrium.' This can probably be expressed as in Figure 3.3.

A Theory of Justice as reflective equilibrium

Which of the above has to be revised, 'our considered judgements' or 'principles of justice,' and in what case? Rawls is silent on this point. Not only that: there is no description whatsoever of the process of changing one or both, specifically when a mismatch does occur.

At a glance, this seems strange, but in actual fact, as suggested a while back, there is 'no alternative.' This seemingly insufficient argument is due to the theoretical status of 'reflective equilibrium.' 'Reflective equilibrium' is not a mere component within Rawls' theory, but rather is the very process that the Rawlsian theory of justice as a whole is following. In other words, 'reflective equilibrium' is not the process followed by anyone appearing in Rawlsian theory, namely the hypothetical parties in the original position or actual citizens. At the same time, neither is Rawls using the term 'reflective equilibrium' to describe the process followed by general normative theory. Rawls is employing the expression 'reflective equilibrium' precisely in order to describe and explain the pursuit of his own theoretical quest. This can be appreciated from the following passage of his:

> I wish to stress that a theory of justice is precisely that, namely, a theory. It is a theory of the moral sentiments (to recall an eighteenth century title[: Adam Smith's 1759 *The Theory of Moral Sentiments*]) setting out the principles governing our moral powers, or, more specifically, our sense of justice. There is a definite if limited class of facts against which conjectured [justice] principles can be checked, namely, our considered judgments in reflective equilibrium...In any case, it is obviously impossible to develop a substantive theory of justice founded solely on truths of logic and definition. The analysis of moral concepts and the *a priori*, however traditionally understood, is too slender a basis. Moral philosophy must be free to use contingent assumptions and general facts as it pleases. There is no other way to give an account of our considered judgments in reflective equilibrium (Rawls 1971, pp. 50–51).

Figure 3.3: The process of reflective equilibrium

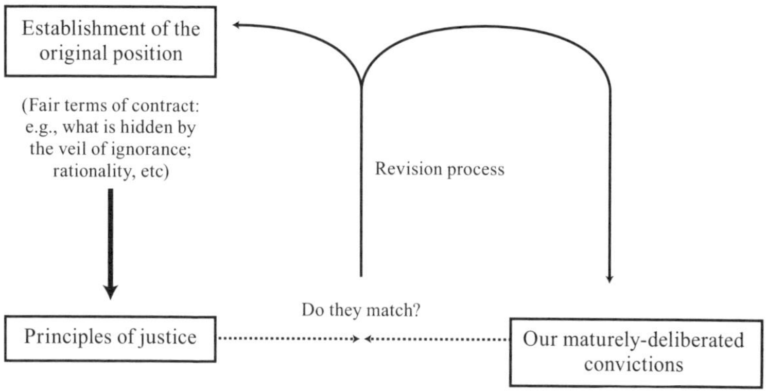

What we need to note is that Rawls differentiates three elements in this passage, namely 'a theory of justice,' 'justice principles' and 'our sense of justice,' and gives to 'reflective equilibrium' the role of mediating them into coherency. Rawls' aim in this work is to develop a theory of justice such as would exhibit the substantive justice principles. Justice principles will govern our sense of justice or our normative judgements. It is impossible, however, to derive justice principles exclusively from any kind of *a priori* moral basis, or conceptual analysis, or seemingly self-evident truths. This is because a theory of justice, if it intends to derive substantive principles instead of just remaining an abstract theory, must take into consideration all empirical facts about society and people, simultaneously making various contingent suppositions. Rawls' hypothetical original position is one example of those contingent suppositions. At the same time, our sense of justice is an independent constituent of a theory of justice, encompassing existing moral concepts and *a priori* beliefs. Each justice principle derived from suppositions on the original position has to be consistent with our sense of justice. When it does not meet our existing convictions, however, it is not only the side of the theoretical structure for deriving each justice principle that is unilaterally revised: our current judgement is also open to amendment. Through this kind of mutual revision, our moral convictions may be said to become 'considered convictions.' 'Reflective equilibrium' is just a term that indicates this process in which a theory of justice crystallises substantive justice principles.

Rawls' own *A Theory of Justice* is also one example of justice theory. Accordingly, 'reflective equilibrium' is the very way that *A*

Theory of Justice has been constructed. Rawls says that reflective equilibrium will by no means achieve a perfect 'philosophical ideal.' In other words, just as is the case with the various theories in empirical science, a justice theory in itself is one that exists as a hypothesis, and so the notion of reflective equilibrium signifies a temporary arrival-point for that hypothesis. That is to say, Rawls' *A Theory of Justice* is a work that presents 'the two principles of justice' as the fruit of such reflective equilibrium, and the major portion of that enormous volume is devoted to an account of the very process that results in reflective equilibrium.

To readers who have been charmed by the social contract theory of the original position, my interpretation of reflexive equilibrium will appear idiosyncratic. In fact, there are many proponents who have agonised in varying ways over the interpretation of reflective equilibrium. Mikio Watanabe, for one, advocates interpreting it not as a binomial relation consisting of 'principles of justice' and 'our moral judgements,' but as a trinomial relationship, with the addition of the 'initial situation' (Watanabe 2000, p. 175). Alternatively, Yasuhiko Itoh understands it as a mediating device between a thought-experiment for rationally deducing justice principles in the original position on one hand, and our existing judgement in an actual, plural-value society, on the other (Itoh 2002, pp. 148–153). Alas, such explanations are flawed in a basic facet. These scholars have interpreted 'reflective equilibrium' as one of the theoretical components within Rawls' *A Theory of Justice*. The reading that I present here, however, is that 'reflective equilibrium' is a process which justice theories in general, including that of Rawls himself, ought to pursue in making adjustments between 'our normative convictions' external to those theories and the theories themselves. This is especially because, if a theory of justice like Rawls' aims to bring about substantive principles of justice, it needs to take into account various factors, not only our pre-existing moral norms or our sense of justice, but also divergent empirical social facts, and the logical appropriateness of the ways by which the theory is constructed. This is the reflexive equilibrium that *A Theory of Justice* itself has followed.

A Theory of Justice as distinct from a contractarian theory

If you understand reflective equilibrium in this way, you will find several points in Rawls' *A Theory of Justice* which hitherto had escaped notice. Firstly, even in that work, Rawls does not rely solely upon contractarian logic, that is, deductive reasoning from the original position. The set-up of the contractarian original position, in his argument, is not given *a priori*: how it is configured, and how to assess its product are also things that are examined within his theory. Contractarian logic comprises no more than one part of the whole of Rawls' theory.

Secondly, *A Theory of Justice* employs two different kinds of argument in regard to the logic of deriving 'principles of justice.' One, it goes without saying, is the argument of social contract theory, which supposes the original position. Here, Rawls asserts that it is precisely those normative principles which the parties rationally choose under conditions of impartiality, namely the veil of ignorance, that constitute principles of justice for us, too. Specifications of the original position are a logical premise for deducing the substantive justice principles. This aspect of Rawlsian argument, therefore, could be marked as a 'foundationalistic' one.

The other is the meta-argument of reflective equilibrium, which is not a mere theoretical component of this book as examined above, but the very theoretical logic followed by *A Theory of Justice* itself. In this argument, both the specifications of the original position and the justice principles that have been temporarily derived from those settings are thrown into the reflective revision process along with pre-existing moral concepts, our current normative convictions, and the like. There is nothing *a priori* in that mix. In reality, what makes up the major part of Rawls' *A Theory of Justice* is a discussion which develops inquiry for the construction of its own theory with critical examinations of utilitarianism, perfectionism and intuitionism. Rawls himself was practising this reflective process.

When, for example, Rawls criticises the utilitarian principle of total utility maximisation, and advocates the difference principle of 'the greatest benefit to the least advantaged,' he does not rely only upon the reasoning that the parties under the veil of ignorance in the original position will make rational choices. If Rawls had followed merely a logic of 'rationality,' then his theory would come to be not cogent with great criticism from Harsanyi and Arrow, as shown in the next section. But even after having received their sharp criticism, Rawls has not revoked his difference principle. This is because, for Rawls, deductive reasoning from the original position is not the crucial logic for the difference principle. What Rawls ultimately bases his argument on is reflective equilibrium between that reasoning and considered moral convictions.

The two meanings of 'justice': justice principles and justice as fairness

Thirdly, with regard to the concepts of 'justice' or 'justice principles,' two divergent meanings should be articulated. One of these is a substantive, normative proposition itself. In Rawls' case, it is presented as two principles: the principle of equal liberty and the principle related to socio-economic equality. It goes without saying that other kinds of normative propositions are always possible. When the expression 'justice principles' is used in Rawls' text, it not only indicates the two principles he presents, but also often signifies other possible normative propositions, as well.

The other aspect is 'justice' when Rawls expresses it in the phrase, 'justice as fairness.' At the beginning of *A Theory of Justice*, we read that 'justice' is 'a normative principle that would fulfil the basic stipulations for fair social cooperation among free and equal persons.' This axiomatic definition of justice is a usage that should be differentiated from the former one. Unlike in the case of his justice principles, this attribution to justice constitutes the starting-point and frame of argumentation of Rawls' quest for a theory of justice. Therefore, this quality of justice is not a subject of his examination. As I showed in the second section of Chapter Two, in *A Theory of Justice*, Rawls first sets out the concept of 'justice as fairness,' then formulates the arguments from which 'principles of justice' can be derived without violating the concept of justice attributed in the first step, and, further, goes on to give evidence to show that this principle is adequate for 'justice as fairness.'

At this juncture, I wish to draw attention to the fact that there are generally two ways of answering the question: 'What is justice?' These correspond to the difference between Rawls' 'justice as fairness' and 'principles of justice.' The 'justice as fairness'-type of answer seeks to address questions such as: 'What is meant by the concept called "justice" in the first place?' 'What kind of social significance does that normative concept have?' 'Why is 'justice' important?' 'Whatever does a theory called a 'theory of justice' investigate?' and so on. These questions we could call 'issues of the functional significance of justice.' Through consideration of what meaning 'justice' has for society, in the sense of how 'justice' should be situated within normative theory, it discusses the theoretical significance (=function) of the 'justice' concept. The part in Rawls' *A Theory of Justice* that discusses 'the theoretical significance of justice' corresponds to this inquiry.

The other type of answer offers substantive principles of justice, and tries to demonstrate that they match the abovementioned functional significance of justice. As these are questions about what kind of normative principle would constitute justice, we can call them 'issues of the constituent concept of justice.' The concrete 'two principles of justice' in *A Theory of Justice* correspond to these.

In Japanese, when the words: '*Seigi to wa nani ka*? (What is meant by justice?)' are used, there is the nuance of asking about the functional significance of justice. On the other hand, when the wording is amended to: '*Nani ga seigi ka*? (What constitutes justice?),' arguably it is more of a question of the constituent concept of justice.

When the question, 'What is justice?' is asked in English, however, the above two nuances cannot be differentiated. Most theorists who have discussed 'justice' hitherto have not made a distinction between them. Though Rawls has not made a particularly clear statement in this regard, he does differentiate between the two by selective use of the expressions 'justice as fairness' and 'justice principles.' This distinction seems extremely important as a way of developing theories of justice, or wider theory relating to normative principles for society. This matter will be taken up again in Chapter Nine, when I examine how the theoretical structure of liberalism is constituted.

As shown below, the notion of reflective equilibrium constitutes the most fundamental structure of Rawlsian theory of justice. Rawls asks about reflexive equilibrium: '[I]s it unique? Even if it is unique, can it be reached?' (1971, p. 50), but adds: 'It would be useless...to speculate about these matters here. They are far beyond our reach' (1971, p. 50). In other words, Rawls himself makes it clear that his justice theory is not perfect, but is in an ever-continuing process of trial and error. Rawls' acknowledgement of the tentative nature of such a theory is a deeply interesting feature of his *A Theory of Justice*. This point, moreover, actually diverges from the general tendency of contemporary liberalism that has been developed since Rawls, as we will see later.

From social contract theory to overlapping consensus

After the publication of *A Theory of Justice*, just as if the prophesy had been self-fulfilling, Rawlsian theory came to follow a developmental route to a new reflective equilibrium. What kind of transformations did Rawls' theory undergo? This is also important to one's appreciation of what *A Theory of Justice* originally meant. One factor that forced a new process of reflective equilibrium upon Rawls was the well-intended but totally unreserved, sharp criticisms directed at *A Theory of Justice* from such people as Arrow (of the Impossibility Theorem), the legal philosopher Hart, and the leading authority in game theory research, John Harsanyi. Out of these, the criticism by Harsanyi was the most severe, levelled at the validity of the maximin rule in the original position, which ultimately prompted the removal of the contractarian composition from Rawlsian theory, while leaving in the original position setup.

Harsanyi's critique

The core of Rawls' theory, seen generally, is the setup of original position in which the parties covered by the veil of ignorance make a rational choice of normative principles of justice according to the maximin rule. However, many scholars have questioned whether this maximin rule is truly rational. The most representative criticism is the 1975 paper by Harsanyi, winner of the Nobel Prize for Economics for his achievements in game theory.

In the early 1960s it had become common sense among game theorists, including Harsanyi, that the maximin rule was inappropriate from the perspectives of both rationality and morality alike. Its defect lies in its complete failure to consider the scale of the probability of the worst-possible situation arising. With the maximin rule, one ought to choose action that avoids 'unfavourable contingencies,' no matter how small the probability of their occurrence may be. Harsanyi claims that this is ridiculous:

> If you took the maximin principle seriously then you could not ever cross a street (after all, you might be hit by a car); you could never drive over a bridge (after all, it might collapse); you could never get married (after all, it might end in a disaster), etc. If anybody really acted this way he would soon end up in a mental institution (Harsanyi 1975: 595).

According to Harsanyi, the principle of maximisation of expected utility is far more rational than the maximin rule in a situation where all kinds of events are equally likely to happen. If one acts according to the principle of maximisation of expected utility, one should calculate for each action the sum of the products of the utility of each event which would follow that action and their probabilities of occurrence. This yields the average of utilities multiplied by the probabilities of events which follow the action one chooses, and is called 'expected utility.' Then one selects the action that has the maximal expected utility. If one expresses the maximin rule by this formulation, it will mean 'assigning probability one to phenomena with minimum utility,' and zero to others. Harsanyi sees that as irrational. There may be some who think: 'If one does not know the probability of something happening, then would it not be better to assume the worst-case scenario?' But if indeed the likelihood were unknown, then it would be rational to presume an 'equal probability' vis-à-vis different phenomena. (Furthermore, in real life, we often act after having calculated the probability of phenomena occurring, rough though that calculation may be. We assume that the likelihood of us being hit by a car or of a bridge collapsing is extremely small.)

If we reconsider the parties' choice in the original position with Harsany's rationale, the result is as follows: because the parties do not know in what circumstances they are placed in actual society, but because they *do* know in what ways people exist in the world in what kinds of circumstances, they may as well think that they have been granted equal probability of being any one of those people. Accordingly, the justice principles the parties should choose are those that would maximise the utility of all people, averaged out with the same weight (this is also 'expected utility'). Harsanyi proved mathematically that this, under certain conditions, matches the principles of utilitarianism.[1]

For Rawls, the criticisms of Harsanyi and others were a serious matter. The maximin rule employed in his theory as a cutting-edge technique ended up being condemned by the very developer of the technique as something already useless and old-fashioned.

From rationality to reasonableness

Still, Rawls was not discouraged. In fact, the role of the maximin rule had been secondary in his original theoretical structure. That will be well understood if one reads a 1958 paper of his, written when he was younger. In it, two principles of justice almost identical in substance to those in *A Theory of Justice* had already been presented, but no mention at all was made of the maximin rule. Basically, what was used was the idea of 'normative principles for fair social cooperation for free and equal citizens,' which I introduced in Chapter Two.

In response to the criticisms from Harsanyi and others, though, Rawls seems to have recognised it as necessary to change his theory to some extent. That process also coincided with a new shift in the problem situation itself which Rawls' theory was attempting to address. This was a shift from the issue of inequalities in social strata in the 1960s to the multicultural situation that became marked from the 1970s onwards.

The 1993 work, *Political Liberalism*, represents Rawls' attempt at responding to the multicultural situation. This situation no longer comprises a contrast between 'the haves' and 'the have-nots.' It is now a difference among 'comprehensive doctrines' for people living under disparate faiths and cultures. Accordingly, 'justice principles' come to mean 'normative principles for fair social cooperation for people with differing faiths and cultures.' The functional significance of 'justice' here is essentially identical to that in *A Theory of Justice*. And its substance, that is, the constituent concept of justice, is basically identical, too. There are a few subtle changes, but the 'two principles of justice' introduced in my Chapter Two are also cited in *Political Liberalism*.

What is greatly divergent is the method of theorisation for deriving concrete justice principles (justice derivation logic). The notions of the original position and the veil of ignorance are left, but they no longer fulfil a central role. The maximin rule has vanished altogether. The thing which is used instead is 'overlapping consensus' among 'comprehensive doctrines,' and 'public reason' for making that possible.

Rawls' 2001 *Justice as Fairness: A Restatement* is a work which deserves to be called a revised edition of *A Theory of Justice*, it having newly reorganised—from a perspective achieved after the 1990s—the main theoretical mechanism in *A Theory of Justice* that was not adequately re-examined in *Political Liberalism*. In it, the comparatively clear-cut formulations of the original position, the veil of ignorance and reflective equilibrium are presented once more. But they have already turned into nothing more than metaphors simply for setting up an impartial viewpoint, rather than as constituents of a contractarian narrative.

> [The original position] is a device of representation modeling reasonable constraints that limit the reasons that the parties as rational representatives may appeal to...[T]he veil of ignorance removes differences in bargaining advantages, so that in this and other respects

> the parties are symmetrically situated. Citizens are represented solely as free and equal persons...[T]he original position respects the basic precept of formal equality (Rawls 2001, pp. 86–87).

In the original position such remodelled, the argument that concretely deduces justice principles is not a rational choice in narrow sense of maximising utility, but a consensus based on the operation of the parties' public reason.

It is true that in his 2001 version, Rawls makes slight mention of the maximin rule, but its significance is explained in a footnote with reference to Harsanyi (1976, p. 39), as follows:

> [T]he maximin rule was never proposed as the general principle of rational decision in all cases of risk and uncertainty...The only question is whether, given the highly special, indeed unique, conditions of the original position, the maximin rule is a useful heuristic rule of thumb for the parties to use to organise their deliberations' (Rawls 2001, p. 97, n. 19).

In this way, the Rawls of *Political Liberalism* (1993) himself dismantles the very root section of the theoretical mechanism he provided in *A Theory of Justice*. That root is the part which I dubbed the 'justice derivation logic' in Chapter Two—the original position, the veil of ignorance, the parties, rational choice, and the maximin rule: the notions that had attracted wide scrutiny are entirely erased in his later theory.

The probable reason why Rawls was able to dismantle this highly controversial portion must be that he considered it would not alter the essential piece of his own theoretical construction. The very foundation of his theory was the part that I termed 'the theoretical significance of justice,' which is the thesis of 'justice as a fundamental normative principle for social cooperation in a fair, well-ordered society' established as his theme of enquiry. This is the part where fundamental ideas about what basic normative principles for society (justice) mean, and what qualities these should have, were developed. This is Rawls' response to the question of 'what is justice?' as a more generally functional notion.

In contrast to this, the part which Rawls amended was that which answered questions as to how to derive normative propositions substantively, and what constituted an impartial perspective. Rawls ceased to use a contractarian structure in relation to this section, amending it to a theoretical structure that appealed to the 'reasonableness' of actual people, not of hypothetical parties.

People's being 'reasonable' means that they think things over and make judgements by the power of 'reason.' Reason is the ability to think reasonably, with which people are assumed universally to be equipped. Rawls' explanation of this concept goes round in circles, but that, too, cannot be helped, because it is a conceptual existence, assumed to exist in the anticipation that people's thinking will indeed be 'reasonable.' This, too, can be called a fiction, but surely it is more realistic than social contract theory.

Such a change in argument by Rawls may be construed as the result of his directly having come to exercise the logic of reflective equilibrium, after basically discarding the initial contractarian fiction.

Chapter 4

What is the 'Difference Principle'? Rawls' Notion of Equality

Contemporary liberalism, unlike classical liberalism, is tinged with an extremely strong egalitarianism. This originates in the fact that the political camp termed 'liberal' in US society after the New Deal of the 1930s has emphasised the value of social equality, namely the overall reduction of class and racial differences, through such measures as government intervention and regulation of economic activity, guarantee of the livelihood and rights of workers, as well as the acquisition of citizenship and raising of the status of black people. However, this egalitarian orientation has long been unformulated as a comprehensive theory. Rawls' 1971 *A Theory of Justice* is the first work to crystallise this liberal tradition. Through its publication, contemporary liberalism clearly consolidated its position as a 'new egalitarian theory.'

Rawls' egalitarianism has as its core the 'difference principle,' which constitutes one portion of his principles of justice. This difference principle has already been introduced in Chapter Two. But Rawls' description is extremely brief and quite ambiguous. Of course, Rawls devotes a considerable proportion of *A Theory of Justice* to developing his account of this principle, but its ambiguity is still not sufficiently resolved. For that reason, things that Rawls has not said are sometimes introduced to the world at large as his 'difference principle.' This chapter intends to present a correct interpretation of Rawls' difference principle, and make clear what his theory of equality comprised.

The challenges of egalitarianism

The collapse of socialism

Around when would equality have started to make its appearance as one of the tenets of human society? Thucydides' *History* gives a detailed account of the fundamental conflict between the group of democratic states centring on Athens and the group of aristocratic states led by Sparta in the age of the Peloponnesian War in ancient Greece, and other mortal combat even within each polis between those championing the commoners and the nobility respectively. Yet, as in either case it was self-evident that nobody challenged the institution of slavery, their ethos of equality greatly differed from that in its present-day sense. In his *Politics*, Aristotle refers to such a situation of conflict as rooted in the opposition between the assertion that those who are unequal in terms of wealth ought to be treated unequally in the political arena, and, conversely, the assertion that, in regard to freedom, those who are equal should be treated equally. Aristotle sees the conflict of opinion over how equality in one sphere should be linked to equality in other segments as the root cause of political chaos in ancient Greece. Judging from this, the question of what kind of equality we ought to seek for a good society had already gained importance in those times.

But the age in which the notion of equality was distinctly presented in an unmistakeable form was the Age of Enlightenment, centred round Rousseau in the eighteenth century. Via the independence of the American nation and the French Revolution, the idea of 'natural equality' formulated in Rousseau's writings went on to become a fundamental element in the constitution of modern nation-states. Moreover, by means of such ideologies as Marxism and socialism, an egalitarianism relating to socio-economic aspects was strongly advocated; and in reality, also, egalitarian social policies steadily went on to be extensively implemented. That has been the underlying trend of social change in the modern age.

Throughout the twentieth century, it was socialist thought that was most intimately associated with egalitarianism. It is a theory that endeavours to achieve equality of distribution among people through the nationalisation of industry and a planned economy. This theory regarded economic activity in a free market as being carried out in a haphazard manner, based on selfish motivations under a system of private ownership, causing differences in people's standard of living. In order to resolve serious problems such as inequality and poverty, socialist theory asserted that economic structure should be radically restructured.

Nowadays, this socialist ideology has largely lost its attraction. On the surface, this has been due to the collapse of the Soviet Union, the prosperity of contrasting market-economy societies, and so on, but one must think that, more fundamentally, the theory itself was flawed. (In this volume, I will omit commentary on this point.)

Here, one must avoid a misapprehension—the collapse of socialist ideology and its mistakes do not necessarily signify the mistakes of egalitarianism itself. Socialism is a philosophy that advocates socialist economics as a means to achieve equality. Though it is true that socialist economics is the wrong way to achieve equality, it does not follow that its objective of achieving equality is wrong in itself.

Present-day egalitarianism is not necessarily advocated in connection with socialism. Rather, it stands in marked contrast to one-time socialism on the following point. While socialism was a theory that stressed the practicalities of how to achieve equality, tending to make light of the issue of *why equality is important*, current-day discussion of egalitarianism conversely concentrates upon why equality is an important value, and what kind of equality is important.

Why 'equality?

So, what sort of answer does egalitarianism give to the fundamental question: 'Why equality?' In his 1755 *Le Discours sur l'Origine et les Fondements de l'Inégalité parmi les Hommes* (Discourse on the origin and basis of inequality among men), Rousseau discusses egalitarianism by assuming a primitive situation, or the 'state of nature,' in which people were equal in politico-social terms, saying that this was the true human form, and further explaining that all kinds of inequalities came into existence amid the process of civilisation, which constituted a fall from that natural state. The idea of the 'state of nature as something intrinsic' is at the root of Rousseau's egalitarianism. And, diverging somewhat from in the case of his *Du Contrat Social* (The social contract), here the state of nature is understood not as hypothetical, but as a primitive situation that actually existed historically. This point is followed in historical materialism, in works including *The Communist Manifesto* by Marx and Engels.

For Rousseau, 'nature' is another name for a transcendental perspective which, being counterposed to reality, could criticise reality and relativise it. It by no means constitutes nature as is, but always 'nature as an idea.' Nobody has ever actually seen it, yet it is represented as something that radiates intense normative implications.

Nature as an idea is the most promising of bases for a norm in modern times. The notion of people being 'innately equal' means that they are born with it, their equality being a kind of 'natural thing' which is simultaneously 'intrinsic.' In short, if something is 'natural,' then it follows that there will be a sense of it somehow being 'original' or 'inherent.' As such, to appeal to a notional 'nature' means to presuppose 'nature' as a kind of ultimate grounds which one neither is able to, nor needs to, trace back any further.

Thus, the United States' Declaration of Independence contained the words, 'the equal station to which the Laws of Nature and of Nature's God entitle them' and 'all men are created equal,' while in the French Revolution's Declaration of the Rights of Man, it was loudly trumpeted that '[m]en are born and remain free and equal in rights.'

It goes without saying that this idea remains current in our society, even today. In school education, legal judgements and the like, 'inherent equality' is frequently mentioned. Yet as far as academic social theory is concerned, caution is now exercised vis-à-vis the seeking of normative grounds in the kind of 'nature' that, as in Rousseau's day, was unreservedly presented as being 'natural.' Nowadays, it is more common for such a move to be criticised as being 'essentialist.' It is seen as inappropriate to discuss some matter by using the argument that the differences between male and female, for example, are inborn. Accordingly, though both the notion of 'innate equality' and its value as an idea are acknowledged, it is not possible to rely upon either of these as theoretical grounds for equality. Of course, this does not mean that the conception of 'nature' has ceased to be represented as a source of value: 'nature' still frequently plays a major role in discussions of environmental issues, individual ways of life, and so on. Once it has been mounted on the chopping board of theoretical contemplation, however, its theoretical power becomes questionable. The notion of 'inherent equality' by itself is insufficient to form a basis for egalitarianism.

Nevertheless, irrespective of how the theory goes, modern society has in reality promoted equalisation in a great many of its aspects. In particular, the abolition of the pre-modern type of class- (*mibun* in Japanese) system and establishment of an education system open to all, as a general rule, has given broad opportunity to young people with ambition and ability, though contingent upon a certain level of financial resources. In Japan, in the early years of the Meiji Era (1868–1912), much read were volumes based on utilitarian liberalism, such as Yukichi Fukuzawa's 1876 *Gakumon no susume* (An encouragement of learning) and Rousseau's *Du Contrat Social*, published in translation in 1877 as *Min'yakuron*.

Of parallel import to the question of the *reason for equality*: 'Why equality?' is the question of the *objectives of equality*: 'What kind of equality?' In the latter case, these have long been largely divided into 'equality of outcome' and 'equality of opportunity.' 'Equality of opportunity' is generally understood to mean that social status is widely open to everyone, though conditional upon academic achievement and qualifications. 'Opportunity' is a concept premised upon the existence of competition. In a marathon, everyone starting together at the same time from the same place constitutes equality of opportunity. It does not also mean 'equality of outcome'—making the time that everyone reaches the finish line the same. That is why the great point of contention in equality theory is whether to aim for equality of opportunity as the objective of equality, or to go so far as to strive towards equality of outcome, as well. And what kind of equality of outcome should be the goal?

Deeply connected with this issue is the question of the market, and governmental intervention into and regulation of it. In modern society, markets have developed in a variety of domains. The market basically is an arena where people all mutually compete with the aim of achieving a good life for themselves, even while entering into agreements; or cooperating with each other; or engaging in friendly rivalry. Markets exist and competition happens in all kinds of areas—there are financial markets, of course, but also markets dealing in educational backgrounds, career advancement, the academic world, sports, the arts and entertainment. The important values which support the institution known as the market include 'freedom,' 'equality of opportunity' and 'fairness in competition.' Equality of outcome, however, is considered unrelated to the market, or rather stands in opposition to it. In fact, because competition only becomes competition when a disparity arises in the outcome, if the market is an arena for competition, then it will directly conflict with equality of outcome.

Of course, the market is not almighty. It goes without saying that social conditions derived according to the market are not necessarily desirable. With the market alone, it is impossible, for a start, to banish poverty, to secure people's health and safety, and to guarantee all persons the opportunity to 'aim for the achievement of what, for each, is a good life.' It would not do for us to disparage equality of outcome just because it went against the competitive market.

Fundamentally, the question of the reason for equality is inextricably linked to the question of what kind of equality is meant, namely the objective of equality. The explanation of the reason *why* something should be made equal is, at the same time, something that supplies an answer to the question of *what* should be made equal, and the opposite also can be said. Contemporary liberalism endeavours to reply to such questions.

Interpretations and critiques of the difference principle

The difference principle

The contemporary lively debates on equality were triggered by the difference principle in Rawls' *A Theory of Justice*. The Rawlsian difference principle was accepted as the newest, up-to-date theory since Rousseau regarding the reason for equality, in other words, why equality should be a desirable value.

As I introduced in Chapter Two, the principles of justice which Rawls presented consist of two principles. In the first, 'an equal right to the most extensive basic liberty compatible with a similar liberty for others' (Rawls 1971, p. 60) is stipulated. In other words, it asserts that fundamental freedoms for people are equal, and that the right to enjoy them ought to be an equally-shared possession. This constitutes the first pillar of the objective of equality in Rawls. Here, what Rawls regards as 'basic liberties' are political freedom, freedom of speech and association, freedom of conscience and thought, freedom of person (liberty from physical oppression and coercion), individual property rights, and freedom from arbitrary arrest. Nowadays, these refer to political and civil liberties with which everyone is well acquainted, and the idea that people are equal in relation to these is one that may be considered to mean that people similarly have these freedoms as their right. British social theorist T.H. Marshall identifies three elements of freedom (or, as he terms it, 'citizenship'): 'civil (legal)', 'political' and 'social' equality (Marshall and Bottomore 1992), and Rawls' first principle corresponds to the first two of these. These liberties are seen as one of the most important values in the majority of contemporary states, and no one disagrees in principle.

The topic of Rawls' second principle is 'social and economic inequalities.' There, beginning with the words: 'social and economic inequalities are to be arranged so that…,' two conditions which would allow the existence of 'social and economic inequalities' are stated.

The first condition, (a), embodies the difference principle, saying: 'the greatest benefit to the least advantaged.' Here, what is especially brought to mind by use of the word 'benefit' is the ability to enjoy 'primary goods.' Primary goods are defined by Rawls as 'rights and liberties, powers and opportunities, income and wealth' (1971, p. 62).

The second condition, (b), insists upon 'equality of fair opportunity.' The drift of (b) may be understood as being that, though various socio-economic inequalities might result from guaranteeing equality of opportunity, as long as the consequent inequalities are an unavoidable side-effect of equality of opportunity, then equality of opportunity should be afforded priority. In actual fact, the concept of 'opportunity,' as I stated previously, is one that originally implies some kind of competitive market and some sort of inequality as a result of competition.

In either case, 'primary social goods' comprised Rawls' reply to the question of equality's objectives, namely 'What kind of equality?'

Of the above, the first principle and (b) of the second principle are normative principles widely accepted as being reasonable in the eyes of people of today. For that reason, there is little discussion about their content. By contrast, the egalitarianism that can be seen in the difference principle of (a) has stirred up all kinds of debate. This is due to there being too much ambiguity in the meaning of the difference principle as blandly described in the text as simply 'the greatest benefit to the least advantaged.' For that reason, the difference principle was interpreted by commentators as they pleased, and it came to be discussed from varying angles, both affirmatively and negatively.

Several main criticisms

Here, too, Harsanyi, who had criticised the maximin rule, was the leader in setting out a critical argument against Rawls' difference principle, which he considered to be asserting that the interests of the least advantaged individuals in society 'absolutely must be prioritised.' Giving two hypothetical examples, Harsanyi argued that the difference principle would lead to an irrational conclusion. The first example concerned two people who had contracted pneumonia—one originally in good health, the other suffering from incurable cancer—the question being which of them should be given an antibiotic of which there was only enough for one person. The other example was the question of whether limited educational resources should be directed at someone who had the potential to become a really superb mathematician, or at someone whose intellectual development was retarded. Harsanyi answered that if the difference principle were followed, then we would have to give the antibiotic to the person with terminal cancer, and direct the educational resources to the person who was developmentally retarded. These actions he criticised as being morally unjustifiable (Harsanyi 1976).

Another promising critic was Arrow, known for his impossibility theorem. While making an issue of the application of the maximin rule as a standard for rational choice, as did Harsanyi in Chapter Three, Arrow, too, criticised Rawlsian theory as having no reason for being deemed superior to utilitarianism; and he particularly suspected that the difference principle would mean 'asset egalitarianism.' In other words, Arrow asserted that the difference principle implies 'that all the assets of society, including personal skills, are available as a common pool for whatever distribution justice calls for' (1973, p. 248), imposing a one hundred percent tax upon income over a certain fixed level, which, of course, would generate the question of production incentives.

Arrow's criticism comes from his interpretation of the difference principle as implying that it equates to asset egalitarianism. Later, I examine whether Arrow's interpretation is correct. In any case, there is no small number of people who took it in the same way as Arrow.

The sociologist J.S. Coleman, for instance, is among them. Coleman was the author of the 1966 *Coleman Report*, which was a pioneering empirical work on the structure of inter-racial educational inequalities in American society. (Until then, in America, it had mostly been sociologists that discussed theories of equality.) He was quick to take note of the importance of Rawls' *A Theory of Justice*, writing a book review in the *American Journal of Sociology* soon after its publication in which he severely criticised (what was interpreted as being) the extreme egalitarianism of its difference principle. Even in a volume penned in his later years, entitled *Foundations of Social Theory*, Coleman states as follows:

> [A]s several authors have pointed out, Rawls' second principle implies eliminating the inequalities imposed by the family, which implies that the state has the right to take children from parents at or near birth (1990, p. 335).

In other words, he regards the difference principle as implying 'the equalisation of all input resources for educational opportunity.' Let me introduce a critique by another scholar, from Japan. Tatsuo Inoue, the representative advocate of liberalism in today's Japan, gives the conception of *A Theory of Justice* a high assessment overall, yet in regard to the difference principle, which he understands as something that 'in principle, permits unlimited exploitation of the high for the sake of minutely increasing benefits to the low' (Inoue 1986, p. 53), he expresses doubts as to whether ultimately it can be justified. Here, Inoue takes the words 'the greatest benefit to the least advantaged' to mean 'other people's benefits should be redistributed until there is no longer any person with the least benefit.'

Diverse interpretations of the difference principle

A certain proportion of such criticism hit the mark, but a considerable amount is based on a misapprehension. Indeed, one might say that the greater part of the responsibility for having been misunderstood lies mainly with Rawls himself. Of course, even in *A Theory of Justice*, he was strongly aware of the fact that it was the difference principle which comprised the core of his own theory of justice, and, moreover, that it was a supremely controversial assertion. For that reason, he has developed various arguments for defending that principle, but they have not been sufficiently organised, and in light of his amount of discussion, he has often written in an ambiguous manner regarding whatever sort of equality constitutes the equality signified by the difference principle.

Oddly, though, other advocates who have debated the difference principle also naturally ought to have noticed that they are basing their various discussions on mutually different interpretations; and, if so, there should have been various opportunities for them to discuss more thematically as to what said difference principle means, but such attempts have been entirely absent. Rawls himself, while knowing that fact, does not display much of a spirit of service in terms of willingness to explain.

So, what kinds of diverse interpretations are there? These can broadly be divided into the following three categories:

1. Prioritised distribution to the least-advantaged

This is the interpretation upon which the aforementioned Harsanyi relied when he argued against the difference principle, which is understood to be a principle that requires us, in allocating goods, to give priority to people identified as worst-off in a situation where a distribution issue has arisen. This can be formulated in the following manner: first, a distinction has been made in advance between people known to be 'the least advantaged' and those who are not. If the former is expressed as D, and the latter as C, and if the respective initial standard of benefit is expressed as u_D and u_C, then $u_D < u_C$. Assume, then, that Δu_D and Δu_C exist as additional allocations of benefit. At this time, we interpret the difference principle as making the normative assertion that Δu_D should be greater than Δu_C. There are few advocates of this view, however.

2. The maximin-type interpretation.

The overwhelming proportion of proponents understands the difference principle to mean a maximin-type choice among differing social states, interpreting the difference principle as a normative rule for the problem of social choice from among multiple social states. According to their interpretation, it is necessary to compare the level of benefit of the least-advantaged under each social state, and select the one which would yield the highest level of benefit for the worst-off. This is the understanding shared by the majority, which Yutaka Saeki in Japan explained in his 1980 book, *'Kimekata' no ronri* (The logic of 'decision-making'), and which has also been adopted by most of the Western advocates introduced in that volume. There is also a detailed introduction of it in Reiko Gotō's 2002 *Seigi no keizai tetsugaku: Rōruzu to Sen* (The economic philosophy of justice: Rawls and Sen). It means that if, for instance, there is one society with perfect free competition and another that is a welfare society, and we assume the income of the most poverty-stricken member of the former to be one million yen, but that of the latter to be two million yen, then we should choose the welfare society of the latter.

This interpretation can be formulated as in the following. Say there are social states $x, y, z, \ldots$, and $x_i, y_i, z_i, \ldots$ represent the benefit which individual i enjoys in each. There are fluctuations in people's benefit within each of the various social states, but we have the individual who receives but the smallest benefit among them represented by $i^*_x, i^*_y, i^*_z, \ldots$, and the respective benefit (least benefit) represented by $u^*_x, u^*_y, u^*_z, \ldots$. What is expressed by u^* is the smallest (minimum) benefit in each society. Then, we compare those minimum benefits $u^*_x, u^*_y, u^*_z, \ldots$ among the different societies, and find the one among them that takes on the largest value. Let us assume, for example, that it is u^*_y. In short:

$$u^*_y \geq u^*_x, u^*_z, \ldots$$

Table 4.1 The maximin interpretation of the Difference Principle

Social state	Individuals and their respective advantage					
	1	2	3	...	Least-advantaged	Least benefit
x	x_1	x_2	x_3	...	i^*_x	$u^*_x = u(i^*_x)$
y	y_1	y_2	y_3	...	i^*_y	$u^*_y = u(i^*_y)$
z	z_1	z_2	z_3	...	i^*_z	$u^*_z = u(i^*_z)$
⋮		...			⋮	⋮

So, we understand the difference principle to be asserting that we should choose the social state *y* in which the value of the least benefit is the highest.

3. Perfect egalitarianism

There are also more than a few people who take the difference principle as substantively advocating perfect egalitarianism. (The above 1 and 2 are not perfect egalitarianism, as differences in benefit can remain among people.) Among the criticisms introduced above, it is those of Arrow, Coleman and Inoue that fit this classification.

Even just counting the main ones, there are this many divergent interpretations of the difference principle. Moreover, each of them asserts that 'the difference principle is such-and-such,' and using this as a basis to discuss Rawlsian theory. The emergence of multiple interpretations of an idea which was so salient a focus of attention from a great many people might be inevitable. Still, it is a mystery why nobody has yet made an issue of the fact that the different interpretations have each gone their independent way.

Below, while clarifying what the difference principle really means, I wish to address the question of the ultimate validity of each of these interpretations. That will mean resolving what sort of thing Rawls' egalitarianism actually is.

What Rawls intended by the difference principle

Mistaken interpretations of maximin

Harsanyi's version, in 1 above, signifies that he takes the difference principle as being 'a principle that stipulates the method of distribution when there is an additional allocation of assets.' This interpretation is one that has simply understood the phrase 'the greatest benefit to the least advantaged' just as if it were a rule relating to how to distribute Christmas presents collected through a charity drive, and to whom. In other words, as this relies solely upon the ambiguous, brief phrase itself (the 'difference principle'), all explanation regarding the difference principle and the very theory of justice which Rawls develops throughout *A Theory of Justice* is completely ignored. As I emphasised in Chapter Two, justice for Rawls meant something that constitutes a fair condition for encouraging people to participate in social cooperation, and in that situation, the focal point is how to divide up the benefits that accrue from social cooperation. Accordingly, in a case that considered a person with superior mathematical potential and a person with an intellectual disability, for example, what is at issue is how to put the former's gift of potential to use so that it would be to the advantage of all people in that society, including the latter. It is not, as Harsanyi imagined, merely a question of how to direct educational resources supplied from the exterior. Rawls' question is not merely about what sort of educational resources should be directed to what kind of people, but also how the various benefits which are individually or socially generated as a result of that resource allocation ought to be distributed. Here, any supplementary goods are not assumed to be granted from the outside. What is at issue is the mechanism of cooperation in the whole of society which could produce goods to be distributed. Harsanyi's interpretation, it must be said, is too simplistic a reading that overlooks such social cooperation.

The problem is the maximin interpretation of 2, above. An overwhelming number of proponents understand the difference principle in this sense, and all of the expository texts on Rawls are dominated by this understanding. Yet this interpretation is clearly mistaken. Most advocates conflate the fact that the maximin rule was employed in the logic by which justice principles are derived in the original position (justice derivation logic) with the question of whether the substance of the difference principle comprising part of the principles of justice is an application of the maximin rule. That is confusing things on different levels, just as if one were to think that, seeing as the president of a state is chosen by democratic voting, that president's individual policy decisions are also determined by democratic ballot. Formally speaking, the rules for choosing the norm called X and the substance of X are seen to be identical.

In actuality, when all is said and done, Rawls himself has realised that such a misunderstanding could arise, and time after time states clearly that it would be a mistake.

Firstly, the following passage can be found in *A Theory of Justice*:

> Economics may wish to refer to the difference principle as the maximin criterion, but I have carefully avoided this term for several reasons. The maximin criterion is generally understood as a rule for choice under great uncertainty, whereas the difference principle is a principle of justice. It is undesirable to use the same name for two things that are so distinct (Rawls 1971, p. 72).

In this text, emphasis is placed on the point that the difference principle is not a rule for choice, but a principle of justice, and by that, it is indirectly stated that 'it is not a rule for choice called the maximin.' But as this may still be insufficient, let me also add other evidence.

The original form of the difference principle is expressed as follows in an early paper by Rawls which predated *A Theory of Justice*, 'Constitutional liberty and the concept of justice' (1963): '[I]nequalities as defined by the institutional structure or fostered by it are arbitrary unless it is reasonable to expect that they will work out to everyone's advantage' (cited in Rawls 1999b, p. 75). Here, it can be seen that the wording is 'to everyone's advantage,' not 'the greatest benefit to the least advantaged.' With the former expression, there is nothing at all to suggest the maximin rule. As the formulation in *A Theory of Justice* can be understood as having made more definitive and specific the concept expressed here as 'everyone's advantage,' the idea of the difference principle can be seen as originally not having been anything which suggested that 'the kind of social state where the least benefit would become the maximum is desirable.'

What requires attention here is the difference between the 'least advantaged' in Rawls' difference principle, and the maximin interpretation of the 'least advantaged' in the various social situations depicted in Table 4.1. The maximin interpretation understands the former in the sense of the latter, but that is not a correct reading of Rawls. This is clear from the following explanation by the man himself.

Rawls' explanation

In the thirteenth section of *A Theory of Justice*, Rawls explains the difference principle in the following way, while referring to his own Figure 6 (my Figure 4.1).

> Suppose that x_1 is the most favoured representative man in the basic structure. As his expectations are increased so are the prospects of x_2, the least advantaged man. In figure 6 let the curve OP represent the contribution to x_2's expectations made by the greater expectations of x_1…Clearly the difference principle is perfectly satisfied only when the OP curve is just tangent to the highest indifference curve that it touches. In figure 6 this is at the point a (Rawls 1971, p. 76).

In this figure, the horizontal axis x_1 indicates the most advantaged person's benefit, and the vertical axis x_2 the least advantaged person's benefit. The forty-five degree line shows a condition in which the expectations of both are equal, in short, a condition of perfect equality. The horizontal lines drawn in the right-hand half, which Rawls calls the 'indifference curve,' show that the higher up the line, the greater will be the benefit of the least favoured person, x_2, while on the same line there is no difference.

Rawls basically uses the same figure in his explanation of the difference principle in his 2001 *Justice as Fairness: A Restatement*. Accordingly, my Figure 4.1 expresses a fundamental idea about the difference principle which has not changed even after thirty years. The following fact is clear from this:

The things with which Rawls concerns himself are not moment-by-moment social situation, but long-term 'institutional structure.' This also can be deduced from the fact that justice principles are normative principles for the basic structure of society, but it is also shown by the way Figure 4.1 is drawn. The curve OP is a type of production-possibility frontier. The kind of basic structure one selects determines what place on curve OP will materialise, how much benefit will be generated through social cooperation, and how that will be distributed.

What Rawls questioned at this time was nothing other than the issue of poverty and social stratification (social class) which hitherto had been

Figure 4.1: The greatest benefit to the least advantaged

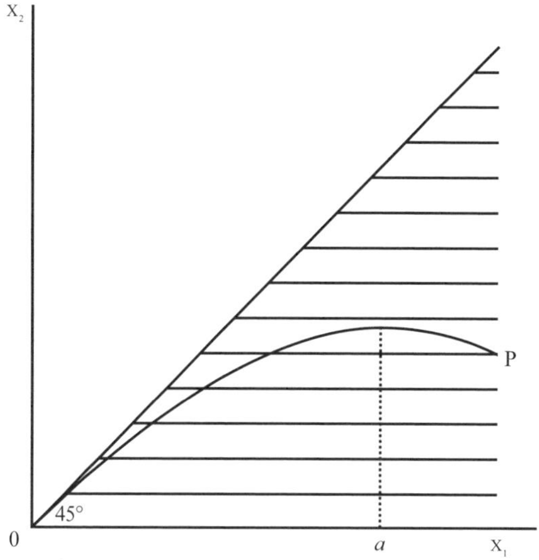

Source: Rawls 1971, p. 76

the focal point whenever inequality was discussed in social theory. This is clear from the fact that, a little after the aforementioned figure, Rawls explains as follows, using the examples of the 'entrepreneurial class' and 'class of unskilled workers.'

> According to the difference principle, it is justifiable only if the difference in expectation is to the advantage of the representative man who is worse off, in this case the representative unskilled worker. The inequality in expectation is permissible only if lowering it would make the working class even more worse off (Rawls 1971, p. 78).

Here, it can be understood that Rawls is citing the unskilled worker as an example of 'the least-favoured person.' In another part, it is written that 'those with fewer native assets and...those born into the less favourable social positions' constitute 'the least advantaged group' (Rawls 1971, p. 100). Such people are those who, in other words, are placed in the most disadvantageous position in a market-competitive society. In its most general sense, that also corresponds to the concept of 'the lower classes' in a capitalist society.

That 'the least advantaged people' in terms of the difference principle are those who are placed in a disadvantageous position in a free society based upon a market economy means that they are not the 'least favoured' in the sense of Table 4.1. And that is incompatible with the maximin interpretation of the difference principle.

The maximin rule as a heuristic device

The maximin interpretation can be considered a misreading that occurred when a forcible attempt was made to formulate Rawlsian theory with a social choice theory framework. Social choice theory is a research field that flourished on the impetus of Arrow's impossibility theorem. Its object of consideration is the theory of choosing what is desirable from among differing social states which have been abstractly conceived. Though I say social states, the sole focus there is upon the aspect of what sort of utility (payoff) people can obtain, its institutional substance being made entirely abstract. Similarly, people simply have an order in which they rank different social states according to the amount of utility which each yields them, irrespective of concrete matters such as to what social stratum they belong or what abilities they possess. As in game theory, one examines in an extremely abstract framework what kind of theory can be constructed vis-à-vis which should be chosen out of given alternatives. The maximin rule was devised as one of the theories of choice within such an abstract framework in game theory.

By contrast, what Rawls is attempting to examine in *A Theory of Justice* is not a theory of choice among abstract social states, but normative principles that should be applied to the basic structure of society. Amid these, it is the difference principle that describes the concrete normative principles relating to the conditions of social and economic inequalities. To start with, Rawls' theory is built using a completely different standard from social choice theory and game theory.

So, finally, let me state precisely how the 'maximin rule' is used in Rawlsian theory. In this volume, up to this point, my explanation has suggested that it is written in *A Theory of Justice* that the parties' choice of principles in the original position is carried out according to the maximin rule, but this is actually quite a simplified description. Precisely speaking, Rawls' mention of the 'maximin rule' in his accounts of the two principles is exceedingly patchy. It begins with the following text:

> *It seems clear from these remarks* that the two principles are at least a plausible conception of justice. The question, though, is how one is to argue for them more systematically. Now there are several things to do. One can work out their consequences for institutions and note their implications for fundamental social policy. In this way they are tested *by a comparison with our considered judgments* of justice. Part II is devoted to this. But one can also try to find arguments in their favour that are decisive from the standpoint of the original position. In order to see how this might be done, it is useful *as a heuristic device* to think of the two principles as the maximin solution to the problem of social justice (Rawls 1971, p. 152. Emphasis added).

This quote very distinctly describes the overall composition of Rawls' theory and the role of the maximin rule within it. First of all, for Rawls, even without bringing out the maximin rule, the two principles of justice are fundamentally defensible. Two streams of thought are present there. One is the view mentioned by '[i]t seems clear from these remarks.' In these expositions are explanations of such things as the basic structure and institutions of society, the conception of justice, the basic values of liberty and equality, primary social goods, social position, what is chosen, and choice by parties in the original position under the veil of ignorance; and within that framework, the two principles of justice are derived (without using the maximin rule). This, in other words, is the part which develops the justice principles by means of a contractarian argument.

The other consideration is what is expressed as 'tested by a comparison with our considered judgments of justice,' this corresponding to 'reflective equilibrium.'

In Rawlsian theory, such a pair of considerations is provided from the beginning. By contrast, the maximin rule is at best simply employed because it is 'useful as a heuristic device.' 'Heuristic' generally refers to an approach using a kind of speculative, provisional formulation, such as would be a guide for the investigation of or solution to a particular issue.

Accordingly, the above means that when an attempt is made, using a simplified model, to assist in an understanding of the way parties in the original position choose justice principles, it is useful to try to see it as an application of the maximin rule in a game-theory-like situation.

In other words, 'choice by the maximin rule' means that one is giving only a modelistic account of how the parties make their selection, and not a substantive description. The parties are not using the maximin rule in actuality. It is just that the maximin rule perspective in the game-theory model is handy for understanding the theory applied there. Such is the significance of the maximin rule for Rawlsian theory.

In this way, one can appreciate that those who hitherto have discussed the maximin rule have been under a double misapprehension. One of these is that they mistakenly interpreted something that originally was only used merely as a heuristic device as being a substantive theory; and the other is that they imagined the maximin rule to have been applied even inside the difference principle.

However, as I stated at the end of the previous chapter, later on Rawls discards the maximin rule even as a logic for deriving principles of justice. This eloquently tells how the maximin rule was not in any way essential for Rawlsian theory.

Asset-egalitarianism and property-owning democracy

Next, let me make clear that the perfect egalitarianism of scholars like Arrow, Coleman and Inoue is a mistaken interpretation. This is seen to be obvious also from the fact that in Figure 4.1, the point *a* actually leaves in situ the inequality between the most advantaged and least advantaged person. However, *A Theory of Justice*, in no small measure, contains the sort of dissertation that would make such an misunderstanding of theirs inevitable.

Firstly, the passage of Rawls that constitutes grounds for Arrow's having called it 'asset egalitarianism' runs as follows:

> We see then that the difference principle represents, in effect, an agreement to regard the distribution of natural talents as a *common asset* and to share in the benefits of this distribution whatever it turns out to be. Those who have been favored by nature, whoever they are, may gain from their good fortune only on terms that improve the situation of those who have lost out (Rawls 1971, p. 100; emphasis added).

Here, in regard to the difference principle, even assets such as inborn talents that have until now been taken for granted as belonging to individuals are plainly stated as being 'regard[ed]...as a common asset.' On this point, there are certain grounds for Arrow's 'asset egalitarianism' reading.

What must be noted here is that no matter what the 'asset egalitarianism' asserted here actually signifies, that claim is not one derived as something chosen by the maximin rule under the veil of ignorance in the original position. For Rawls, the normative assertion called 'asset egalitarianism' is independent of the original position, it corresponding rather to 'our considered moral judgements' which appear in the process of reflective equilibrium. That is, it is a thesis of 'the moral groundlessness of the arbitrariness of luck,' that being why it forms the additional foundation of this assertion.

> [E]ven if [the liberal conception] works to perfection in eliminating the influence of *social contingencies*, it still permits the distribution of wealth and income to be determined by the natural distribution of abilities and talents...and this outcome is *arbitrary from a moral point of view*. There is no more reason to permit the distribution of income and wealth to be settled by the distribution of natural assets than by historical and social fortune (Rawls 1971, pp. 73–74; emphasis added).

From a moral standpoint, both historical and social fortune, as well as inborn abilities and talents, are purely arbitrary things. In other words, morally, they are uncalled for. They lack justification. There is no reason why people of ill-fortune should be disadvantaged in terms of allocation; or, conversely, any reason why fortunate people should be advantaged.

Rawls intends to say that 'fortune cannot be morally justified.' This judgement is not a normative principle derived in the original position, but one that Rawls presupposes as 'our' moral judgement. Surpassing Rawls' intention, this became the point of departure for the theory of 'luck-egalitarianism' which constitutes the main current in contemporary egalitarian theory, which I will discuss in the next chapter.

Be that as it may, one must finally determine what 'asset egalitarianism' signifies here, and the relationship between it and the difference principle.

Rawls calls a social system which has a fundamental structure based on the difference principle a 'property-owning democracy,' and in his 2001 work, *Justice as Fairness: a Restatement*, he describes its characteristics in the following manner:

> [T]he background institutions of property-owning democracy work to disperse the ownership of wealth and capital, and thus to prevent

> a small part of society from controlling the economy, and indirectly, political life as well...By contrast, welfare-state capitalism permits a small class to have a near monopoly of the means of production.
>
> Property-owning democracy avoids this...by ensuring the widespread ownership of productive assets and human capital (that is, education and trained skills) at the beginning of each period, all this against a background of fair equality of opportunity. The intent is not simply to assist those who lose out through accident or misfortune (although that must be done), but rather to put all citizens in a position to manage their own affairs on a footing of *a suitable degree of social and economic equality* (Rawls 2001, p. 139; emphasis added).

The idea of property-owning democracy was originally conceived by a scholar named J.E. Meade, and Rawls already invokes it to explain the import of the difference principle in *A Theory of Justice*. So, this means that the above passage gives an extremely precise account of the notion of egalitarianism which Rawls endeavoured to present while employing the terms 'difference principle' and 'property-owning democracy.' One could say that these constituted something like the following:

Firstly, Rawls certainly did not intend to advocate that 'all assets should be allocated equally.' The proof lies in the fact that even in all of his writings championing the dispersal of productive resources, he by no means says that these 'should be distributed equally.' The expressions used in his writings are limited to 'to disperse,' 'ensuring the widespread ownership,' and 'fair equality of opportunity.' And he goes only as far as to say 'a suitable degree of...equality' and 'continuously to neutralise the tendencies leading over time to even greater inequalities in terms of social position and wealth, and in the ability to gain benefit from opportunities that can be obtained by exerting political influence.' Moreover, property-owning democracy is deemed to be something that 'allow[s] private property in productive assets' (Rawls 2001, p. 139).

Secondly, the idea at the core of what Rawls intends to mean by the difference principle is that even if people are not gifted with abilities or resources, they should be given opportunities as nearly equal as possible to people who *are* thus gifted, and that is the condition for fair social cooperation involving free and equal people, and for them mutually to be fully-qualified, equal members of the same society. This is clear even from Rawls' initial statement in *A Theory of Justice*, namely: 'A very important primary good is a sense of one's own worth' (1971, p. 92). Rawls calls this feeling 'self-respect' or '*self-esteem*' (1971, p. 440). Again, in *A Restatement*, the difference principle and property-owning democracy are claimed to be superior in terms of moral theory, in comparison with laissez-faire capitalism, state socialism, and 'welfare-state capitalism,' and on that occasion, Rawls primarily stresses '*mutuality*,' which means continuous and mutually-beneficial concern among people. In Rawls' view, welfare-state capitalism thinks that it needs merely to guarantee a fixed standard of living.

In this way, what Rawls sees as important is 'to put all citizens in a position to manage their own affairs on a footing of a suitable degree of social and economic equality' (Rawls 2001, p. 139.) One could say that mutually cooperating so as to enable all to have such autonomous ability is the idea at the heart of his egalitarianism.

Thirdly, Rawls' argument on 'asset egalitarianism' is thus understood to be something not advocating perfect egalitarianism, but asserting that, from a moral perspective, even such an individual asset as native aptitude does not belong to individuals as an inalienable right, and must be utilised for the sake of society as a whole, to the extent that justice requires.

The above is the substance of the egalitarianism which Rawls constantly had in mind all the way from *A Theory of Justice* to his *Justice as Fairness: a Restatement* of later years, and it embodies Rawls' answer to the questions of 'What should we make equal?' (the objectives of equality), and 'Why equality?' (the reasons for equality). That answer is, naturally, far removed from perfect egalitarianism, and is also totally different from the maximin-type interpretation that is the prevailing belief. Moreover, this egalitarianism is also completely unrelated to luck-egalitarianism, which is considered in the next chapter.

Part II

Theories of contemporary liberalism

Chapter 5

Luck-Egalitarianism and the Intensification of Liberalism

From the Difference Principle to a pure theory of equality

The pursuit of an axiom

For contemporary liberalism, Rawls' *A Theory of Justice* occupies a similar position as does Newton's *Principia* for classical physics or Adam Smith's *An Inquiry into the Nature and Causes of the Wealth of Nations* for economics. Everything began from there, as from the Big Bang.

Again, though Rawls was no 'guru,' neither was Newton nor Adam Smith. Spurred by *A Theory of Justice*, various writers proceeded further to develop theory relating to justice, equality and freedom. But this stream gradually grew into something divergent from Rawls' own theory. Theory has a basic tendency to be steadily radicalised, and come to be tinged with a more radical and a kind of dogmatic hue. This, too, is extremely common in terms of the prevailing developmental process in scholarship. As trends go, it is not rare for ideas and theoretical conceptions that at first are presented as groundbreaking or prototypical to be further refined and fundamentalistically reconstituted as they undergo examination and discussion by successors. Because subsequent theorists compete as to how further to ensure the internal consistency of the logic, the tacit struggle over the 'inheritance' of theories and ideas easily can, and often does, lead to the victory of the more rabid, unequivocal and candid.

In the case of contemporary liberalism, this process has taken a shape made up of the formulation and development of several doctrines. Examples of such doctrines include 'the priority of justice over the good,' 'neutrality,' 'autonomy,' 'anti-consequentialism' and 'the moral groundlessness of the arbitrariness of luck.' These serve as a kind of 'axiom' in the respective theories.

An axiom, as can be understood by Euclid's axioms in geometry, is a proposition with the premise that it holds true for the theory in question, though no reasons for it need be given within that theory. Merely by laying down just five axioms made up of propositions such as 'there is one and only one straight line that joins two points,' Euclidean geometry creates a system of geometry that can be endlessly deepened. With only these five axioms presupposed, we can logically derive such 'theorems' as, for example, 'the sum of the internal angles of a triangle equals 180 degrees,' or 'in a right triangle, the square of the length of the hypotenuse is equal to the sum of the squares of the lengths of the other two sides.'

The production of theory through a way of framing similar to that in Euclidean geometry is called the axiomatic method. This is the method usually adopted in mathematics, and it is also a common one used in natural sciences when composing 'theory.' Some social theorists consider the axiomatic method to be a 'desirable form of theory' even when investigating social theory, as well. For example, in his book entitled *Ethics*, the Dutch philosopher Spinoza has derived ethical norms that we humans should observe, while at the same time 'proving' the existence of God by constructing an axiomatic theory. Though not as blatant as that, Hobbes' *Leviathan* also has a strongly axiomatic tinge.

Usually, however, it is difficult to compose social theory axiomatically. Instead, there are visible attempts to develop theory with a composition that is as axiomatic as possible. Social thinkers who aspire to present their theories in axiomatic fashion, all the while keeping an axiomatic theoretical structure in mind, and seeking 'a proposition that would be a likely candidate for an axiom' as a preparatory task, start from several (often unspoken) premises, without explicitly presenting them as axioms, and attempt to derive various propositions as kinds of 'theorems' from them. Descartes' *Discourse on the Method of Rightly Conducting the Reason, and Seeking Truth in the Sciences* starts from the establishment of an indubitable method or foundation for us to gain knowledge, that being the famous thesis: 'I think, therefore I am.' Alternatively, Kant's philosophy sets up the concept of 'universally applicable moral laws,' variously examines the conditions which these should fulfil, and, having done that, presents the renowned 'categorical imperative' which states: 'Act only in accordance to that maxim through which you can at the same time will that it should become a universal law' (Kant [1785] 1993, p. 30).

The methods of Descartes and Kant are nowadays called 'foundationalism,' and are deemed to be rather unfavourable. *Foundationalism* may be considered to mean a methodological attitude which believes that there are things called 'indisputable, certain truths,' and that, taking these as ultimate grounds and as a point of departure, it should be possible to compose an irrefutable theory.

The term 'foundationalism' is generally attached a negative nuance. This dismissive connotation mainly comes from the viewpoints of postmodernism and deconstruction, which criticise the main current of Western philosophy beginning with Plato, accusing it of 'smacking of the metaphysical.' But, strictly speaking, for every sort of theory and knowledge, it is inevitable to presuppose certain elements which are 'indubitable' and 'self-evidently true,' so the distinction between what is foundationalism and what is not is quite fuzzy. For that reason, there are times when it is used simply as a label when criticising others (as has been the case with such labels as 'bourgeois' of times past, or the recent 'essentialist'). Yet though it is fairly sweeping, surely there exist 'self-conscious' pursuits which deliberately have sought unquestionable grounds and tried to compose a theory with those grounds as a foundation. One probably could call those attempts 'foundationalism.' In that sense, contemporary liberalism has shifted in a far more foundationalistic direction, having transcended the methodological standpoint which Rawls has taken.

As already shown in previous chapters of this volume, Rawls' theory as a whole is not organised in foundationalistic way. But it is true that the part concerning his social contract theory is, at least in appearance, constructed in a foundationalistic manner. The part that uses the maximin rule to explain the choice of principles from the original position is especially so. Furthermore, partially because of this, Rawls is generally interpreted in a foundationalistic way, and this is by no means unrelated to the fact that foundationalistic contemporary liberalism has evolved so colourfully.

'Luck-arbitrariness' in Rawls

As we saw in the previous chapter, the egalitarianism in Rawls has been actually quite mild. Nevertheless, many writers have tended to read an extremely strong egalitarianism into Rawls' work. The main reason for that lies in the fact that Rawls advocated the 'moral groundlessness of the arbitrariness of luck' when he explained the Difference Principle.

Indeed, as we have already seen, this does not mean that Rawls educes a perfectly equal distribution of final products and assets from this. Why, then, might he have advocated that the 'distribution of wealth and income determined by a natural lottery/distribution of abilities and talents' is 'arbitrary, from a moral standpoint'?

My guess is that what Rawls had in mind here was probably the assertions of libertarianism. In the view of libertarians, whose representative advocate is Robert Nozick with his 1974 book, *Anarchy, State, and Utopia*, each individual is given, as a natural right, 'things which originally belong to him,' and each person's rights are inalienable, except in cases of exchange or relinquishment on a voluntary basis. Only distribution and ownership based on this principle constitute 'justice,' and anything in opposition to it is 'injustice.' This is called 'entitlement theory.' Even among libertarians, opinion is divided as to 'what are natural rights.' But at the minimum, talents and inherited assets are, as a matter of course, counted as constituents of innate rights. In libertarian perspective, the difference principle is tantamount to an attempt to justify a ridiculous infringement of rights.[1]

This view should not be considered merely as the specialised ideological standpoint of a narrow libertarian camp. Its normative appeal seems to have enjoyed wide credence in American society as if it were a 'self-evident principle,' so to speak. (Unless I think thus, I honestly cannot understand why such extravagant praise is directed at Nozick, whose theory is just too naïve from our commonsensical perspective.) Rawls had to resist its 'self-evident' nature, an unconsciously-held moral conviction among American people.[2] In order to secure a theoretical free hand as to how to allocate the goods produced through talents, inherited assets, and other properties seemingly owned by natural rights, he severed the connection between 'the rights of ownership' and 'the owner.' That was the objective of the 'moral groundlessness of the arbitrariness of luck' thesis. A glimpse of this can also be had in the following passage:

> In justice as fairness men agree to share one another's fate. In designing institutions they undertake to avail themselves of the accidents of nature and social circumstance only when doing so is for the common benefit. The two principles are a fair way of meeting the arbitrariness of fortune (Rawls 1971, p. 102).

The justice as fairness that Rawls is considering was to present a normative principle for distribution from the viewpoint of morality as an independent domain, contrary to such arbitrariness of fortune. Here, in particular, I beg attention to Rawls' use of the expression 'common benefit.' It is clear that he does not intend to forbid people absolutely from exploiting 'natural contingency and social fortune' (Rawls 1971, p. 96), thereby giving rise to social and economic inequalities. As long as it was of 'common interest' from a justice perspective, as well, then it would be permissible from moral viewpoints.

What is even more important is that, conceptually, a clear-cut distinction has been made between situations which would be of 'the common interest' and of 'the accidents (of nature).' In other words, accidental contingencies include both ones which would be of common benefit and others which would not. Just because things are accidental, it does not follow that all will immediately be deemed 'not of common benefit.' Conversely, neither does it follow that all things of common interest will be 'things which are not accidental.' Both are different situations, and they can arise independently.

It follows, then, that the question that constitutes the first criterion for Rawls' justice as fairness is whether something is 'of common benefit,' not whether it is 'non-accidental.' Just because a social circumstance is accidental, that does not mean that it is immediately 'contrary to justice,' it being regarded in such a light only when it is not of common benefit. Accordingly, though Rawls claims that accidental natural contingency and social fortune are 'morally arbitrary,' he is not saying that their use for personal purposes constitutes being 'incompatible with justice' merely for that reason.

Still, the theories of equality in contemporary liberalism touched off by Rawls continue to be duly assembled, with the question of whether something is 'morally arbitrary' as their greatest criterion. A theory of 'perfect equality in relation to things that are due to morally arbitrary fortune' comes to be newly developed by Dworkin and others. Such a theory is called 'luck-egalitarianism' (about which I shall explain in detail in the next section). In direct translation, this would be *un-byōdō-shugi* in Japanese, but I render it as *sekinin-byōdō-shugi* (responsibility-egalitarianism) because of the greater weight afforded to 'responsibility,' as something standing in opposition to luck.[3]

Sen's capability approach and critique of welfarism

In one sense, it was the 1979 lecture (published in 1980) by Amartya Sen, 'Equality of what?' that launched the discussion. In that paper, Sen posed a fundamental issue of egalitarianism, namely: 'What should we make equal?' Although Sen himself did not advocate luck-egalitarianism, the foundationalistic quest for equality was triggered by his paper, later going on gradually to spawn the various arguments of luck-egalitarianism.

It was in that paper that Sen first presented his now well-known concept of 'capability.' He argues that if it is desirable to equalise something, then this will be neither the level of people's subjective utility, nor the distribution of what Rawls calls primary social goods (though these are not subjective). He concludes that what should be achieved is the equalisation of basic latent potential.

Sen applies the term 'welfarism' to the setting-up of a criterion for social desirability based solely upon the method of allocation of something on the level of utility that constitutes subjective satisfaction or benefit. In his paper, Sen criticises equality-related utilitarianism, welfarism and Rawls' difference principle, respectively.

Utilitarianism is one type of welfarism, as it is a principle calling for the maximisation of total or average utility. Moreover, it expresses a kind of egalitarianism. This is because utilitarianism is based on a procedure of counting each individual's welfare equally, and seeking its total sum. In other words, in the aspect that each person's utility is treated equally, without discrimination, it is clearly egalitarian. It is certain that, when Bentham extolled utilitarianism, he had egalitarianism in this sense in mind. Even today, when prominent social theorists like Harsanyi and R.M. Hare champion utilitarianism as a desirable socially-normative principle, there is the view that utilitarianism in this sense offers a criterion for bringing about an unbiased judgement.

Still, it is also well known that, by focusing solely upon the average of utility, and ignoring the mode of allocation of utility, utilitarianism is not completely egalitarian. There is no necessity to provide a detailed introduction of Sen's critique of utilitarianism here. In his paper, Sen's primary goal was to criticise welfarism and its most egalitarian version, welfare egalitarianism, rather than to attack utilitarianism. Welfare egalitarianism is a normative principle promoting the equalisation of the level of people's utility. Clearly, this is far more egalitarian than utilitarianism which concerns itself with the maximisation of the sum total or average of utility. Nevertheless, Sen criticises it. The greatest reason for this lies in the fact that even though welfarism is egalitarianistic, it is concerned only with '*utility information*.' But in Sen's view, utility information alone is all too insufficient in terms of data about the people's situations that should be equalised. While giving thought to the problems of equality and discriminatory wages for persons with disabilities, Sen says that judgement as to what constitutes as good life must take into consideration not only the degree of utility, namely that person's happiness and desire-fulfilment, but also certain objective factors, such as whether that person is 'hungry, cold, or oppressed' (Sen 1980, p. 154); and he argues that *non-utility information* which also includes objective factors is essential to egalitarianism.

Based on this premise, Sen further takes issue with the fact that when explaining the difference principle, Rawls removed people with physical or mental disabilities from the group of 'the least advantaged' in his consideration. In actuality, the issue of the treatment of such people is placed outside of the themes of Rawls' *A Theory of Justice*. As to the reason for this, Rawls says only that 'hard cases' can 'distract our moral perception by leading us to think of people distant from us whose fate arouses pity and anxiety' (Rawls 1975: 96). As we saw in the previous chapter, the people whom Rawls had in mind as examples of the least advantaged were those from a disadvantaged social stratum such as unskilled labourers, or those who were in an unfavourable position in regard to their talents or natural attributes. At any rate, probably because he first prioritised the construction of a kind of systematic theory, Rawls seems to have endeavoured to limit to a certain extent the parameters of its application.

For Sen, this limitation of Rawls is not correct. A theory of equality also needs to include people with disabilities in its field of vision. So, the focus of Sen's criticism is directed at the concept of 'primary social goods' which comprises Rawls' egalitarianism. As primary social goods are considered on an objective level, the criticism aimed at welfarism as being based solely upon utility information does not apply. Rather, Sen conversely uses the term 'fetishism' to criticise the hyper-objective nature of primary social goods. That is to say, in the concept of primary social goods and the difference principle, no thought is given to the fact that the same amount of goods can signify different things among different people, such as those with disabilities and those without them.

In Sen's mind, when the marginal utility of people with physical disabilities is small, utilitarianism will force discriminatory disadvantage upon them. Again, the difference principle does not take into account the urgency of the needs of a person who is physically disabled.

> [U]tilitarianism would do nothing for him; in fact it would give him *less* income than to the physically fit. Nor would the Difference Principle

> help him: it will leave his physical disadvantage severely alone…If we still think that he has needs as a cripple that should be catered to, then the basis of that claim clearly rests neither in high marginal utility, nor in low total utility, nor—of course—in deprivation in terms of primary goods (Sen 1985, pp. 159– 60; emphasis added).

What Sen is asserting here is that because people have 'degrees of urgency or needs' such as make their receipt of preferential treatment a natural 'right,' then it would be socially desirable for such needs to be satisfied.

Such objective needs Sen conceptualised as 'basic capabilities.' Focusing not upon 'utility' as the level of satisfaction enjoyed, nor upon the goods to be enjoyed, but upon the ability to enjoy them, Sen expounds his normative conviction that what society should do is to guarantee such basic capabilities for those people such as the disabled or the poor who lack them in their present condition. Capability, or functioning, is the ability to carry out the kind of activities that would have value for people, and, apart from the question of whether those activities are actually carried out, it means that opportunities for activity have been opened up as alternatives.

Yet one must pay attention here to the fact that a concept like this 'capability' of Sen's does not signify a solely empirical thing. The notion of basic capability itself has encapsulated an *already normative conception*. This is because what is at the basis of a 'demand for rights' is our 'idea' that 'there are needs that naturally should be met.' Sen makes this ambiguous, and for that reason there are many people who think as if the 'functioning' which should be fulfilled had some kind of empirically objective existence, but that is a delusion.

I will not pursue Sen's equality theory further in this volume.[4] In any case, due to this discussion of Sen's, which was presented in a form that critiqued Rawls' difference principle, investigation was begun into 'what should be equalised,' and that went on to become the main theme of equality theory.

The expansion of luck-egalitarianism

Dworkin's theory of equality of resources and compensation for brute bad luck

Following Sen, legal philosopher Ronald Dworkin's *What is Equality? Part 2: Equality of Resources* was published for the first time in 1981, and it was a great step in a new development. This was the first work in which the 'responsibility' concept had been explicitly adopted in equality theory.

Dworkin, in turn, criticises various types of welfare- (=utility) egalitarianism. According to him, an individual's utility could be considered in terms of subjective success over that person's entire life (this is called 'the conception of a good life'), but that measure depends not only upon what the person achieved, but under what manner of distribution of resources it was achieved. People who have but meagre resources probably have a tendency to derive great satisfaction even from small achievements. Accordingly, equalising utility alone, without thought to the distribution of resources, cannot be morally desirable.

Given this situation, Dworkin goes on to develop resource-egalitarianism, using a model such as the following: first, suppose that a group of people are thrown into a market society and start life without any presumptions whatsoever. Say their level of basic talent is identical, their only differences being in their tastes, risk-preferences and conceptions of a good life. At this stage, the first condition of egalitarianism is to equalise the resources that people have when they enter the market. Conversely, as long as people are equal in resources and talents for their lives in a market society, the inequalities which would arise as a result are morally permissible, in Dworkin's opinion. The reason for this is that if the starting-point is equal, then anything which arises as the result of competition in a fair market is always due to self-responsibility. In an actual market society, however, (1) there are diverse differences in talent and ability; and (2) there is also the issue of luck. Dworkin expands his model to enable it to deal with these issues, as well.

The first device is the *auction*. With an auction, people are able to redistribute resources according to each person's preference and conception of a good life. All participants in market society gather at the resource auction house, bringing the same amount of bidding slips corresponding to their initial equal amount of resources. The auctioneer displays a certain price system, and under those terms all of the bidding slips are tendered, and, assuming that all of the resources are sold out, the resulting state of distribution of resources will, in a substantive sense, represent an equal distribution, according to Dworkin. That is because he thinks that the outcomes of spontaneous transactions in a fair market are also fair, if the initial conditions are fair. He further establishes a criterion called the 'Envy Test,' in which nobody covets any other person's bundle of resources over her or his own (Dworkin 2000, p. 67). Because the result of the auction yields a distribution that clears (satisfies) this test, the distribution yielded is, Dworkin asserts, substantively equal.

The second device is *insurance*. Dworkin regards differences in innate abilities and circumstances (problems of handicap) as being issues of '*brute (bad) luck*,' the same as disasters and accidents over which one has no control.

Brute bad luck is 'natural luck,' and it happens regardless of the will and choice of the person concerned. On the other hand, there is another type of luck called 'option luck.' If the risk of contracting cancer increases due to smoking, then the degree of increase is option luck. To smoke or not to smoke is up to the individual in question. Accidents that happen when people are driving are also option luck.

In our actual society, insurance markets, including motor vehicle insurance, accident insurance, life insurance, catastrophe insurance and so on, have developed in response to different kinds of misfortune. And if, on the odd chance, one should be visited by misfortune, an insurance payout is then made according to the premiums one has paid. This insurance payout can be considered as compensation towards bad luck.

Dworkin suggests that the amount of social compensation as an egalitarian response to such brute bad luck as being born with a disability can be determined by thinking of a *hypothetical insurance market* (not an actual one).

> If (contrary to fact) everyone had at the appropriate age the same risk of developing physical or mental handicaps in the future...but the total number of handicaps remained what it is, how much insurance coverage against these handicaps would the average member of the community purchase? We might then say that but for (uninsurable) brute luck that has altered these equal odds, the average person would have purchased insurance at that level, and compensate those who do develop handicaps accordingly, out of some fund collected by taxation or other compulsory process but designed to match the fund that would have been provided through premiums if the odds had been equal (Dworkin 2000, pp. 77–78).

In Dworkin's way of thinking, it is possible to set an appropriate level of compensation towards 'innate bad luck' as the amount of insurance coverage which people in society would likely see as appropriate, to be paid vis-à-vis the risk of 'future misfortune.' Of course, this insurance system is not one that could be set up in reality. It will always remain hypothetical. In one sense, it plays a theoretical role similar to that of Rawls's establishment of the original position. Hypothetical though it may be, if an appropriate judgement could be derived from it, then that would be, Dworkin supposes, very fitting for us in reality, too. But we should be reminded that Dworkin has not derived or shown a substantive judgement—namely, an appropriate amount of compensation for each person's innate misfortune. He has only described its outer framework.

What Dworkin is emphasising is a basic principle relating to what should be compensated so as to satisfy the conditions for egalitarianism. He formulates this using the concepts of 'brute (bad) luck' and 'option luck.'

> [T]he bare idea of equality of resources...would not argue for redistribution from the person who had insured to the person who had not if, horribly, they were both blinded in the same accident. For the availability of resources would mean that, though both had had brute bad luck, the difference between them was a matter of option luck, and the arguments we entertained against disturbing the results of option luck under conditions of equal antecedent risk hold here as well (Dworkin 2000, p. 77).

The normative principle underlying Dworkin's egalitarianism says that, under conditions of equal antecedent risk, inequalities in outcome arising from option luck need not be remedied, but it is the inequalities arising from natural luck that must be remedied. This is the normative principle at the foundations of Dworkin's egalitarianism. The concept of option luck is linked with 'self-responsibility.' In earlier papers on equality theory, Dworkin does not engage in much discussion where the notion of 'responsibility' is brought to the surface. But in his 2000 Introduction, subtitled 'Does Equality Matter?,' he states that in contrast to 'Rawls's difference principle, which prescinds from any consideration of individual responsibility,' he adopts 'the hypothetical insurance approach, which attempts to make as much turn on such responsibility as possible' (p. 5). It would not be untoward to say that what lies at the base of Dworkin's argument on equality of resources is 'luck-egalitarianism' in which 'individuals should be relieved of consequential responsibility for those unfortunate features of their situation that are brute bad luck, but not from those that should be seen as flowing from their own choices' (Dworkin 2000, p. 287).

The brute/option distinction

Some scholars regarded Dworkin's distinction between 'brute bad luck' and 'bad option luck' as giving a ground-breaking and unequivocal answer both to 'What should we equalise?' (the issue of the objective of equality), and 'Why should things be equal?' (the question of the reasons for equality). Originally, in social theory, these two problems were not necessarily addressed in close connection with each other.

Marxism, for example, responded to 'Why should things be equal?' with a 'theory of exploitation.' This was based on the labour theory of value, which argued that the value which by rights should belong to the worker is unjustly appropriated by the capitalist: in other words, there is exploitation. Because resolving this 'injustice' was considered to be the road to achieving equality, it was the very abolition of private ownership of the means of production that would bring about an equal society. In this theory, however, there is too large a gap between the 'abolition of private ownership' as a means, and 'equality' as an objective. This is because it is unclear as to what kind of equality would materialise, and to what extent, for the simple reason that private ownership had been abolished. To that end, experimental attempts to create socialist societies were actually made in the twentieth century, but the outcome was merely the emergence of a new classed society that was far distant from an equal society.

The 'brute/option' dichotomy would not provoke such a slippage between the reason for and the objective of equality, because this very dichotomy is simultaneously a reason and an objective. Disasters and inequalities that have arisen through option luck are things that have happened due to personal responsibility, and so they may be left as they are. Conversely, the things that are not the result of choice should be equalised. In this way, the reason therefore provides the objective.

As may easily be imagined, the brute/option distinction instantly became tied to the concept of 'responsibility.' The reason why it is unnecessary to rectify or compensate people even though misfortune has arisen as a result of their choice is that it boils down to 'self-responsibility.' Notions such as the ideal of equality which have to do with the desirable state of society are connected with the concept of society's moral responsibility. But events which have occurred within a particular individual's own responsibility are clearly not society's responsibility. In like manner, the brute/option distinction is understood as a division between 'one's own responsibility' and 'society's responsibility,' and, at the same time, that simultaneously defines the 'target of equalisation' in terms of society's responsibility. Accordingly, it was thought that if we explained what kind of things constituted brute luck, then the question of what should be equalised would naturally be settled.

The currents of actual argument did not converge in as neat a manner, however. Firstly, critical arguments arose against Dworkin's resource-equality theory. A disputant named Richard Arneson, for one, raising the example of the case in which a young person who had been born and raised in an Amish community decided to leave it and live in a modern metropolis, argued that equality of resources would not be sufficient (Arneson 1989). As is common knowledge, the Amish people who inhabit the Appalachian Mountains in Pennsylvania eschew such tools of modern civilisation as electricity or petroleum, and even now tenaciously preserve a seventeenth- to eighteenth-century lifestyle. They are placed, of course, outside the field of vision of such ways of life as going on to university and becoming a business-person, doctor or lawyer. Let us suppose that a young person who grew up in such a community wishes to discard that traditional lifestyle and live in a modern, civilised society. Here the problem arises that, because he or she has not received the standard education necessary for making a living in a modern, civilised society, it will be difficult for him or her to make a go of it when thrown into the midst of a market-type competitive society. Dworkin considered that the idea of a hypothetical insurance market could deal with people with disabilities, but that was because being born with a disability was seen as being brute bad luck. Whether being born into an Amish community can similarly be seen as brute bad luck is a tricky question. At least, it did not cross Dworkin's mind.

The question of whether someone has received standard education or training depends not so much upon the choices made individually by the person involved, but rather on what kind of child-rearing practices the person's parents and local community chose. In like matter, that person's 'conception of a good life' and 'preferences,' namely what sort of way of life she or he considers desirable, and what she or he likes and dislikes, are influenced by the way that person was reared as a child. From this, Arneson points out the inappropriateness of policies of equally distributing resources based on whether the individual is responsible or not, instead advocating the principle of 'equality of opportunity for welfare.'

Introduced in this way, Arneson might appear not to be a luck-egalitarian, but in actuality, he is. He states that if 'equality of opportunity for welfare' is realised, then there is no problem, because the inequalities that actually arise 'can be attributed to various factors within the locus of control of each individual.'

It was a Marxist, G.A. Cohen, who more obviously advocated luck-egalitarianism. While giving a completely novel definition of 'exploitation,' he speaks of the notion of equality in the following terms:

> A person is *exploited* when unfair advantage is taken of him, and he suffers from (bad) *brute luck* when his bad luck is not the result of a gamble or risk which he could have avoided. I believe that the primary egalitarian impulse is to extinguish the influence on distribution of both exploitation and brute luck (Cohen 1989, p. 908; emphasis in original).

This egalitarianism of Cohen's ultimately comes down to an issue of dividing what needs to be equalised according to a criterion of the existence or nonexistence of responsibility: in other words, whether it is something that arose as a result of individual choice. Cohen asserts that preferences and values—even a taste for luxury, for example—must be respected if their formation was not the individual's fault. For Cohen, '[t]he right cut is between responsibility and bad luck, not between preferences and resources' (1989, p. 922).

Roemer's equality of opportunity: the circumstances called 'effort'

Another work that further promoted luck-egalitarianism was a short 1998 publication by John E. Roemer, called *Equality of Opportunity*. Roemer is a scholar who has developed a very radical and provocative approach to the problems of social class and inequality by employing techniques from mathematical economics. His 1996 publication, *Theories of Distributive Justice*, which also appeared in Japanese translation, is one that thoroughly utilises a mathematical tool-set, so it is difficult for people to read unless they have more or less specialised in the study of mathematics at university level. By comparison, in *Equality of Opportunity*, mathematics is used only in one portion, and overall, it is written in a readily-comprehensible manner.

'Equality of opportunity' is a concept generally used as distinct from simple 'equality,' but this concept originally had a particular problem. By way of example, we use 'educational equality' to refer to all people having an identical level of education; but conversely, we say 'equality of educational opportunity' or 'opportunity is open' when everyone is given the right to receive an education without suffering discrimination due to social status or sex, even if the resulting level of education is not identical. Yet many people have long harboured doubts as to whether a lack of blatant discrimination allows us to say that 'opportunity is equal.' The fact that children from poor families often have to forgo advancement to university for economic reasons, for example, suggests that the opportunity for tertiary education is closed to children from poor families. If people who would like to go on to university if possible have to abandon the idea because of poverty, then we cannot say that they have 'equal opportunity,' can we? Such doubts naturally arise.

So, in order to lessen the incidence of people giving up entering higher education for economic reasons, efforts such as various scholarships and exemption from tuition fees have been made in many countries. That without doubt has softened the impact of economic difference in university entrance, and has greatly expanded opportunities for children from poor families to receive higher education.

If we grant sufficient scholarships according to the income of students' family of origin, for example, then can we expect that opportunity among different social strata will be completely equalised? The answer is no. In fact, children's average scholastic ability and aspirations towards proceeding to university differ according to their family's social stratum and economic level, resulting in inequality in educational level. In the United States, especially, one cannot ignore the difference by race.

This actually became an enormous social problem in America from the 1960s onwards. Contemporary society is one in which social position and income are largely determined by academic background. (This is just speaking in average terms, though, and I draw your attention to the fact that there is certainly no shortage of people who have achieved a high social standing and income despite a low level of education.) Accordingly, if one does nothing to address race-related differences in scholastic ability, then the interracial disparity in education as well as in income will remain forever. This is not merely a grave issue for the idea of equality, but also a hotbed of such social problems as racial discrimination and confrontation. In order to address these problems, a policy of affirmative action is implemented in the majority of American universities. Under this measure, the student-admission policy takes into consideration not only academic prowess demonstrated by entrance test scores and other data, but also race and sex, in an attempt to guarantee, to a fixed extent, an admission ratio of students from minority backgrounds who used to have a low level of advancement to higher education. This policy became widespread from the 1970s, and the proportion of black and other ethnic-minority students proceeding to tertiary education actually improved significantly. On the other hand, however, there was also criticism that this might be 'reverse discrimination,' and lawsuits were also mounted.

Here, the crucial point is the question of what constitutes 'fair equality of opportunity.' In terms of pure theory, it is a problem such as the following: now, let $x_1,\ldots,x_n$ represent factors that influence people's level of education. These could be their economic standing, social stratum or race of their family of origin, or the person's own scholastic ability, aspirations, and so on. Then, simply by removing only the influence of their economic level, would this make for 'equality of opportunity'? Would it not be odd not to remove influence factors such as academic ability, aspirations, race, and so on, as well? On the other hand, though, if students could enter the same university in spite of having quite different scholastic ability, doubts would arise as to whether that could be called 'fair opportunity' after all. Moreover, if one thought to remove all of the influence factors, then that would result in the equalisation of the level of educational achievement itself. If that were the case, where would be the sense in thinking of 'equality of opportunity' and 'equality of outcome' as two different things? Alternatively, should one consider 'equality of opportunity' to have been achieved when, for some reason, a distinction was made between factors that should be removed and those which did not need removing, and the influence of the former was actually taken away?

It was Roemer's *Equality of Opportunity* that endeavoured to supply an answer to this difficult problem, using the logic of luck-egalitarianism. Roemer divides the various factors that impact upon educational achievement into 'differential circumstances' and circumstances for which people 'should be...held accountable,' and then asserts that removing the influence of the former or giving compensation for its impact will mean 'levelling the playing field,' that is, achieving equality of opportunity in education. In this argument, the issue that is particularly focused upon is that of 'effort.'

We well know that our scholastic ability is affected by the quality of our own effort. In Japan, there are some nostalgic sayings long current, such as '*yontō goraku* (four win, five lose)'—a phrase exaggerating the severity of the so-called 'examination hell,' in which a candidate who slept for only four hours per night would pass, but would fail if sleeping for five or more hours. This saying reflects the common understanding that if one devotes oneself to the effort of studying, then one's academic ability will improve and one's chances of passing the entrance examination to a difficult school will grow. In reality, this is not a mistaken assumption (though *yontō goraku* is a joke). Of course, there is no guarantee that one's academic prowess will necessarily improve just because one has made efforts, but the probability is high. One could say this is a social reality shared by all countries, not only Japan.

While there are some children in the world who put all their energy into the effort of studying, there are also those who do not do so, instead spending their time at leisure. According to whether they make efforts, naturally there will emerge a disparity in their median scholastic ability. Is it permissible, then, to regard the decision to make the effort of studying or not as a choice based on individual will? Many people will probably think that it is clearly a personal choice. Roemer is a little different. He says that even in relation to whether to make efforts, there is some involvement not only of individual accountability, but also the effect of circumstances. Let us call the overall amount of effort the 'level of effort.' I will call the part of this that is subject to circumstantial influence the '*propensity for effort*' (Roemer does not give a name to this), and the other part which is ascribed to personal responsibility, the '*degree of effort*.' People who have been raised in advantaged circumstances and those born with favoured natural attributes probably embody a propensity to make strenuous efforts themselves for that very reason. For example, Roemer states that in American society, the reason why 'Asian' children perform well at school is because of discipline (circumstances) at home by which they would be punished severely unless they studied. Conversely, the absence of effort on the part of children from other groups becomes the fault of a laissez-faire approach to child-rearing at home.

In this way, Roemer roughly divides the factors leading to certain social outcomes into circumstances and personal responsibility. And he thinks that differences in circumstances can be collected into some kind of qualitative '*circumstantial type*,' and differences in the propensity for effort emerge for the very reason that their circumstantial types are dissimilar. In relation to effort, these circumstances are envisaged as operating by means of a mechanism such as in Figure 5.1.

Accordingly, Roemer asserts that, among the inequalities in people's socioeconomic situations, the disparity brought about by

Figure 5.1: Equality of opportunity in Roemer

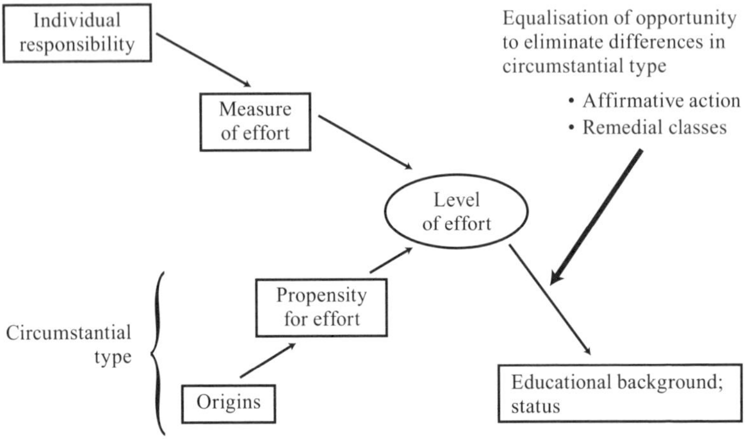

differences in the 'propensity for effort' which ultimately arises due to 'differences in circumstantial type' is not the fault of the individual, and therefore 'equality of opportunity' will be realised just by compensating socially for that disparity.

The measures Roemer has in mind for achieving such equality of opportunity are remedial classes and affirmative action. Firstly, hold remedial classes for students whose effort is insufficient due to their circumstances, and improve their academic ability. As for any gap in educational standard still remaining, forcibly enable people originating from all circumstantial types to reach an identical educational standard through affirmative action. In this way, Roemer thinks, equality of opportunity relating to educational standards is achievable.

In commonsense terms, it is idiotic to suggest that society should compensate even for unfortunate circumstances resulting from neglect to make sufficient efforts. If one goes along with Roemer's idea, then it will become necessary to come to the salvation of students who failed subjects because they were too lazy to study, or third-generation business owners who ruined the family business because they had a leisurely upbringing, or the like. It is natural to think there is something odd about that idea. But the logic of luck-egalitarianism, which argues for 'making equal what is nobody's fault,' had sufficient charm to make great authorities in mathematical economics like

Roemer, who tried to be faithful to logicality, become addicted to its argumentative idiosyncrasies.

Analytical Marxism

The work of Roemer and Cohen generally is derived from Marxist concerns and aims, along with that of the mathematical social theorist, Jon Elster, author of a book entitled *Making Sense of Marx*. Their works are called 'analytical Marxism.' Analytical Marxism plays one part in contemporary liberalism, but strictly speaking, it is different from liberalism. To say the least, Marxism is an ideology which has criticised the nineteenth-century system of liberal capitalism head-on. Yet between today's analytical Marxism and contemporary liberalism there is a greater proportion common to both than there are differences and conflicts.

Analytical Marxism is definitively divorced from old-time Marxism on the following points: (1) it has discarded the scheme at the root of Marxism, namely the setting-up of the concept of 'exploitation' based fundamentally upon the labour theory of value. Roemer's early effort, *A General Theory of Exploitation and Class* (1982), has great merit. In that volume, while expanding a mathematical model that Japanese economist Michio Morishima developed in his *Marx's Economics* (1973), Roemer thoroughly demonstrated that the labour theory of value cannot be sustained; (2) it also completely discards the 'revolution' myth and 'materialistic view of history' that constituted the apocalyptic and romanticist side of Marxism. Neither is 'historical necessity' or 'the dictatorship of the proletariat' discussed; and (3) the epistemological and philosophical doctrines of Marxism are also thrown out. Nor does it analyse people's social or political consciousness by employing the concepts of the 'base/superstructure' model, 'false consciousness,' or 'ideology,' premised upon a 'materialistic dialectic.'

So, what makes it 'Marxism,' then? Perhaps its advocates themselves have simply dubbed it thus, and the reasons are not always clear. But the following kind of elements could vaguely be given as components of its convictions. Firstly, there is the basic recognition that society is divided by unequal social classes with differing life-opportunities and levels of benefit. Secondly, there is a judgement that this inter-class disparity is based on some kind of 'exploitation.' And thirdly, the inter-class inequality based on this exploitation is somewhere connected with the basic structure of contemporary capitalist economic institutions, and unless this economic structure is changed, it will be impossible radically to remedy that inequality.

These three points are not necessarily shared by contemporary liberalism. The following point is common to both, however, namely that among the inequalities in society there exist some things which are normatively 'unjust,' and a social system that qualifies as just is one from which unjust inequalities have been expunged. Accordingly, one of the most important tasks for normative social theory is to hammer out theory relating to what constitutes an unjust inequality.

Unlike Marxism, contemporary liberalism does not always use the concept of 'exploitation.' Nowadays, 'exploitation' means nothing much above 'unjust distribution.' It is merely another name for 'inequalities which should be removed.' As such, analytical Marxism and contemporary liberalism may be said to be supported by a concern for issues with an extremely high degree of commonality.

Overlooked consequences

In the eyes of many advocates, luck-egalitarianism—which splits social and economic inequalities into those which can be reduced to personal responsibility and those which can not, and assumes that it is the moral responsibility of society to take some kind of measures to equalise or compensate for those for which individuals cannot be held accountable—appeared very attractive. For egalitarianism, it seemed to be something that offered an extremely clear-cut theory.

There was a great misapprehension here, though. There are two problems: the first is a radical misunderstanding regarding the theoretical effectiveness of the concept of 'responsibility.' This misunderstanding is not limited to liberalism, but has permeated throughout moral theory. The other issue is one stemming from the fact that egalitarianism is 'foundationalistically' constituted. This, too, is not limited to liberalism, and is something that has long been present in the greater part of egalitarian theory. Let me explain, starting from the second issue.

The side-effects of luck-egalitarianism

The notion of responsibility has exceedingly strong moral implications. In reality, though, the decision to ascribe responsibility for something to somebody is one that is also accompanied by dangerous side-effects. Let me give examples of some of the side-effects of luck-egalitarianism deemed undesirable in commonsense thinking.

Firstly, as anyone would easily realise, all of the inequalities and misfortunes such as could be ascribed to personal responsibility are, under luck-egalitarianism, left alone by society. People may drive too fast and have traffic accidents, or become ill due to smoking or neglect of their health. But according to the theory of luck-egalitarianism, society need do nothing to save them; society does not, at least, have the moral obligation to do so. However, we may conceive also that the speeding, the smoking, and so on are the fault not of individual people but of their 'circumstances.' If that be the case, the story should differ. So, the normative criterion given by luck-egalitarianism is rather arbitrary.

Secondly, when equalisation or compensation measures are taken on the basis of luck-egalitarianism, many people will be forced to carry out actions that are not to their liking. In Roemer's opportunity-egalitarianism, for instance, students whose effort is insufficient because of their circumstances will be forced to raise their level of effort through remedial classes; while children whose academic achievement is inferior due to their circumstances will have to receive schooling until they reach an average educational standard, even if that is repugnant to them.

Thirdly, luck-egalitarianism means that individual disposition and behaviour will be classified according to the 'presence or absence of responsibility.' At this juncture, while it would be embarrassing to be characterised as 'accountable,' on the contrary, by no means would it always be gratifying to be deemed 'not accountable,' either. Roemer's discussion, for example, is premised upon the idea that we can identify people as belonging to divergent groups according to their type of circumstances. It is obvious that this probably implies a discriminatory way of looking at things. Though the effort-level of the group which Roemer calls 'Asian' is high, that is deemed to be due to mere 'circumstances,' not the 'responsibility (merit) of the individuals in question. Yet there is nothing that wounds personal self-esteem so much as having a high degree of effort attributed not to the inherent character of the person concerned, but to that person's circumstances. To continue on this track, this would probably equate to saying that someone who won an Olympic marathon did not deserve it in any way, victory being due to the winner's innate constitution, her or his coach, and an advantageous training environment. Relieving a person who has gained a lofty position of any responsibility for having attained it conversely implies an evaluation of the 'circumstances' of the gaining of that position as being 'unjustly advantaged.' In this appears the risk that the concept termed the 'circumstantial type' will easily become a sort of stigma.

Indeed, a scholar named Elizabeth S. Anderson has incisively pointed out that there is such a risk of stigma in the egalitarian theory in contemporary liberalism. Anderson variously discusses the fact that despite the intentions of luck-egalitarianism, it will ultimately bring about injustice both to the victims of option luck and the victims of brute luck. In particular, she indicates that when people in the latter category who have mental or physical disabilities are socially regarded as 'not being responsible' for their plight, there is a danger of 'rais[ing] private disdain to the status of officially-recognised truth' (Anderson 1999, p. 306.) There is always a possibility of attaching an insulting stigma through pity rather than compassion. And in a society that practised luck-egalitarianism, she imagines, something akin to a 'State Equality Board' would be set up, from which the following kind of letter might be sent to people with disabilities.

> To the disabled: Your defective native endowments or current disabilities, alas, make your life less worth living than the lives of normal people. To compensate for this misfortune, we, the able ones, will give you extra resources, enough to make the worth of living your life good enough that at least *one* person out there thinks it is comparable to someone else's life (Anderson 1999, p. 305; emphasis in original).

Of course, this is a fanciful tale which Anderson inflated to ridicule luck-egalitarianism, yet it is a spine-chilling fiction also resembling the world of Orwell's *1984*.

Egalitarianism as ethics of sentiment

Fourthly, as can be appreciated from the fact that there are fears of such stigma and unwilling coercion, luck-egalitarianism is completely steeped in the evils of 'foundationalism' which makes absolutely no attempt to see what kind of consequences would arise if such logic were carried through. Egalitarianism itself is surely a sublime and beautiful notion. When egalitarianism is put into practice, however, it often causes preposterous calamity. Stigma and compulsion are one example, and this relates to deprivation of such major values as personal dignity, freedom and basic rights. Still fresh in memory is the way that the socialism of old, in the name of equality, trampled these down with not an iota of remorse.

This is not the only evil. Another serious problem with foundationalistic egalitarianism exists: that is, egalitarian measures often markedly reduce the 'total amount of all value that should be equalised.' In order to put equality of resources into practice, those resources have to exist. Resources for compensation are needed in order to compensate people visited by brute bad luck. Furthermore, in order to implement egalitarianism as a policy, it is necessary to set up administrative organs and hire people. Where on earth do such resources spring from? (As we saw in the previous chapter, Rawls' difference principle signifies point *a* in Figure 4.1, but the joint production of a fixed value is presupposed there, and the problem indicated here is avoided.)

If we think using Roemer's equality of opportunity, for example, people classified as the type with low propensity for effort would be, for that simple reason, guaranteed to receive the same average status and payoff as people typed as having high propensity for effort. As there is disparity within each respective type according to people's 'degree of effort,' it does not mean that there is no incentive at all to work hard. Under Roemer's compensation measures, however, people deemed to be of the type with high propensity for effort—'Asian' children, for instance—would ultimately only be able to obtain the same level of status and payoff as other groups, no matter how hard they worked, so clearly they would be likely to reduce their degree of effort. For people in the low-propensity-for-effort category, on the other hand, there would be no merit in raising their effort level, either. The overall level of effort thus would shrink. As a result, economic activity clearly would head for decline.

Egalitarians have a tendency to avoid head-on consideration of the aspects in which egalitarian policies damage people's incentive. The (unconscious) reason for this is that thinking about factors relating to the private desire called incentive is not being faithful to the lofty notion of equality. What lies here is none other than their ethics of sentiment as theoreticians. Devotion of intellect to the internal purity of theory is given the greatest emphasis. Yet the question of what purpose theory serves in the first place is ignored. Originally, the theory of egalitarianism does not exist only for the sake of the ideal of equality, but as part of a normative principle for social structure. There are many different kinds of values and ideals which a society as well as a normative theory of society should respect. Then, in the question of what kind of values must be respected in what ways in normative principles, clearly equality is no more than one of these (though, of course, one of the important ones). If, only for the sake of egalitarianism itself, people have to lose many of the numerous other benefits they should actually be able to enjoy, it would be exactly the same as throwing the baby out with the bathwater.

The illusion of 'responsibility'

The difficulties of conceptualising responsibility

I pointed out in the previous section that a risk of stigma arises on the premise that people can always be classified according to their circumstantial type, and social outcomes can be divided into those which are ascribable to individual responsibility and those which are not. If this division could not be made, then it would be impossible to implement luck-egalitarianism in the first place, and the danger of stigma would accordingly vanish. Yet if luck-egalitarianism were implemented superficially, in spite of such a division actually being impossible to effect, but on the pretence that it *were* possible, then the result would probably be ridiculous injustice.

Conclusively speaking, it is impossible in principle to categorise the social realm by the presence or lack of responsibility on objective criterion. 'Responsibility' is a 'constructed concept,' as are 'rights' and 'obligations,' and these are not things which exist in a materially objective manner, as do stones or water, as I argue in my 1995 book *Seidoron no kōzu* (The theoretical structure of institutions). It is something that is put together in society through some kind of popular consensus (often silent). The question of how to put it together is a vital challenge for society, but this does not mean that it already exists objectively, as a given. It is thus impossible to seek the grounds for egalitarianism in responsibility, or the lack of it.

Certainly, in the long history of thought relating to norms till now, the concept of 'responsibility' has been indispensible to moral theory. The view that the 'responsible subject' could be the very target of moral evaluation was a self-evident axiom that enjoyed wide acceptance. Luck-egalitarianism has been founded on the idea that it might be possible to incorporate 'responsibility' not only as such a classification criterion for individual morality, but also as a standard for the morality called social justice. It judges that it is moral for people's situations to be determined according to their level of responsibility, and that it is wrong for there to be no connection between responsibility and outcome.

All of the moral theories heretofore have adopted the pattern of 'explaining morality by way of responsibility.' In other words, when assessing people in moral terms the notion of 'responsibility' has been used as an 'explicans.' This is a common practice in the everyday world, and moral theory has adhered to that without modification (which I call the 'pseudo-second-order theorisation of first-order theory,' where 'first-order-theory' means the theoretical knowledge about society of everyday persons, which exists empirically irrespective of whether it is true or not, and 'second-order-theory' is the objectively true theoretical knowledge which should be pursued by scientific investigation, but may not necessarily be established as such.) In its role as an explicans, responsibility is seen just as if it were 'already objectively there.'

Yet the 'responsibility' that was supposed to exist 'objectively' in this way was laden with extremely troublesome problems. Here, let me simply explain just two of them: the issues of determinism and free will. Firstly, if one thinks along the lines of the world being decided deterministically, then it will appear as if there is no room for responsibility to be involved. If, like Roemer, one thinks that even the propensity for effort is determined by circumstances, then it would probably be not at all odd to imagine that the remaining 'degree of effort' is also actually decided by some factors. If that be the case, then everything is the fault of circumstances, and personal responsibility is nowhere to be seen. At the end-point of luck-egalitarianism, only perfect equality in all quarters would constitute justice.

Responsibility also involves a way of thinking that presupposes the presence of free will, yet free will is a very bothersome concept which is not readily understood. For example, I much enjoy smoking, and even if my lifespan may be somewhat shortened, I have no intention at the moment to quit. Here, 'not to quit' is certainly my own will. But whether this constitutes 'free will,' I do not know. It is obvious that an addiction to tobacco built up by a habit of many years' duration is the underlying cause, and this is also often called a 'nicotine addiction.' There are also suggestions that it might be influenced by genetic traits. If so, then my smoking might be nothing more than the manifestation of an inclination imbued in my flesh, and not 'free' will. If one is going to consider the concept of 'free will' to be something along the lines of 'the will to do something, on the condition that one can have the will to do anything, with no constraints,' then there can be no such thing as 'free will.' Not only is our will based on physiological conditions: it is also regulated by our diverse knowledge and accumulated beliefs and values.

The issue of determinism and free will vis-à-vis responsibility troubles philosophers even today. One named Thomas Nagel, a follower of Rawls' line, for instance, debates how it might be possible to redeem the concept of responsibility when a deterministic world where people's actions ultimately are not under their control appears plausible. But his argument is full of confusion. With the idea that responsibility presupposes individual autonomy, Nagel especially attempts to theorise autonomy in a form that does not conflict with causal determinism, but as he thinks of autonomy as approaching free will, he is led to the glum conclusion that the expansion of our objective knowledge erodes our autonomy (Nagel 1979).

Alternatively, the young Japanese ethicist Kazunobu Narita has recently posed a concept called 'control necessary for responsibility,' which he defines as follows:

1. Either (Subject) S rationally exercises her or his (practical) ability, resulting in the emergence of will in response to rational judgement, and that will is manifested by (Action) A; or else,
2. (Subject) S fails rationally to exercise her of his (practical) ability, resulting in the emergence of will, and that will is manifested by (action) A, [in these cases the control necessary for responsibility is carried out] (Narita 2004, p. 227).

In simple terms, when, after due consideration (this indicating the exercise of 'rational (practical) ability), a certain Action A is carried out as a result of the decision that A should be done; or, conversely, when a certain action is carried out as a result of the will to do it, but in the absence of such consideration, then the control necessary for responsibility is present; therefore, the doer has responsibility vis-à-vis Action A. It is immediately obvious that the conceptualisation of this is extremely curious. It means that regardless of the intention to exercise what constitutes rational (practical) ability, if the doer acts willingly, then he or she has responsibility for that action; but if, on the contrary, there was no willingness present, then the doer will not be responsible. Accordingly, in the case where, for instance, a young child was playing with a cigarette lighter and a fire broke out, then the child would be responsible if she or he had had the will to 'set alight' to something; while conversely, if a drunken adult were to fall asleep with a cigarette still burning and a fire started, then, because there had been no will to 'set alight' to anything but the original cigarette, then that adult would not be responsible. This is contrary to our everyday usage of the concept of responsibility.

'Responsibility' is something that is socially constructed

It does not matter whether the above usage conforms to everyday terminology, for first of all, Nagel and Narita's premises contain radical misapprehensions. They, like many other scholars, adhere to two mistaken impressions, namely: (1) that responsibility can be established in relation to actions; and (2) that it is possible objectively to distinguish actions for which someone is responsible from actions which are not. These impressions are based on the presumption that responsibility is not something created by our own initiative, nor is it a 'construct' (to use the current jargon). They follow our everyday view of morality (first-order theory), as is. But in the end, these are nothing but misapprehensions, because such 'responsibility' does not objectively exist. Our quotidian knowledge and theory relating to society is mostly created as a kind of fiction, in other words 'an imaginary' as in the case of Benedict Anderson's *Imagined Communities*, and 'responsibility' is also one example of that.

The everyday concept of responsibility has the following kinds of qualities. Firstly, we impart responsibility not only to actions, but also to positions and roles that are not accompanied by actions. For example, top business executives and government ministers who are not directly connected with incidents and mishaps involving their organisations are often saddled with the blame. This is because we are employing a concept of responsibility in the social context surrounding the action, not according to the causal structure of the action itself. Responsibility is a notion to do with social relationships. Ascribing the responsibility for a certain happening to someone means nothing other than reconfirming or restructuring our normative understanding of social relationships. The reason why we never morally praise or berate dogs or babies, let alone grass or trees, is that we do not acknowledge them to be 'responsible subjects.' In this way, the question of who, or what, to recognise as such a responsible subject is just the one of the normative structures of society, and should be established through public consensus. In our society we do not ascribe responsibility to children or persons who are mentally impaired, simply because we have decided not to do so. We consider people who have the 'capacity for responsibility' to be 'autonomous individuals,' 'individuals who have free will,' or the like. But such descriptors have conveniently been chosen for the concept of 'responsibility as something objective, and as a certain explicans.' 'Autonomy' and 'free will' are simply operating as unexplained independent variables.

In contemporary social custom, it probably can be said that what we envision in an 'individual with the capacity for responsibility' is the quality of 'having the capacity for rationality and mature deliberation.' Notions like mature deliberation and rationality are not at all clear, but essentially one can presume that the individual has the capacity to give some thought to what is right, what to do, or what will happen if she or he carries out a particular action. Naturally, it is entirely another story whether the person actually does give it some thought, and whether a correct judgement is reached as a result of that thought. In many cases, people who cause accidents or commit crimes probably at that point either have not engaged in mature consideration, or have made a wrong decision. Still, that is no reason for us to relieve them of responsibility on a daily basis. If they are presumed to have a rational capacity for mature deliberation, then that will be sufficient to establish them as subjects whose responsibility can be queried. This is an 'assumption,' of course. Nobody could precisely measure a person's capacity.

Accordingly, the issue of conflict with causal determinism can be interpreted in the following manner: firstly, when questioning someone's responsibility for an action vis-à-vis some event, we have the tendency to make the action's being the 'cause' of that event into a condition for culpability, but this relies upon an individualistic legal view with a background in modern scientific thought. In non-modern societies it was not unusual for 'black magic' and 'curses' to be made grounds for culpability, or for a whole clan with no direct connection to be made responsible. Even today, as I have already stated, there are occasions where 'occupying a responsible social position' becomes grounds for culpability, this having no connection with the action and the causality of the event. 'Culpability' therefore is essentially independent of 'causality.'

In addition, the idea that because actions are culpable, it must follow that they are 'free from everything,' or 'could have been something else' merely means that, in everyday terms, it is possible to assume that the 'doer of the action in question has a moral character with the ability to choose actions after mature deliberation.' In actual fact, in a causal sense, it is not implied that the action in question 'has not been prescribed by anyone or anything else.' Still, as the next chapter will show, in European thought since Ancient Greece, the concept of 'freedom' developed in connection with the morality of character and eligibility for membership of society, and 'freedom' in the sense of 'not constrained' meant not only not being socially constrained by other people or the law, but also implied not being physically restrained. Because of this, moral theoreticians mistakenly imagined that as a particular action was culpable, it might have to be free from causality as well. In other words, the aporia between culpability and causality is no more than a thing that moral theoreticians themselves have created by reading 'freedom for the sake of culpability' as 'freedom from causality.'

Following this line of thought, the age-old problems surrounding 'free will' or 'freedom of will' can be understood to mean not that 'will is causally autonomous,' but that it is 'morally autonomous.' In other words, this implies that 'the possessor of will is a subject such as can reflect upon her or his own existence, and the moral significance of her or his actions.' Consequently, 'responsibility' and 'freedom' are almost synonymously connected through the catalyst of 'morality,' and to be 'free' in this sense means to be a 'subject who can take responsibility.'[5]

In this way, the concept of 'responsibility,' as with rights and obligations, is a socially constructed institutional concept, not one that has natural existence. What is clear in either case is that the matter of when, and what kind of, responsibility can be ascribed, and to whom, is a social agreement: something that is established by consensus. It is an institutional notion for understanding, situating and linking social events in a social space to yet other events, and specifying how they relate to the individual. The term for this is a 'socially constructed concept.' Accordingly, to presume 'responsibility' is already in itself a moral judgement. It would still be the same to use the notion of 'desert' instead of 'responsibility' to consider ideal ways of distribution.

Contemporary egalitarians completely err on this point, together with the majority of moral philosophers up to now. If responsibility could be objectively identified, then it would probably be possible to ground a normative judgement as to what should be equalised in the presence or absence of objective responsibility. In actuality, however, the very matter of where whose responsibility lies is itself a normative judgement. This is the same as the way in which the concept of 'needs that should be met' previously had presupposed a normative judgement, even in Sen's equality theory of basic capability.

As such, a plan to construct egalitarianism by tying it to luck and responsibility inevitably will fail. Though luck-egalitarianism, which makes its reference point the 'moral groundlessness of the arbitrariness of luck' in the explanation of Rawls' difference principle, appeared at first glance to be a logical construction, in reality, one cannot help saying that it was nothing more than a house of cards.[6]

Rawls' equality theory, however, is vastly different from this foundationalistic egalitarianism in the following points. Firstly, in Rawls' case, because the reasons for equality are based on the reasons for 'justice,' namely the 'fair conditions for free and equal citizens to participate voluntarily in social cooperation,' they avoid being mired in fundamentalistic egalitarianism. In contrast, Dworkin's luck-egalitarianism, by tying the presence or absence of 'responsibility' to 'what should be equalised,' combines the objective of equality and reasons for equality, and while this is attractive, it is also the cause of its difficulties. Secondly, the difference principle which champions equality is included in Rawls' second principle of justice, and he says that the first principle, which extols the 'most extensive system of equal basic liberties,' takes priority of over the second. Accordingly, equality of basic liberties is advocated first, before equality in the narrow sense relating to economic wealth. And thirdly, the 'benefit' which should be considered in equality is composed of 'primary goods,' but the thing which Rawls defines as the most important primary good is 'self-respect.' Therefore, the kind of equality that gives rise to stigma and compulsion, as luck-egalitarianism does, should be thought to have been purged from Rawlsian theory from the outset.

In this fashion, according to Rawls, the things that it was vital to equalise were 'liberty' and people's 'dignity.' In the next chapter, I will thus consider how contemporary liberalism discusses 'liberty' and 'dignity.'

Chapter 6

Reasons for the Value Called Freedom

Nothing in modern social theory has had more importance than the value called freedom. Marx, an advocate of egalitarianism, also characterises the ideal communist society as one where 'the full and free development of each individual' is actualised. In turn, Martin Luther, who appears to have promoted religious reformation in a fundamentalist manner completely unrelated to freedom, has a brief treatise, *Concerning Christian Liberty*, in which he argues that '[a] Christian man is the most free lord of all, and subject to none' (1520). This demonstrates how exceptionally strong the appeal of the value called freedom is.

In modern times, the value of freedom seems almost indubitably self-evident. Liberalism is a standpoint which attaches the greatest emphasis on 'liberty,' and Rawls, too, in his first principle of justice, insists that people should enjoy extensive and equal freedom. Why, though, is this so? Rawls' arguments presuppose that liberty is unquestionably the supreme value, and he has not reiterated his reasons for liberty.

Still, we may wonder, though: whatever kind of freedom is socially desirable to be guaranteed for people, and why? What are liberalism's views on that matter? In this chapter, I shall explore this anew.

The principle of self-determination

The factorisation of bioethics

In Japan, bioethics problems have tended to focus on brain death and organ transplantation, as seen in Chapter One, but in America's case, the greatest issue has been around the pros and cons of abortion. In the bioethics debate over abortion, at one time, the question of 'personhood' was actively discussed. The 'personhood' debate is a discussion that seeks to answer the question: 'what constitutes a being that has a personality?' Such a debate was freshly conducted because it was expected that, if a definition for the concept of a 'person' could be established, then a social consensus as to what constitutes a 'person' would be established; and since, in general, 'one must not kill any person,' this would perhaps enable us to obtain a resolution of the convoluted argument over abortion.

During the past twenty to thirty years in the United States, the pros and cons of abortion have continued to be bones of contention in an extremely heated political conflict, and the issue has polarised public opinion. It has been one of the principal points of controversy in every presidential and national assembly election, and, as is similarly the case in Japan vis-à-vis political figures' visits to Yasukuni Shrine, which venerates the war-dead, and the problem of historical recognition of Japan's actions, the mass media tend to enjoy taking up the words and deeds of politicians regarding this issue. The vehemence of conflict has intensified to an abnormal extent: various personal attacks have been carried out on medical practitioners who perform abortion procedures, even to the extent that some of the latter have been murdered.[1]

Thinkers who have endeavoured to solve this problem by means of the personhood debate have held the view that opposition to abortion is based on the logic that 'a foetus is a person, so abortion, which means taking the life of a foetus, is equivalent to homicide.' As such, if one can demonstrate that a foetus (at least, before a certain trimester) is not a person, then there will no longer be any basis to argue against abortion. Here, the following seem to be conjectured: if a foetus is not a person, then abortion is nothing more than an issue of how a particular woman treats her own body; and how one treats one's own body, as one does one's other possessions, becomes purely a question that ought to be left up to one's free will. If the established general norm were applied that one has the right to deal with one's own possessions according to one's will, then it would be logical that abortion, too, which constitutes taking the life of a foetus that is not a person, be permitted as something entrusted to free choice.

The majority of early publications on bioethics took up this personhood debate as their main theme, and they proposed various criteria for differentiating 'persons' from 'things which are not persons.' Not surprisingly, though, this personhood debate strategy has had no success, simply because there can be no reasonable grounds whatsoever for unambiguously determining at what specific moment between the instant of conception and birth a foetus could be said to change from being 'not a person' to being a person. Whether the personhood debate is right or wrong is not the issue here, however.

What is important is that the premises of 'self-determination logic' were widely shared as grounds for the view that the personhood debate had significance.

There is nothing more frequently utilised or mentioned than the logic of 'self-determination' in any of the various discussions around bioethics today. This is because it has been expected that if it were possible to apply this logic of self-determination to complex and seemingly difficult-to-solve issues in ethics, then it might be possible to exert authority such as could solve an overall problem by breaking down the composite of the problem into all of its simple elements, just as in factorisation. In other words, 'self-determination logic' is nothing other than a generic term for a theoretical attempt to solve a complex issue like bioethics by demarcating social spaces into domains that should be entrusted to self-discretion for each individual, based on a notion of freedom which has already been generally established in modern society. Therein, of course, has lain the basic premise of liberalism, namely that it is a good thing for as broad a domain as possible to be left up to self-determination. In early bioethics, there was prolific advancement of such projects.[2]

The harm principle and discretionary space

The idea which has formed the basis for this kind of self-determination logic is the approach dubbed the 'harm principle' by J.S. Mill. In his *On Liberty*, it is expressed as follows:

> The only part of the conduct of any one, for which he is amenable to society, is that which concerns others. *In the part which merely concerns himself*, his independence is, of right, absolute. Over himself, over his own body and mind, the individual is sovereign (Mill 1973, p. 484; emphasis added).

In other words, no other person, nor society, may interfere in those actions of a person which concern that individual alone. The principle claims that this represents the desirable way for a society to be. Society can forbid or restrict behaviour that might harm others, but people have the freedom to decide for themselves in regard to actions that would not do so. In this sense, it would probably be better to call it the 'do-no-harm principle' rather than the 'harm principle.' It is a 'principle of self-determination vis-à-vis behaviour that is unrelated to others.' Furthermore, from the standpoint of this principle, interference by other people or society in behaviour unconnected with others would be strongly criticised as 'paternalistic.'

This is very lucid reasoning. There seems to be absolutely no room for objection. In actual fact, however, problems can hardly ever be solved by means of this principle. Especially in regard to controversial problems of social ethics, Mill's principle is almost powerless. The reason for that will soon become apparent, but let me offer a little explanation.

There is the problem, for example, of whether it is permissible to make human clones.[3] The argument that it is permissible asserts that a certain person's action of cloning her- or himself should be left up to the free choice of the person involved, according to Mill's principle. This is because even though it would mean obtaining the help of a medical practitioner, voluntarily-donated egg cells, and a woman to be the 'incubator' (in some cases, the person herself), fundamentally the cloning can be regarded as concerning only the cloner her- or himself. Yet most people tend to oppose human cloning. From the standpoint of the harm principle, this appears irrational. Actually, most recent Japanese ethicists who have discussed cloning technology have emphasised that there is no rational basis for restricting it, the reason being that they think that the harm principle applies in this case. (The same people sometimes oppose the medical use of embryonic stem cells. This involves a slightly different ethical principle, taking issue with the ethicality of doctors or scientists who are not the individuals concerned exploiting things that belong to other people, or those people themselves, for such impure objectives as academic glory or commercial gain.)

Certainly, if quizzed as to the reason for their opposition, there would be few people able to expand their rationale in a theoretical manner. But, aside from the question of whether there *are* theoretical grounds, the following fact is clear: namely, that many people do not view somebody's creating a human clone as being 'an act that concerns only that person.' Perhaps this simply means that a lot of people could be mistaken. Though human cloning really relates to just the person in question, it might be misunderstood as being related to many others. But, *who on earth could determine* that creating a human clone would relate solely to that person?

What sort of thing is meant by 'to relate solely to that person,' in the first place? On this issue, Dworkin, in an argument justifying liberalism, tried to reinforce the harm principle by making a distinction between 'external preferences' and 'internal preferences.' People often take an interest in the condition of others who are unconnected to themselves, and they have their likes and dislikes. One example of this is the view that another person's belief in a different religion is 'mistaken.' Such preferential judgements to do with other people's matters are called 'external preferences.' Dworkin asserts that external preferences ought not to be taken into consideration when examining social desirability or normative principles.

It must be said, however, that this assertion, rather than supplying grounds for the harm principle, is merely restating a conceptual division to support it. Indeed, the boundaries of what constitutes an external preference are extremely fuzzy. It may be an external preference to feel repugnance at other people's belief in a religion that one loathes, for instance, but would it still be an external preference to say that one hated seeing posters soliciting recruits to that religion posted up on street corners? Still more, one could not always advocate the banning of interference in the sort of religion that believes it right to slaughter followers of a different faith from its own, on the rationale that it is an 'external preference.'

Of course, even if one accepted the harm principle, there are some powerful counter-arguments against cloning. Above all, when an individual *A* makes a human clone, this will cause the birth of a new personality, *B*, so *A*'s act has not constituted an 'act relating only to *A*.' In response to this, there is a discourse in defence of cloning which says, 'in cases where parents create a child in the usual way, the parents' action is involved in the birth of a separate individual, and that, moreover, is permitted; so there is no reason for only cloning to be prohibited.' That in itself constitutes one argument, but in this case, one must pay attention to the fact that the harm principle is not being utilised as a reason for defending cloning. It is rather an argument developed upon the recognition that cloning is '*not* an act relating solely to the person concerned.'

Whatever the case, it is clear that the following problem is inherent here: namely, what kind of action in general is one relating only to that person? Who will make that decision, on what authority? For the principle of self-determination and the harm principle, it is the major premise that these will be objectively determined. As yet, however, nobody has succeeded in setting forth such objective criteria.

Actually, the same problem as this arises in connection with the notion of 'rights peculiar to each individual.' Libertarian advocates, represented by Nozick, think that every person has some kind of inviolable domain of rights. These could be the right to manage one's own assets and the right to dispose of them freely, or the right to self-management over one's own body. Libertarians consider that only when there is perfectly spontaneous agreement on the part of the original person in question is it permissible for others to intervene in such a rights domain, or for one to be able to hand it over to another.

This argument is very simple and easy to understand: social space is distinctly partitioned into inviolable domains belonging to each person, and only through the procedure called agreement are changes in the domain permitted. It is a theoretical structure that could be called the acme of individualism. Yet this argument is premised upon there being firm settlement as to 'what constitutes an inviolable domain peculiar to each person.' In response, many libertarians—following the example of the seventeenth-century thinker, Locke—consider that what is at its core is justly-owned land, and the products obtained by the work of individual labour upon it. In this response, a particular social model is implicitly assumed. That is, it is a 'community composed solely of independent farmers' where each farmer makes his farming business on justly owned land in complete independence, so that any products obtained by his business unmistakeably belong to him.

This premise is not valid, however. Firstly, the 'just ownership of land' is historically hard to justify, because one cannot imagine that the ownership of land today has been shaped since the dawn of humankind solely by means of just original ownership and its fair transfer. Next, libertarian principles can tell us nothing about how the products of the land should be distributed in cases where joint farming such as 'tenant farming' is present, in which different persons participate in one farming business. This difficulty becomes all the greater in the case of present-day general production activity. Our society is composed of an extremely complex economic structure. Its various products are produced by means of the 'joint production' of large numbers of people. The idea of dividing up jointly-produced goods and services into inviolable domains proper to each individual has been an impossible one from the start. (In reality, our joint-production economy adopts various ways of distributing benefits jointly produced, both within and between productive organisations. But none of these distribution systems should be considered as 'inviolable.' The question of what kind of normative principle should be applied is the very research subject of Rawlsian liberalism, as seen in this volume.)

The personhood debate in bioethics, together with libertarian philosophy as a normative social theory, were types of fundamentalist individualism that have shared the limelight since their development mainly in 1970s America. In one sense, they might be understood as attempts to return to the initial principles of modern social theory in order to supply answers to the difficult ethical questions that beset contemporary society in its pluralistic complexity. These theories presuppose the existence of undeniable answers to the questions of 'what constitutes action related only to a particular person' and 'what constitutes a person's own inviolable domain,' yet these presuppositions can never be established.

Sen's liberal paradox and its significance

Now, let us ponder the issue of the principle of self-determination from a different angle. One of the achievements of Amartya Sen, winner of the 1998 Nobel Prize in Economics for his theoretical contributions to the problems of equality and poverty, was his 'liberal paradox' theorem in his early career. Generally, this is understood to be an extension of Arrow's impossibility theorem which says that it is impossible to derive social decisions under a certain reasonable set of conditions. This in itself is correct, but when this theorem and the controversy around it are put to the test, problems latent in the view of establishing a discretionary sphere come to the surface.

Lady Chatterley's Lover

Sen's theorem says that when at least two individuals are allowed a discretionary space for each, there will be no general method that would lead to a social decision. Let me explain its substance by means of the example that Sen himself employs.

Assume that there are two men, 'Mr *A*, the prude,' and 'Mr *B*, the lascivious' (Sen 1970, p. 80), and that there is to be social choice as to whether Mr *A* should read D.H. Lawrence's *Lady Chatterley's Lover*, or Mr *B* should read it, or neither should read it. The prudish Mr *A* would prefer that neither read it, but thinks that if someone had to read it, then it would be better if he himself read it, as there would be greater harm in letting the lascivious Mr *B* read it. Mr *B*, on the other hand, thinks that both should read it, but if only one of the two were allowed to read it, then it would be better for society to make the moralistic Mr *A* read it, rather than Mr *B* himself. (I draw your attention to the fact that each man, conscious of the other, has made a choice contrary to his own frank preference.)

As the possibility that 'both read it' is excluded in advance, the social circumstances that could eventuate would be of the following three types: (even if 'both read it' were added to the alternatives, the main thrust of the argument would not change.)

> x: only Mr *A* reads it
>
> y: only Mr *B* reads it
>
> z: nobody reads it

In regard to these three social states, by assumption, Mr *A* and Mr *B*'s order of preference would be as below. (Social states to the left would be more strongly preferred.)

> Mr *A*: z, x, y
>
> Mr *B*: x, y, z

As in Arrow's case, the question here is how a single social preference ordering could be derived when the above kind of order of preference was given for two individuals. In other words, the possibility of a social choice function which could determine an order of social states commonly applicable to both Mr *A* and Mr *B* is an issue.

Here, Sen places the following conditions on the social choice function:

(1) (Acyclicity) Social preference orderings must not be cyclical.
(2) (Pareto principle) If all parties' preferences are identical regarding the ordering of two alternative social states, x_1 and x_2, then social preference ordering also must follow that ordering.
(3) (Unrestricted domain) Any set of individual preference orderings must be included in the domain of the social choice function.

These conditions are quite similar to those in Arrow, but are looser than the latter: specifically speaking, the 'non-dictatorship' and 'independence of irrelevant alternatives' terms have been removed. Instead, in Sen's theorem, the following 'liberal' condition is added:

(4) (The 'Liberal' condition) There are two or more individuals such that for each of them there is at least one set of two social states whose social preference ordering will be determined according to

Figure 6.1: The liberal paradox

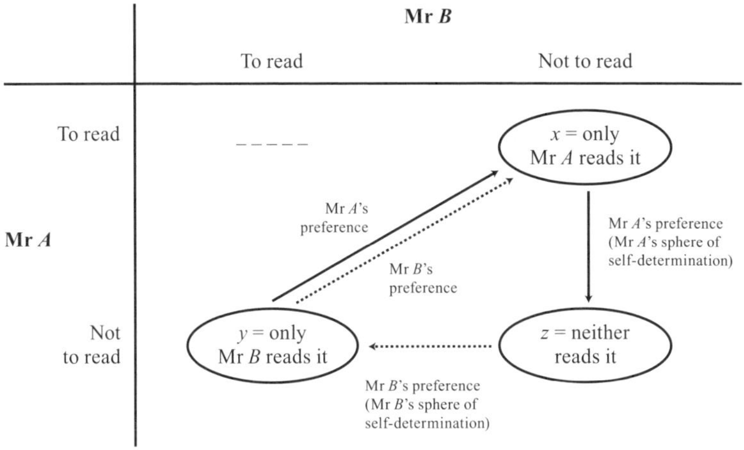

> her own order of preference. In other words, the social preference ordering vis-à-vis these pairs must follow the preference ordering of the individual in question. This will constitute the 'discretionary sphere' for the individual.

Let me explain the meaning of these conditions using the above example of *Lady Chatterley's Lover*. The sets of possible social states which Mr *A* and Mr *B* are facing are expressed as in Figure 6.1.

The arrows indicate the respective preference orderings, with the alternative at the arrowhead being the more preferred.

Here, assume the two individuals' 'discretionary sphere' such as would fulfil the Liberal condition (4) to be as follows: firstly, as for Mr *A*, let the choice between '*x* and *z*' be left to his discretion, because the difference between *x* and *z* is only a matter of whether Mr *A* reads or does not read, and there is no alteration in Mr *B*'s state. For the same reason, as for Mr *B*, let the choice between '*z* and *y*' be at his discretion. These are each indicated in the figure by solid lines and broken lines, respectively. What Sen calls the 'Liberal condition' means specifically embedding such a 'discretionary sphere' within social choice. (Sen's condition is very loose, however, and even when there are three or more members, it will suffice to establish an ordering of alternatives as the 'discretionary space' for only two of them.)

In this way, if Mr *A* and Mr *B* are allowed a respective discretionary pair, then, as can be understood from Figure 6.1, the social ordering

$x \rightarrow z \rightarrow y$ will be obtained. There are, however, two arrows pointing from y to x. These show that both Mr A and Mr B prefer 'x over y.' The preferences of all parties (that is, the two men) are identical as regards y and x. Accordingly, by condition (2) (Pareto principle), this ordering must also be reflected in the social ordering.

If these are linked together, though, the cycle '$x \rightarrow z \rightarrow y \rightarrow x$' is generated, contravening condition (1). This is the 'liberal paradox.' The theorem which Sen proved is a general theorem such as the following:

> Sen's theorem: there is no social choice function such as will satisfy all conditions (1) to (4) simultaneously.

To avoid misapprehension, let me add two further points of explanation. Firstly, for a certain specific set of individual preference orderings, this theorem will not preclude the possible existence of a social choice such as would derive an acyclic social ordering, having satisfied conditions (2) and (4). In actuality, in Figure 6.1, if the preferences of both men vis-à-vis x and y were diametrically opposed, then the social ordering '$y \rightarrow z \rightarrow x$' would probably be easily derivable. What 'does not exist' in this theorem is a social choice function such as would 'always' enable acyclic social ordering for any set of individual preference orderings.'

Next, the reason why it should be inconvenient for a cycle to arise is that if there were a cycle, then a unique social choice would not be obtainable. This will be clear from Figure 6.1. One might think that, in cases of more than four possible social states, even if a cycle should arise in its lower ranks, it could be considered unproblematic as long as the single highest-ranking state were selected. However, a social choice function such as would allow a cycle to arise in a low rank for a certain set of individual preference orderings should also allow one to emerge in regard to different sets in upper rankings, or throughout. Therefore, it should not be good for cycles to arise anywhere, after all.

How can the paradox be resolved?

If a discretionary sphere were allowed, that would make social choice impossible. Sen's theorem says so. This was an impactful theorem not only for self-determinists, but also for social theorists who had desultorily considered 'freedom' to be precious. For that reason, during the two or three years following the theorem's publication, many scholars developed various arguments around it. Mostly, the focus of concern was upon attempting somehow to derive an acyclic social ordering and make social choice possible by relaxing any of Sen's four conditions.

To place the focal points of the issue here, on the premise that adherence to acyclicity in condition (1) would not be shifted, there would be three possible means of solution, namely, relaxing either condition (2) Pareto optimality; or condition (3) non-restrictedness of domain; or condition (4) the Liberal condition.

Relaxing the Liberal condition means ignoring at least one of the discretionary arrows in Figure 6.1. If Mr *A*'s discretionary rights are not taken into consideration, then the acyclic ordering '$z \rightarrow y \rightarrow x$' will be obtained. Similarly, if Mr *B*'s discretionary rights are erased, then the social ordering '$y \rightarrow x \rightarrow z$' will be obtained. Some scholars have thought that, rather than indiscriminately applying the Liberal condition to every discretionary sphere, it would be permissible to remove it from the conditions for constituting social ordering, if the actual content of the sphere does not deserve to be treated so. Indeed, there is ample room for discussion vis-à-vis what should be recognised as being a right in terms of discretionary sphere. That being said, it still does not lead to a resolution of the paradox, because the Liberal condition can be read as a condition to be applied when we set up the sort of discretionary sphere whose content has not been at all problematic.

Conversely, it is Nozick who has argued from the perspective that the right to self-determination is an absolutely inviolable precondition, thus making the idea of relaxing the Liberal condition preposterous. He states that individual rights are an absolute precondition to any kind of social choice, and that social choice can only be carried out within the parameters delimited by individual rights. If we apply this idea to the *Lady Chatterley's Lover* example, both Mr *A*'s individual right 'not to read' and Mr *B*'s individual right 'to read' will be preserved. In this case, as the only alternative that will fulfil these two rights conditions is *y* (Mr *A* does not read; Mr *B* does read), consequently *y* will be socially selected. Nozick's assertion means, in a sense, relaxing condition (3) and narrowing the range of choice in advance (Nozick 1974).

Nozick illustrates this claim with the following allegory: 'If I have a right to choose to live in New York or in Massachusetts, and I choose Massachusetts, then alternatives involving my living in New York are not appropriate objects to be entered in a social ordering' (1974, p. 166). In reply, Sen counters with: 'But one can also argue that if I believe that it is a better society which—given other things—lets Nozick decide where he wishes to live, then I must *assert* that it is socially *better* that Nozick should be permitted to live in Massachusetts as chosen by him' (Sen 1976, p. 231, emphasis in original).

This counterargument probably has a weightier significance than Sen himself realises. He is frankly saying that the very question of whose discretionary sphere will be recognised, and where, constitutes a social state. In other words, while there initially appeared to be only two alternatives, 'Nozick will live in New York' or 'Nozick will live in Massachusetts,' a further meta-social state will be set up, namely 'whether Nozick's living in New York or in Massachusetts belongs to his discretionary sphere, or not.' In generalised terms, the question of 'to whom the right to decide belongs' will be added as a constituent element of a set of social states. By extension, any number of further additions can be made of a variety of elements, such as 'rights,' 'obligations,' 'decision procedures,' and the like. 'The right to determine a right,' would be followed by 'the right to determine the right to determine a right,' and so on, *ad infinitum*.

This, of course, is half in jest. Its material significance is enormous, however—by which I mean that it illustrates that the basic composition of the social choice theory of 'determining the social preference ordering from a given set of individual preference orderings on social states' is nothing more than a fiction. The assumption of something called a 'given set of social states' is meaningless for actual society, from the outset. In reality, any set of social states that could be the object of our investigation of desirable society is not given in advance of our investigation. We may always conceive of a new social state which hitherto has not been imagined.

Let us not encroach upon this point now. What is clear is that if, like Nozick, one thought that something constituting a discretionary sphere could unconditionally be established, then something akin to Sen's liberal paradox would cease to exist; or else, even if it did exist, it would be nothing but a trivial paradox, from Nozick's point of view.

Sen's solution strategy and its tricks

Sen himself has proposed a method for resolving the paradox: to relax condition (2)'s Pareto principle. Condition (2) stipulates that if all parties hold the same preference ordering of two alternatives, then social ordering should reflect that. In that sense, it would be easier to understand if we called it the 'unanimity rule.' Sen asserts that, 'in order to enable social judgement while avoiding the application of the unanimity rule, it is desirable that there be such *individuals as would be prepared to amend their own preference orderings*' (Sen 1982, p. 314). In other words, he says that a desirable solution would be the presence of '[a] person...[who] wants only a part of his total preference to count such that it can be combined with everyone's preferences over *their* respective 'protected spheres (= discretionary space) [without conflict]' (1982, p. 314, emphasis in original). This is the sort of individual who thinks, 'my own preference need not carry weight in social judgements as regards any part in which a contradiction arises.' Sen calls such an individual 'a person who respects the rights of others,' and he proved that the presence of even one such individual would enable the existence of a social choice function such as would satisfy conditions (2) to (4), and also yield an acyclical social ordering.

On this basis, Sen coined the term 'Paretian epidemic' for the rise of inconveniences due to seeing the unanimity principle as absolutely inviolable, and he emphasised that it was precisely the existence of 'a person who respects the rights of others' that was vital for checking the spread of the epidemic and obtaining a fitting social judgement.

Sen's strategy for resolution appears to mean that 'the very presence of the kind of individual who possesses public-spiritedness in the form of respect for others' rights makes possible the realisation of the public value as a unique social determination, built upon respect for mutual rights.' Sen intends that it be interpreted as such. There is a problem in this interpretation, however. I draw your attention to the following two tricks.

Firstly, here, the 'person who respects the rights of others' is essentially 'an individual who is willing to suppress her or his own preference for the sake of social judgement.' This certainly may be one personal virtue, but assuming such an individual means assuming an individual who will repress her- or himself for the sake of a collective judgement, and this would, in the first place, render meaningless the basic problem-establishment of social choice theory, namely, the derivation of social judgements vis-à-vis random combinations of given individual preferences.

Secondly, we should note, it is not specified at all here '*who* respects *what kind* of rights of others.' In the *Lady Chatterley's Lover* example, irrespective of whether it is Mr *A* or Mr *B* who respects others' rights, the conclusion to Sen's solution strategy is 'only Mr *B* reads it.' In terms of outcome, this is identical to Nozick's assertion, but for a different reason. Its being the same as Nozick means that the result is one that has respected self-determination, so Sen's solution will appear plausible. It can be thought to be so, however, just because the question was 'whether to read the controversial but well-reputed novel that D.H. Lawrence wrote.' Sen's solution looks good for the very reason that we are thinking on the basis of a norm that already says it ought not to be forbidden to read this novel. What would happen if what Mr *A* and Mr *B* were squabbling over was not this problem, but 'whether to smoke marijuana,' 'whether to maltreat animals,' 'whether to make human clones,' or the like? One could hardly say that choosing 'only Mr *B* will do it' would be desirable.

The idea of compartmentalisation

Many of the scholars who confronted Sen's liberal paradox developed their arguments with a focus upon the issue of 'how to resolve the paradox.' That may well be interesting as an intellectual quest, but it is a mistake to think that that in itself is directly connected with an investigation of the problem of normative principles. The problem-establishment in social choice theory has been put together on an extremely mechanical pattern. All of the concepts which constitute that theory: social states, individual preference, discretionary sphere, and so on, are exceedingly abstract, and their substance has not been specified in any manner. Accordingly, setting up problems on this pattern and solving them is no different from working out a logical puzzle. Especially, even if a social choice function which could always elicit an acyclical social ordering had been established, it would merely mean that a formal algorithm for deriving a social determination had been found—in other words, a computer programme such as would automatically output some kind of 'correct social determination' if one were to input something like individual preference orderings on social states as 'data.' Arrow's impossibility theorem and Sen's theorem teach us that such a programme does not exist. If anything, it probably should be considered a welcome discovery.

Accordingly, there is no necessity whatsoever to agonise—as many writers have done when faced with Sen's liberal paradox—over whether there is no way of resolving it. We had better think that, under the sort of circumstance in which the discretionary sphere and unanimity principle were set up merely in a formal manner, it would apparently be quite impossible to arrive at a social determination which could satisfy us. What the liberal paradox means is that it would not be possible for us to derive a desirable social determination by using a formal logic such as would be applicable anytime and anywhere.

What is even more important in relation to Sen's theorem is that each of the conditions stipulated as prerequisites within it are not prerequisites for us in reality. In other words, all of the questions—what should one recognise as whose discretionary sphere; when, and to what extent, should the unanimity principle be observed; and, when, and to what degree, should people's personal preferences be respected—themselves are the objects of social choice. Sen happens to remark, 'if I believe that it is a better society which…lets Nozick decide where he wishes to live' (1976, p. 231). This means that the very issue of 'who should be allowed what right of self-determination' is the target of people's 'preference,' and therefore is also something that should be socially decided.

In actuality, such a pattern of questions around the discretionary sphere parallels the problems besetting the 'luck-egalitarianism' seen in a previous chapter. Luck-egalitarianism is premised upon the ability of people's circumstances in society to be divided into those which have resulted from their environment, and those arising through their own responsibility. This division is something that *is objectively given*, and about which there is *no social choice necessary*. Accordingly, society merely needs to compensate for consequences that are due to situations which do not belong to people's sphere of responsibility, and for the results of brute bad luck. This was the basic structure of luck-egalitarianism.

Self-determination logic, too, considers that the social world can be *incontestably* divided into that which constitutes the discretionary sphere, and that which does not. On that premise, it asserts that other people and society should not intervene in matters belonging to the discretionary sphere.

Common to both theories is a way of thinking that could be called the '*idea of compartmentalisation*.' This is a way of thinking which argues that, as society has a pre-determined discretionary sphere where individual persons should freely take responsibility, normative social theory can find such a discretionary sphere and, based on that fact, construct normative principles. It says that the task of social theory is to recognise accurately what belongs to the personal sphere and to prohibit unjust interference in that personal sphere; and to let society take responsibility for problems that cannot be resolved within personal spheres.

Such an idea of compartmentalisation has widely permeated among American theorists since the 1970s. It is shared not only by libertarians, but also by self-determination theorists who believe in the harm principle, and many advocates of liberalism. Indeed, in one sense, it is probably an attempt to respond particularly to the pluralistic situations which I will examine in the next chapter. This is extremely similar to the resolution policy after the Thirty Years' War, which partitioned the Western European world into sovereign states by means of the Treaty of Westphalia, and, while acknowledging autonomy in relation to religious issues within each state, did not make the question of religion a point of contention between states. Compartmentalisation is an ideology that endeavours to apply this idea not to a state level, but to the level of the individual.

Nowadays, though, this view of a world segmented into sovereign nation-states has ceased to hold true. The reason, simply speaking, is that we have come to have enormous interest in things that are happening inside other states and societies, and it is considered that we *should* be concerned. The same goes not only for economic or military situations, but also for socio-cultural situations such as poverty or human rights.

The same, or even more, can be said in regard to the individual level. Compartmentalisation on the individual level is inherently invalid, because the question of what 'relates only to oneself' and what belongs to the personal sphere of self-autonomy, or what belongs within an individual's range of responsibility, is not something given *a priori*, but something that society decides. More precisely speaking, we first deliberately consider in what spheres of individuals other people or society ought not to interfere, or for what we should penalise or reward individuals from a normative viewpoint; and, thereafter, we institutionally establish what constitutes the discretionary sphere and the range of responsibility.

It is the same with 'rights' and 'responsibility,' too. These are all words which express *institutional notions*, and, in a sense, are things that we humans have wilfully created, and with which we have ordered our own society. They are by no means things which have been naturally determined *a priori*.

Liberalism's three freedoms

The meaning and reason of freedom

There is no room for doubt, however, that freedom has important value in the present day. As I have stated above, however, the question of what kind of freedoms should be allowed us is one which we ourselves should decide, and its answer is certainly not something which should be given from without. Moreover, there must be reasons for advocating those respective freedoms. In the case of liberalism, of course, since 'liberty' remains its core value, as its nomenclature shows, the way its grounds are attached must be interrogated. As the institutional establishment of some kind of freedom means setting up a political authority to deter its violation and punish actual acts of violation, there has to be sufficient reason for it.

In European society, the importance of 'freedom' has been recognised from ages past by a wide range of people as being more or less self-explanatory, as can be seen in Luther. The origins of such an emphasis on 'freedom' can be traced back to the world of Ancient Greece. There, the primary feature of persons deemed suitable for membership of society was that they were not 'slaves,' but 'free persons.' The war with Persia, too, was signified as being a fight between 'tyranny' and 'freedom.' As I have mentioned already, in his arguments on democracy in the age of the Peloponnesian War, Aristotle finds egalitarianism in the form of 'those who are free and equal should be treated equally.' At that time, important significance had already been attached to 'being free.'

Socrates and Plato did not discuss 'freedom' to any great extent, however. Neither did Aristotle assert the value of 'freedom' as his own argument. Indeed, the primacy of freedom is something that was not established until recent times. It goes without saying that it is hard to find anything in the traditional social thought of Japan and China that expounds freedom. The Chinese character-compound currently used for 'freedom' ('*jiyū*' in Japanese pronunciation) has been used since Ancient China, but it meant merely 'behaving as one wishes,' and it was not imbued with a social value such as that of today. In Japan, the present-day meaning of *jiyū* is one which gained currency from the Meiji era onwards as a translation for 'liberty,' 'freedom' and '*Freiheit*.'

One great element behind the fervent discussion of 'freedom' in modern times probably was the striving by the intelligentsia for liberation from previous thought-control by the Catholic Church, and from a feudalistic political system. It was the same with Japanese youth of the Meiji era, also. In early modern period thought which aspired towards a theory for the rational ordering of society, 'freedom (*jiyū*)' tended to be justified as being a 'natural right (*shizenken*).' The same applies in Hobbes and Locke, and their legacy is carried on even today by libertarians, starting with Nozick. By contrast, in the tradition of German idealists such as Kant and Hegel, the grounds for 'freedom' are given in terms of it being an 'internal necessity,' so to speak. In other words, individuals are said to be 'free' as proof that they are rational and moral beings that have free will.[4] In discussions around liberalism today, too, such different ways of supplying grounds for freedom are invoked both implicitly and explicitly. Normally, it would be proper to review such grounds painstakingly, but here I wish to limit my examination to the minimum necessary for understanding the theoretical composition of contemporary liberalism.

The three freedoms

The first important point is that there are various contents and grounds to 'freedom.' In one kind of liberalism, for example, 'freedom' exclusively indicates the right of self-determination. In other cases, the word 'freedom' is used more to mean mainly freedom of thought and belief, or political freedom. This is closely connected also to religious toleration and multiculturalism. In yet another case, 'freedom' also principally means individual autonomy.

For the time being, it would probably be appropriate to divide the substantive notion of 'freedom' into the following three broad types for consideration:

1. Freedom from constraint
2. Freedom as autonomy
3. Open freedom

It goes without saying that this classification is only tentative. With that in mind, let me explain the features of these three concepts.

Freedom from constraint is what Berlin, in his essay, 'Two Concepts of Liberty' (1969) calls 'negative freedom'—freedom in the sense of not being restricted by society or any other person. It is the freedom meant by the principle of self-determination and the harm principle, and Sen's allegory of *Lady Chatterley's Lover* corresponds to freedom in this sense. It thinks that the question of what kind of novel a certain person reads or does not read—just like whether to have toast or cereal for breakfast—belongs within the bounds of that person's right of self-determination.

The concept of 'freedom' in libertarianism is largely this freedom from constraint, but it has also widely permeated into liberalism. Much of contemporary liberal thinking places great value upon 'each person's conception of a good life' being autonomous; and it tends to consider it wrong for society to intervene paternalistically in that. It is thought that, regardless of what each individual's conception of good might be, as long as it is something that does not infringe upon the harm principle, then enabling and supporting its pursuit is the primary moral duty of society. For this kind of liberalism, freedom from constraint is seen as important because, as in the formulation of Mill's harm principle, it is thought that 'the individual in question is sovereign in matters pertaining to him- or herself.' At its base is the idea of a '*sovereign self*,' which says that there is no possibility that anyone other than a particular individual, or society, will be capable of better judgement for that individual's sake in regard to that individual's business. It is *paternalism* to interfere in these things, which is wrong. Moreover, if one thinks on the basis of Bentham-style individualism, which says that 'all that exists is the individual, and social desirability relies solely upon the individual's situation,' then it will mean that guaranteeing freedom from constraint would be expected to form the heart of society's normative principles.

The viewpoint that emphasises freedom from constraint has extremely high congeniality with the idea of compartmentalisation already mentioned. The 'rights-based approach,' in particular—asserting that people inherently have 'rights' proper to themselves that nobody can violate, and that it is exceptionally important in terms of social desirability that such rights be preserved and guaranteed—constitutes one of contemporary liberalism's major theses.

By contrast, there is a moral philosopher named Joseph Raz, who is typical of scholars who expound *freedom as autonomy*. He asserts that individual autonomy is the primary value for a person, saying, 'The autonomous person is a (part) author of his own life' (Raz 1986, p. 408), and '[a] person's life is autonomous if it is to a considerable extent his own creation' (1986, p. 369). For Raz, the morally primary values are 'self-creation' and 'being an author of one's own life'—in short, pursuing personal virtue and excellence. Accordingly, normative principles relating to social institutions come to be put together from the perspective of how to enable and support such individual autonomous activity. In other words, social and political freedom constitutes the most fundamental condition for this autonomy, and that is why freedom has an intrinsic value in itself (Raz 1986).

As can be appreciated from this, the idea of freedom as autonomy clearly differs from simple freedom from constraint in the following aspect: namely, individual conceptions of the good have to be unconditionally respected in the case of freedom from constraint, regardless of their substance, whereas freedom as autonomy makes an issue of the goodness of the conceptions of the good. The morality theory that places great value upon individuals' cultivating virtue in moral or other aspects is called '*perfectionism*.' The idea of freedom as autonomy is one type of perfectionism.

There is a tendency among advocates of contemporary liberalism, starting with Rawls in *A Theory of Justice*, to view perfectionism as something different from liberalism. This is because perfectionism is obviously the kind of theory that intervenes in the 'individual's way of life,' and is thought to be incompatible with liberalism, which emphasises the self-determination of the individual's way of living.

Nevertheless, there is certainly no dearth of liberal theories of the type in which to respect individual autonomy, as does Raz, means respecting not merely an individual's way of life as is, but the way that an individual's life *ought to be*.

Tatsuo Inoue, who represents Japanese liberalism, for example, has developed the following kind of theory of the self as a 'self-interpretive being,' which is clearly perfectionist.

> My autonomy lies in the following kind of ability to carry out the 'twin responsibilities' which in principle cannot be diverted. One is the ability to discharge, through self-interpretation, the responsibility for interpreting and pursuing the guiding values of my own life, which, because I cannot imagine that I have the freedom not to choose, I cannot even assert that I have chosen freely. Another is the ability to discharge the responsibility to know myself through interpreting such values (Inoue 1999, p. 159).

Inoue calls this kind of autonomy 'interpretative autonomy,' and the liberalism that respects interpretative autonomy 'robust liberalism.' One could say that here, one ideal image of liberalism is being attractively and loftily extolled. But I beg your particular attention to Inoue's deft use of the word 'responsibility.' Here, 'responsibility' is a notion which connects the individual to a value that transcends the individual. The concept of freedom as autonomy is tacitly directed towards some kind of value in a higher-order situation that surpasses the individual.

Furthermore, it has become a regular view in philosophy to think of moral responsibility and freedom as being inextricably linked. In theoretical terms, Kantian moral philosophy is renowned for having the opinion that an individual's behaving morally means adhering to 'moral law' and 'internal necessity,' and that this itself constitutes an inherent 'freedom' at the same time. Though there is something of a logical trick in 'necessity' and 'freedom' being linked together, the connection between freedom and morality is not an odd one. As I touched upon in a previous chapter, we think on a daily basis that the subject that can take responsibility has to be a free being from the outset, and, conversely, freedom is accompanied by responsibility. In modern society, the subject of moral and legal responsibility is assumed to be a free individual. Accordingly, it could be said that the idea of freedom as autonomy is something that coincides well with our everyday moral considerations.

While still sharing the name of liberalism, the difference between freedom from constraint and freedom as autonomy vis-à-vis which of the freedoms ought to be respected generates a huge disparity in the content of the normative principles that society should adopt. Especially sharp opposition around the question of the extent to which a government or society is allowed to interfere with the individual will arise. If one regards freedom from constraint as foremost, then, as long as this is not restricted by the harm principle, it will not be a desirable thing for society to intervene in the individual's way of living. That would become the target of criticism for being 'paternalism.' By contrast, if one sees freedom as autonomy as being primary, then it will be more desirable for society to intervene actively in order for people to 'enhance their own autonomous virtue.' This means that society should support people so that they can take on ways of living in which they become the 'authors of their own lives.'

Finally, as for *open freedom*, this is what initially was called 'freedom of conscience,' and is the freedom that is expressed in institutional settings as 'freedom of thought and belief' and 'political freedom.' Conscience is the working of the mind when individuals autonomously carry out normative judgements using the power of reason, while adhering to their own convictions. Open freedom argues that such workings of people's hearts must not be hindered or repressed by society; and, accordingly, this means that nobody must penalise individuals or compel them in a prescribed direction due to the latter's thoughts and beliefs or political assertions.

Open freedom has already been widely established as an institutional norm constituting the fundamental element of most present-day constitutional political systems, and cannot always be uniquely attributed to contemporary liberalism. It is not the case, of course, that communitarianism does not value open freedom. As can be understood from the fact that the word 'liberal' has signified 'toleration' all along, classical liberalism was from the outset something that advocated this open freedom. Moreover, the legacy of its ideological origins lives on in the way present-day liberalism has developed an argument that also emphasises 'toleration' towards multicultural circumstances.

This open freedom is subtly different from freedom from constraint and freedom as autonomy in the following aspects. Firstly, open freedom presupposes that people live their religious or moral convictions in their respective ways. What is at the heart of its openness is the fact that it is open towards differing beliefs such as would form the basis of conscience. By contrast, the target of consideration by freedom from constraint is all unadulterated conceptions of the good, which could encompass even selfish ways of living that could not be supported by conscience. Freedom as autonomy, in turn, can be called more interventionist than open freedom, in regard to the content of conscience.

Secondly, the social freedoms which social institutions should guarantee have different foci. Open freedom, it goes without saying, has a focus on classical political freedom and freedom of religion, thought and scholarship. Guaranteeing to the maximum extent that people will live according to their own conscience constitutes the first condition of a normative principle. With freedom from constraint, on the other hand, the main purpose is to guarantee to the maximum degree that each person will freely pursue his or her respective conception of the good. That requires a far broader-ranging social liberty than political or religious freedom, and strives as far as possible to remove paternalistic interference from the government or society. Conversely, freedom as autonomy does not merely tolerate society's intervening in a certain type of belief in order to foster it, but rather supports that intervention positively.

In sum, though liberalism admittedly is an ideology that endeavours to protect the value of freedom, such freedoms are not singular. Their being regarded as indispensable for people's goodness of life, and their protection being seen as society's most important moral duty, are points in common, but they diverge as to what kind of freedoms are in question. This difference is due to dissimilar ideas about what sort of freedom is most essentially important for people's goodness of life.

The three freedoms and normative principles

Rawls' first principle of justice stipulates that basic liberties should be equally and most widely guaranteed, but what is actually placed at the core of those basic liberties is 'freedom of conscience.' In other words, the kind of freedom to which Rawls gives most weight as a normative principle for society is neither freedom from constraint, nor socio-economic equality, but open freedom.

In relation to the choice of justice principles in the original position, Rawls establishes that:

> [equal liberty of conscience] is one of the fixed points of our considered judgments of justice… [I]t seems evident that the parties must choose principles that secure the integrity of their religious and moral freedom (1971, p. 206).

He continues as follows:

> [the parties]… do not know…what their religious or moral convictions are, or what is the particular content of their moral or religious obligations as they interpret them…Further, the parties do not know how their religious or moral view fares in their society, whether, for example, it is in the majority or the minority…[T]he question they are to decide is which principle they should adopt to regulate the liberties of citizens in regard to their fundamental religious, moral and philosophical interests (1971, p. 206).

In other words, the main object of principles of justice is, above all, the equal guaranteeing of people's religious and moral freedom. While this reason is formally explained in Rawls' book as a choice in the original position, it is fundamentally based on the fact that such freedom is hard to shift in terms of 'our considered judgements.' Justice as fairness originally is something that determines fair terms in order for people to participate voluntarily in social cooperation, and as social cooperation primarily is something that makes up a political community, equal political freedom and the freedom of conscience that lies at its core are indispensable.

One thing worthy of note here is that Rawls' parties greatly emphasise 'religious or moral convictions... [and] their moral or religious obligations' (Rawls 1971, p. 206). It is precisely because of such people that open freedom, with freedom of conscience at its nucleus, is vital.

Considering this point, it would perhaps be better to see the primary focus of Rawls' justice as fairness as already having presented, at the stage of *A Theory of Justice*, a response from moral theory towards the problem of religious and moral pluralism. The idea that the issue of socio-economic inequality was paramount in his thinking might possibly be a mistaken reading on our part. Yet, on the other hand, it is also true that *A Theory of Justice* does give the impression that its overall composition centres upon the 'difference principle.' One of the probable reasons that come to mind as to why the problem of religious and moral pluralism became the central theme of Rawls' later work, *Political Liberalism*, could be that he intended to rectify the bias in the impression given by this point.

On the other hand, as Dworkin's liberalism makes the rights-based approach one of its pillars, it leans far closer to freedom from constraint than Rawls, but still, in a recent work, Dworkin writes that it is justified by the principle of 'authenticity' especially to preserve

> freedom of religious commitment, freedom of expression, access to the widest available literature and other forms of art, freedom of personal, social and intimate association, and also freedom of nonexpression in the form of freedom from surveillance (Dworkin 2000 (originally 1987), p.160).

What he calls the authenticity principle here is an individual's authenticity as a personality—in more readily-understandable terms, this means a normative principle that the maintenance of the nucleus of a certain person's personality must be respected. Accordingly, Dworkin, too, is thought to have gradually come to attach importance to the significance for the individual of religious and moral convictions and open freedom.

In spite of the weight given to open freedom by such major advocates, contemporary liberalism gives the strong impression that it centres upon freedom from constraint and the logic of self-determination. The reason for its being thus seen seems to be that the idea of compartmentalisation, which pivots upon freedom from constraint, provides the simplest solution to the question of how to construct a basic normative principle for society. Firstly, under this premise, there is no need to worry about interpersonal conflicts of interest, or opposition between religious or moral beliefs. At most, there would only be the problem of how to adjust 'negative externalities' such as environmental pollution accompanying economic activities, or the nuisance caused by noise leaking from mobile telephones or headphones on trains. Ultimately, it would suffice to insist upon the simple rules of 'to cause as little trouble as possible to others' and 'to make appropriate recompense for any trouble caused to others.' Secondly, according to the above premise, each person would never be bothered by the question of by what kind of moral norms or culture she or he ought to live. That would be something that belonged to the 'private sphere,' and not an issue in which society or social theory should interfere. Thirdly, there would be no need to agonise over conflicts that might exist among various freedoms, or between freedom and other values. Even if there were such conflicts, they would be things that each person ought to resolve on a personal level.

In this manner, if freedom from constraint is made the sole issue, the burden falling upon theorists who have to consider normative principles will be remarkably small. The theorists will need only to concern themselves with the job of establishing boundaries between people, so to speak; then, after that, to devote themselves to witnessing people living according to the principle of mutual non-interference in internal affairs; and, if they were to see someone intending to 'invade' by trying paternalistically to interfere, or if there were such action, those theorists would merely need to say, 'That is unjust!' The personhood debate and self-determination theory have been advocated on that pattern.

In contrast to that, in the case of freedom as autonomy, the burden for theorists is a little greater. Before anything else, they first have to posit the value of 'autonomy' theoretically. In that work, there is a need to clear the following kinds of hurdles. Firstly, if liberalism firmly maintains the 'neutrality' thesis which I will discuss in the next chapter, then the value of autonomy will have to be posited without depending on any sort of religious or cultural background belief.

Secondly, they will also have to demonstrate that the value of autonomy takes priority over any other value which is religiously or culturally founded. If not, even if they presented a normative social principle based on the notion of freedom as autonomy, it would be something meaningful only to those people who believed that notion to have supreme value.

On the other hand, one can understand that many challenges remain for theorists to solve, when they try to think of a normative principle based on open freedom. Firstly, interpersonal conflicts over religious or moral beliefs are still left. There are some people who think, based on religious conviction, that abortion and human cloning are 'evil' and should be prohibited, while conversely there are others who think that 'to prohibit them is evil,' based on the theory of self-determination. Merely to advocate open freedom and toleration when there are such conflicts of belief will not constitute a guide to how best to think as to 'whether abortion should be banned' or 'whether human cloning should be allowed.' Secondly, it is not clear how the notion of open freedom is connected with action choice on an individual level. Should every sort of individual person's belief be respected, *because* it is a 'religious belief'? Or is the establishment of limits justified for some reason? If it is the latter, then what sort of reason is behind it?

In this way, the various ideas of freedom give rise to different theoretical conceptions as to which normative principles should be established in society, and what fundamental rules they should follow. They are tested in the question of what kind of theoretical conceptions can actually be presented towards the challenge of multicultural situations which liberalism sets itself. From the next chapter onwards, I shall examine liberalism's strategy towards this issue.

Chapter 7

Comprehensive Liberalism and Restricted Liberalism

From social stratification to culture

The issue of cultural pluralism

As I have already stated, Rawls' *A Theory of Justice*—especially as illustrated by the 'difference principle'—discussed justice as fairness with a focus on the problem of hierarchical inequality; from that time on, though, the focus of contemporary liberalism has shifted to a quest for principles of justice in today's culturally-pluralistic circumstances.

'Cultural pluralism' refers to a situation in which diverse people live according to different cultures within one society. Ordinarily, the presence of a variety of cultures is a very good thing. One can enjoy food, music and sport from countries all over the world. It is undeniable that we have entered a pleasant era, yet rather serious problems are emerging here.

Two movements, ideological and academic, are connected with the establishment of the concept of 'culture' in social theory. One, led by the German romantic nationalist philosopher Johann Herder around the end of the eighteenth century, advocates the notion of 'culture' as something distinguished from 'civilisation.' In contrast to the image of technical, material and unilinear evolution attached to the term 'civilisation,' the value of things spiritual or intellectual, or unique and diverse, is emphasised by use of the word 'culture.'

The other movement was the establishment of cultural anthropology in the United States in the early twentieth century. Until then, during the nineteenth century, anthropology had been developed as a discipline studying the customs and people of non-Western societies, but in its initial stage it was overwhelmingly under the influence of Spencer's social evolution theory. The latter attributes the phenomenon in which customs, political structures and material civilisation diverge greatly among various societies to their differing stages in a unilinear process of evolution. After the dawn of the twentieth century, however, this social evolution theory quickly declined; and instead, the concept of '*Kultur* (culture),' which had previously been established in German-speaking countries to facilitate understanding of the differences among societies, spread to social research in the Anglophone sphere. 'Culture' is an inclusive concept in which each respective society's idiosyncratic particularities are represented as a unity which exists independently from its natural environment and genetic inheritance. The work of anthropologists such as Bronislaw Malinowsky, for one, who is famed for his research on 'Kula exchange' in Trobriand Islanders (*Argonauts of the Western Pacific* (1922) and *The Scientific Theory of Culture* (1944), as well as Frank Boas, Ralph Linton, Ruth Benedict, Margaret Mead and the like, bolstered the establishment of such a concept of culture.

Both of the above movements stressed the fact that 'cultures' do not necessarily have 'varying degree of merits' on an evolutionary level, or anywhere else, but only have 'differences.' 'Cultural pluralism' involves such 'differences.'

As could be expected, it was after the turning point of 1968 that cultural pluralism came to be recognised explicitly as a problem for social theory to solve. The thing which symbolises that is the transformation of the racial discrimination issue in the United States. Until then, inter-racial legal and social discrimination, and inequalities in income and status in the social stratum were the problem. Such blatant discrimination as buses exclusively for blacks, restaurants which barred blacks and the denial of voting rights went unchallenged, and as non-whites were not blessed with favourable educational backgrounds and occupational opportunities, the problem of poverty was serious, too. These were racial discrimination problems in terms of issues of social hierarchy.

These were gradually improved by the civil rights movement and the like, but, at the same time, discrimination problems kept shifting to another phase. One example which illustrates this is the term 'black nationalism.' Here, nationalism does not refer to the creation of a nation, but to a movement to have culture developed by the black community recognised as one of the rightful cultures in American society. Slogans such as 'Black is beautiful' were also voiced. The word 'Negro,' which had been in general use in academic writing until the beginning of the 1960s, became discriminatory and was replaced by 'Black,' then that, too, was deemed problematical, so employment of the expression 'African-American' or 'Afro-American' came to be recommended.

The substitution of the once-used 'race' by the term 'ethnicity' was also due to 'culture' having become the focus of the issue. While 'race' had a strong image of a group prescribed by biological bloodlines, 'ethnicity' means belonging to a group formed by such cultural traditions as language, religion and lifestyles. The United States, which hitherto had been a 'multi-racial' state, came to be described as a society consisting of multi-ethnic groups.

The period when racial issues were thus in the process of transformation also coincided with the time when appeals from feminism and the gay-rights movement for the elimination of sex-related discrimination began to proliferate, and cultural issues were raised from that area, also. Such ways of life that involved non-marriage or same-sex love, for example, came to be advocated as having the same value as other ways of life, and deserving of equal treatment. It was asserted that the choice of a way of life is not the choice of individual acts, but a kind of cultural choice, and that each culture must be respected equally.

In the terminology of liberalism, this is called 'the goodness of life' for each. Not only minority-group cultures in such forms as race, ethnic group and ethnicity, but also cultures more generally, as in each seeking the goodness of life, assert their respective citizenship rights.

The difficulties of pluralism: a struggle between gods?

What issues might pluralism involve? In my view, there are at least the following three problems.

Firstly, there is the question of equality among divergent cultures. Even within one society, different cultures are not necessarily treated equally. The most salient example is language. It hardly bears repeating, but the national language of Japanese society is Japanese (though there is no stipulation in statutory law). Formal documents, starting with the Constitution, are written in Japanese; school education is conducted in Japanese; and in the subject called 'national language (*kokugo*),' Japanese is taught. In one sense, this is only natural, and usually nobody takes issue with it. Seen from the viewpoint that there should be equality among different cultures, however, this is a complete departure. From the outset, Japanese society has had Ainu and Okinawan languages, as well as various dialects in every locality, and it also is home to people with a mother tongue such as Korean, English or Portuguese. Such languages do not enjoy treatment equal to that of standard Japanese.

The same applies to education relating to culture. At Stanford University in the United States from 1987 through to the early 1990s, serious conflict happened to arise over the issue that the content of classes in philosophical history were biased towards Western philosophy, and an America-wide dispute over 'political correctness' was unfolded (Sacks and Thiel 1998), but *all* cultural transmission, including education, is culturally biased.

Secondly, there is the issue of cultural freedom. It is not unusual for certain lifestyles which could be seen as constituting one idiosyncratic culture to be prohibited or restricted by law. In Japanese society, plural marriage (polygyny or polyandry) is banned, and the teaching of just one particular religion in public educational situations is not permitted. When it comes to conventional regulations and intra-group rules that are not legally binding, though, these are far more numerous. Dress codes, table manners, language use and the like are all part of culture, but there, only a certain set of behavioural styles is endorsed and others are prohibited.

Thirdly, there is the problem of conflict between a discriminatory culture within an individual group and universalistic norms established in the society as a whole. Examples of discrimination include the Japanese Sumo Wrestling Association's ban on females climbing into the tournament *dohyō* (sand ring); nor are females allowed in tunnel construction sites. Speaking as a general rule, such discrimination probably should be prohibited. If the emphasis is on the perspective that this practise is part of the cultures of all-male sumo wrestling and tunnel-boring, however, it would become necessary for such cultures also to be respected.

In a range of aspects, there is a great difference between advocating the raising of the status and rights of a 'culture' and those of an individual. For example, the problem of inter-racial inequality took issue with inter-racial disparity in the higher-education ratio and average income, but on that occasion there was the tacit view that 'the same value-standards' could be applied to different people, reflecting the premise that being well-educated and having a high income are values that all people espouse. Accordingly, the elimination of inter-racial inequality would mean that the distribution of people in terms of their position in the social hierarchy would be the same, regardless of their race. Roemer's idea of 'circumstantial type' introduced in Chapter Five also equates to this.

By contrast, if one considers the notion of equality between cultures, it does not necessarily presuppose thc same quantitative scale as that of equality on an individual level, but rather is at times in opposition to the establishment of an identical yardstick. This is because measuring improvement in status on an individual level with the same yardstick means assimilating into a 'majority culture' that sees that scale as something of value. Though it would be a really splendid thing for young black Americans who grew up in poor families to become the owners of large businesses or leading figures in government through their own efforts, in one sense it means assimilating into majority Anglo-Saxon culture, and does not necessarily reflect an improvement in status for black culture.

The difficulty of such a problem, where cultural pluralism has posed questions, has a completely different complexion from 'interest-pluralism' in which there are divergent interests among individuals. Interest divergence means something like a conflict of interest between a merchant and a buyer purchasing a carpet in a Persian market. There is one party who finds advantage in a high price, and another for whom a low price is more advantageous. It is no simple matter to find a right point of settlement, but both parties understand that they will have to reach agreement at some price. If making a transaction is more advantageous than not making one, then it will not be impossible to find a point of settlement somewhere.

With cultural differences, things often do not proceed in such a way. The best example is that of language. It will be difficult for someone who speaks only Japanese and someone who speaks only English to agree as to 'which language to use as a common tongue.' In the case of religion, too, when Religion *A* believes in a god called *a*, but Religion *B* believes that *a* does not really exist, and that the god that does exist is one called *b*, then it will be hard for someone from *B* to respect someone from *A*.

This is a situation akin to the old days of confrontation over whether to champion capitalism or communism. The first half of the twentieth century was dominated by political or armed struggles and antipathy among various beliefs such as nationalism, imperialism, Christianity, nihilism, anarchism and the like—conflicts that went beyond the level of discussion. By analogy with religious wars, sociologist Max Weber called this a 'struggle between different gods' (2007, p. 44). (His speech, entitled 'Science as Vocation (*Wissenschaft als Beruf*),' addressed to students in Germany after its World War One defeat, in which he expounds the value of devoting themselves to scholarship, is well-known.) Cultural pluralism in our age, too, has an aspect of being a 'conflict of gods.'

The basic theses of liberalism

Contemporary liberalism is a theoretical movement that endeavours to present some kind of 'answer' to such issues of cultural pluralism. It goes without saying that this is an extremely ambitious project. The reason why so many intellectuals are attracted to liberalism lies here.

We have already taken up Rawls' *A Theory of Justice* and Dworkin and others on luck-egalitarianism, introducing and examining the features of the theories of contemporary liberalism, but as the focus of such discussion was upon the problem of hierarchical inequality, there has not yet been sufficient explanation as to liberalism's theoretical strategy vis-à-vis cultural pluralism. In this chapter and the next, I shall illustrate what kind of answer contemporary liberalism has in readiness for cultural pluralism issues, and add my own considerations in that regard.

The theses

As a starting-point for this—though there is some overlap with things I have previously mentioned—let me cite the 'principal theses' which characterise contemporary liberalism. This does not necessarily mean, though, that there is any one faction of liberalism which upholds all of these theses. Liberalism encompasses a range of variations, and there are differences in respect to which of the below-mentioned theses they regard as important. If one were challenged to explain the characteristic assertions of liberalism, however, citing the following major theses, A to E, would generally suffice as an answer.

A. Neutrality toward cultures and conceptions of the good
The assertion that political power must be neutral toward every culture and people's conceptions of the good is one which is shared widely (though not universally) in liberalism. This thesis was first presented in Dworkin's 1978 paper entitled 'Liberalism,' and in no time it was popularised as *the* core thesis characterising liberalism. In Dworkin's words, this is expressed as: '[t]he government [must] treat its citizens as equals,' which he derives from the thesis that: 'government must be

neutral on what might be called the question of the good life' (1985 [1978], p. 171). In other words, it was a position that formed one of the pillars of egalitarianism.

Subsequently, in a 1980 monograph, *Social Justice in the Liberal Nation*, legal philosopher Bruce Ackerman insisted on the 'neutrality' thesis for a slightly different reason. In Ackerman's case, this is predicated upon the idea that in order for political power to be legitimate, it must be justified by 'neutral conversation.' For conversation to be neutral means that none of the assertions of any individuals or groups involved (also including those in power) depend upon their having privileged moral authority as to what constitutes the good. In other words, this means that political powers which are established merely by chance or by the operation of political influence of a particular moral authority are not legitimate, because they are not neutral toward people's conceptions of the good or workings of reason. (This argument is reminiscent of Habermas' discursive ethics, but as Habermas is not considered a liberal theorist in the narrow sense, I have not made it a subject of investigation in this volume.)

In an embryonic condition, such an argument originally can be seen in Rawls' *A Theory of Justice*, but it was Dworkin and Ackerman who used and formulated the term 'neutrality.' Out of the three freedoms discussed in the previous chapter, having 'freedom from constraint,' in particular, in mind, they expressed the equal guaranteeing of that freedom as 'neutrality.' Naturally, neutrality towards 'people's good' also connotes neutrality towards the 'culture' that forms the basis of conceptions of the good. The notion of such 'neutrality' would appear in anyone's eye to have extremely straightforward persuasiveness as a solution to cultural pluralism. When confronted with the existence of different cultures in mutual opposition, political authority must treat each culture from a neutral perspective. Liberalism advocates that this should be positioned at the core of normative principles which society should follow.

B. The rights-based approach

The ideology which says that there are 'rights' that nobody could deny, and that the normative structure of society must be assembled on that basis, is the '*rights-based approach*.' This is deeply connected with freedom from constraint. Such a right is naturally thought to be of universal value, and something which transcends individual culture. The most typical notion is that of 'basic human rights.' However, in the field of positive law, rights tend to be seen as historically and culturally stipulated by actually-existing laws, and the concept of 'universal rights' could be ascribed more to the world of legal philosophy or political philosophy than positive law. Dworkin, for example, establishes a '[fundamental] right to equal concern and respect' (1977, p. 273), but it is thought that the 'right' on this occasion must not be restricted to a positive legal system of statute laws granted by states or the government. Dworkin says: 'Our constitutional system rests on a particular moral theory, namely, that men have moral rights against the state' (1977, p. 147). In other words, people have universal rights that exceed the framework of the state, and the state bears the moral responsibility to respect that.

C. The priority of the right (the just) over the good

This forms the very root of Rawls' *A Theory of Justice*, and is one of the basic theses widely preserved in contemporary liberalism. Originally, the word 'just (*seigi*, in Japanese)' rather than the word 'right (*sei*)' was employed in this thesis, and the latter has been stated as taking precedence over the good. Seeing that this particular 'right' is frequently used interchangeably with the word 'rightness,' it indubitably means 'that which is correct,' rather than signifying *a* right (*kenri*). As such, it is not strange for this 'right' to be progressively replaced by the word 'just (*seigi*).'

From the first, the good and the right have been two contrasting values in ethics, 'the good' being a value restricted to the intra-individual, while what is meant by 'the right' is a supra-individual, more universal kind of principle in ethics that should be followed in choices of action. In either case, they were things connected with ethics that individuals should obey. By contrast, what liberalism problematises is not individual ethics, but the morality of society. As I mentioned in Chapter One, it is the great achievement of Rawls' *A Theory of Justice* to have separated social morality from personal ethics and posited it as an independent subject. Moreover, 'the just,' as a value expressing social morality, is hypothesised as something that transcends 'the good' of divergent individuals and cultures. Accordingly, the thesis that 'the just takes priority over the good' can immediately be accompanied by a theoretical construct that responds to cultural pluralism with a value called 'the just.' This is because 'just(ice)' is another name for a 'universally-applicable normative imperative' that transcends conflict between disparate cultures, as will be seen in Chapter Nine.

D. A society which serves individual welfare

Liberalism, which typifies individualistic social theory, generally considers that 'society exists primarily in order to serve the welfare of the individual.' Already, the thesis of 'what is good for society can only be conceptualised through what is good for the individual' has been posed in Bentham's utilitarian ideology. Liberalism has converted this to a stronger thesis. Here, the word 'welfare' is in mind, but it would not matter if this were to be replaced by 'the good' or 'conception of the good.'

This thesis is not the sort that would always be advocated by any theory as long as the latter were to posit social morality as its thesis. It is also possible to discuss social morality not only from the perspective of how society serves the welfare of its members, but also from that of how its members serve society, or else from the perspective of some kind of transcendent values of society itself. From the viewpoint of some groups within Christianity, or from Islam, social morality will probably be more of a matter to be discussed in terms of a relationship with 'God.' But they are essentially culturally bound.

By contrast, concepts such as 'welfare in individual terms' and 'individual conceptions of the good' will be seen as universal and surpassing cultural differences. This is because the concept of individual welfare—though possibly differing in the content of respective 'welfare' and 'conceptions' in each case due in part to cultural factors—is regarded as representing values at an individual level in general, not a particular cultural level. In that sense, this thesis also constitutes an answer to cultural pluralism.

E. Compartmentalisation

As seen already, this is a thesis represented by self-determination theory and libertarianism. This term expresses the thesis that people have an inviolable domain in which neither society nor others should be allowed to interfere. In this case, if one sees that inviolable domain as a 'private sphere,' so to speak, and assumes that nobody can raise objections towards its content, then, as we will see in the next chapter, it will attract criticism from feminism and the like for 'separation of public and private.' For certain camps in liberalism, however, *compartmentalisation* is an extremely attractive thesis, because as the inviolable domain which it conceptualises is something which is universally established, indeed transcending culture, it can be considered to comprise a powerful theoretical foundation which is capable of addressing cultural pluralism.

The aforementioned five theses of liberalism mutually overlap in some places, but each of them forms a basic assertion for creating a universalistic solution to issues of cultural pluralism. Of course, their respective validity must be subjected to serious scrutiny, but from the fact that so many assertions are included in liberalism, it will be clear how powerful the theoretical framework it has prepared is vis-à-vis the problems of pluralism.

Liberalism criticised by communitarianism

Liberalism tends to take the attitude of not interfering in issues of individuals' way of life or of virtue. This is especially true when it emphasises freedom from constraint. It has a tendency to see any kind of social or political intervention in the cultivation of specific qualities as something unjust. It is difficult, however, to regard people's way of life and virtue as being completely unrelated to social desirability. Irrespective of how the desirable society is conceptualised, most people probably would think that each individual shouldering the burden of that desirable society should need to have some kind of moral qualities. This sort of feature has become one of the foci of criticism directed at liberalism from communitarianism. Here, let me briefly consider the points of contention in this critique.

Sandel's criticism of the 'unencumbered self'

Strictly speaking, it is not correct to suggest that liberalism never problematises the morality of the individual. While there are certain liberalisms unconcerned with the problem, there are more which tacitly lay down the premise that for a desirable society, each individual is a morally autonomous personality. This is especially the case with Rawls' *A Theory of Justice*. However, Michael Sandel's *The Limits of Liberalism and Justice* (1982) takes issue with the question of whether this tacit premise really does have logical symmetry. Sandel calls into doubt whether the manner of establishing the parties in the original position under the veil of ignorance could ever qualify them as moral personalities.

According to Sandel, a party under the veil of ignorance will be established as an 'unencumbered self.' An 'unencumbered self' is an abstract self, so to speak, that has been stripped of historical and social individuality. The opposite concept to the unencumbered self is the 'situated self,' which Sandel explains as being the self by which we understand ourselves 'as members of this family or community or nation or people, as bearers of this history, as sons and daughters of that revolution, as citizens of this republic' (1982, p. 179).

Sandel particularly takes issue with the following passage from Rawls, which characterises the parties in the original position.

> The parties regard moral personality and not the capacity for pleasure and pain as the fundamental aspect of the self. They do not know what final aims persons have and all dominant-end conceptions are rejected (Rawls 1971, p. 563).

What Rawls wants to say in this text is that the parties who select principles of justice in the original position under the veil of ignorance are independent of individual interests, of course, but not only that: they are also unmoved even by something like an ultimate aim in life such as would be assumed that people have in common. This is what is meant by 'dominant-end conceptions are rejected.'

In Rawls' thinking, as the task of the parties is to discover principles of justice which transcend variously-differing conceptions of the good, the parties must not be caught up by particular conceptions of the good. Instead, they form their own identity at the point where each is a personality that adheres to a universal morality. Rawls' parties in the original position are the embodiment of the autonomous, universally-moral personality such as was conceptualised by Kant.

These parties remain 'hypothetical' people to the bitter end, but Sandel challenges the very manner that the hypothesis is set up. The focus of his criticism is upon the following question: if the parties in this hypothetical original position were unencumbered selves, then, regardless of however cosmetically moral Rawls says the personalities are, could they be expected really to be capable of making moral judgements?

> [T]he deontological self, being wholly without character, is incapable of self-knowledge in any morally serious sense. Where the self is unencumbered and essentially dispossessed, no person is left for *self*-reflection to reflect upon (Sandel 1982, p. 180; emphasis in original).

In the above text, the 'deontological self,' as contrasted with the kind of self that chooses action as the means to some end, means one that acts only in accordance with the sort of universally normative principles that Kant envisaged. What Sandel wants to say is that the parties who have such deontological selves in the original position do not substantially possess the moral capability for self-reflection.

'Teleology' is the name for an ethical theory based on the idea that individual behavioural choice is rationally carried out with the aim of achieving some goal, while 'deontology,' by contrast, is one based on the notion that behaviour is chosen according to normative obligations assigned to the behaviour itself. Generally, utilitarianism is deemed teleological, while Kant is seen as deontological.

In sum, the question that Sandel poses is whether people who are nothing but 'unencumbered selves,' cut off from any social or cultural background, truly could have the ability to make moral judgements. If anything, in actual society, it is precisely because people are 'situated selves' that they can support society, and liberalism misconstrues this point.

Strictly speaking, since Rawls does not think that a liberal society is made up of individuals who are unencumbered selves, Sandel's criticism is misconceived to some extent, but it is pertinent in that it points out the flaw in the construct of the original position. Yet, as the logic of the original position for Rawls occupies only a secondary role, as I have already stated, Rawls seems not to have considered Sandel's criticism to be one that dealt a serious blow to Rawls' own theory.

Taylor's criticism of 'procedural liberalism'

Theoreticians who take issue with liberalism's assumptions about individual morality also include the Canadian philosopher Charles Taylor. Taylor has developed his own unique philosophy which is opposed in various ways to liberalism, one being the following kind of critique of 'procedural liberalism.'

What Taylor calls 'procedural liberalism' is the standpoint that 'sees society as an association of individuals, each of whom has a conception of good or worthwhile life and, correspondingly, a life plan. The function of society ought to be to facilitate these life plans as much as possible, and following some principle of equality' (1995, p. 186). As such, Taylor thus argues that 'a liberal society should not be founded on any particular notion of the good life. The ethic central to a liberal society is an ethic of the right rather than the good' (1995, p. 186).

This procedural liberalism that Taylor discusses is actually too extreme a standpoint when seen from the general idea of liberalism, but one could say that it does express rather precisely one of the poles of contemporary liberalism. Out of the characteristics of liberalism as listed above, one can regard this as focusing around the three pillars of (A) Neutrality toward the conception of the good, (B) The rights-based approach, and (D) A society which serves individual welfare.

The major point in Taylor's criticism of procedural liberalism is the question of the 'viability' of social communities. In Taylor's view, the idea of procedural liberalism is fundamentally incompatible with what civic-humanists ever since classical Greece (Taylor himself included) have thought about society. 'In order to have a free society, one has to replace this coercion with something else. This can only be a willing identification with the polis on the part of the citizens, a sense that the institutions in which they live are an expression of themselves' (Taylor 1995, p. 187). Taylor calls this feeling 'patriotism,' and criticises procedural liberalism that does not demand patriotism, saying that it has no prospect of existence because the people who support the society in question do not exist.

It would probably be unthinkable for people who stand on the premise that academic theory must be inherently universalistic to suggest a word like patriotism. Taylor dares to employ this term, though, in an attempt to challenge procedural liberalism. Certainly, there seems to be nothing as unconnected with the ideological traditions of liberalism as patriotism, or anything so diametrically opposed to it. If one follows the aforementioned 'society that serves individual welfare' thesis, then it should be that society serves the good of each individual, not that each individual serves society. Society is something that exists as a means for each individual, not an objective.

In Taylor's eye, however, procedural liberalism without patriotism has no prospect of existence. A free society is in itself a 'common good' for people, not a mere instrumental means. The very notion of being free is not merely a common good: the feeling that one is sharing that society with people—we-consciousness, solidarity, identity based on that, and so on—all exist as things of common value. In order for such a free society to keep on existing, there is a need for contribution, service and sacrifice from the citizens' side aimed at maintaining and developing that existence. And what underpins these citizen's activities—not through coercion but from spontaneous motivation—is a 'feeling of identification with the free society in question,' which is expressed by the word patriotism.

Actually, if we assume that liberalism consists solely of the aforementioned theses A to E, we will see that nothing is assumed there in terms of each individual's moral virtue. Liberalism can also be said to be trying to conceptualise 'social desirability' even for a society composed entirely of people who pay no heed whatsoever to others or to society. Such a purified view is called '*atomistic liberalism*.'

From the beginning, *atomism* in social theory has meant a 'theory that conceives of a social order without demanding or presupposing any consideration for others or a morality such as cooperativity on the part of the individuals who constitute the society.' The individual in atomism is morally *solipsist*. In other words, she or he is the sort of person who thinks: 'I have no moral responsibility of any kind to others,' or 'the circumstances of other people and society bear no relation to my conception of the good.' There is also a more extreme, ontologically solipsistic way of thinking that says: 'I cannot prove that any persons other than me exist; therefore, it is the same as if they did not exist.' But 'solipsism'—which hitherto in philosophy has generally amounted to the assumption of a solipsistic individual—has been considered an argument that ought to be overcome. The major reason for solipsism having been thus seen is that one cannot assume any morality in a solipsistic individual. In this aspect, atomistic liberalism deviates one hundred percent from existing philosophical tradition, though this is rarely noticed. It is probably inevitable for atomistic liberalism to be regarded as having no prospect of viability.

Incidentally, the theoretical standpoint that views as desirable the sort of society supported by people with the kind of 'patriotism' that Taylor mentions is called '*Republicanism*.' In Republican society, people personally participate actively in the political process in their own political community, and support it not only through speaking out, but also by contribution, service and sacrifice. 'Republicanism' is often understood to be the antithesis of 'monarchy' because it clearly stands in opposition to forms of government such as absolute monarchy, but in contemporary political theory, it is more usually regarded as one type of communitarianism in conflict with atomistic liberalism.

The common feature in such criticism as the above from Sandel and Taylor is that for the individual assumed by liberalism, 'society' does not exist. For individuals in that position, what constitutes their own life-goals, values and identity does not contain any self-awareness towards their own existence being socially situated; commitment or solidarity towards the group to which they themselves belong; or concern for or a sense of responsibility towards others. Individuals' conception of the good is formed without relation to society, and society and others are absent from its content. This is the point of criticism by Sandel and Taylor.

By contrast, Sandel and Taylor assert that the self is a social being in the first place, and that the society and other people surrounding each person are indispensable elements contained in that person's conception of the good, and a desirable society is supported precisely by those individuals who have the sort of conceptions of the good which incorporate those elements. Such identification of the '*sociability of the good*' is the nucleus of communitarian criticism of liberalism.[1]

Comprehensive liberalism and restricted liberalism

Rawls' *Political Liberalism*

In spite of such criticism as the above, not all scholars who champion the liberal cause advocate atomistic liberalism. In recent years, especially, even inside the liberal camp, there has been no dearth of remorse over atomistic liberalism or similar fundamentalist liberalisms.

Actually, it is a mistake to imagine that liberalism has never given a thought to the morality of personality. In his *On Liberty*, Mill, for example, not only presents the harm principle, but demands public morality of people as something which supplements the former, as follows:

> [T]he political education of a free people [requires] taking them out of the narrow circle of personal and family selfishness, and accustoming them to the comprehension of joint interests, the management of joint concerns — habituating them to act from public or semi-public motives, and guide their conduct by aims which unite instead of isolating them from one another. Without these habits and powers, a free constitution can neither be worked nor preserved (Mill 1973, p. 591).

In order for a liberal society to exist, the people must have public morality, so Taylor's criticism does not hit the mark in relation to any liberalism that holds such a view.

Taylor, too, acknowledges that there can be the type of liberalism such as has a 'proper place for a common good, hence patriotism' (Taylor 1995, p. 195). The society assumed by that type of liberalism regards 'rights-based control' or 'law-based control' as being a common good, consisting of the kind of people who base their identity upon it. There, the society is supported by citizens' moral and political capability, meaning assurance of the restoration of people's rights and equal treatment. This is just what Taylor calls '*patriotism*.'

As if in response to Taylor, in 1989 Dworkin published a paper called 'Liberal Communities' (reproduced in *Sovereign Virtue*, 2000), expressing the conception of 'liberal civic republicanism.' This is neither something which hypostasises the community in a personified manner, as communitarians do, nor, on the other hand, is it composed of solipsistic individuals, as in atomism: it is a political community where liberal individuals participate positively. (By the way, it is a misapprehension on Dworkin's part to say that communitarians understand the community in a personified way, and it seems to be a manifestation of an individualistic theorist's phobia about hypostatised views of society.) There, people have an interest in their own community achieving liberal justice, and when that does not fulfil its responsibility for justice, the critical value of their own lives is lost. In this manner, their own goodness of life is integrated with the justice of the community. That makes a liberal community.

This, too, is probably what Taylor calls patriotic liberalism. Taylor would probably be critical of it in his own way, too, but it is hard to criticise it for lacking viability.

The idea that public morality among people who support a liberal society is important is also distinctly embedded in Rawls' *Political Liberalism* (1993). As I have already stated, after the publication of *A Theory of Justice*, and especially in *Political Liberalism*, Rawlsian theory has demonstrated such new developments as could be described as unexpected from the perspective of many writers. It goes without saying that the abandonment of a contractarian framework was a surprise. What was even more shocking was that Rawls himself situated his own theory not as a 'comprehensive doctrine' but as a 'political conception.' '*Comprehensive doctrines*' are the sort of religious, philosophical, and moral theoretical doctrines that give an interpretation of the world that surrounds us, define the significance and value of our lives, and support and regulate our daily lives. To borrow Rawls' own words, comprehensive doctrines 'belong to what we may call the "background culture" of civil society. This is the culture of the social, not of the political. It is the culture of daily life, of its many associations: churches and universities, learned and scientific societies, and clubs and teams, to mention a few' (1993, p.

14). He calls his own theory 'political liberalism' because the very liberalism he presents is not such a comprehensive doctrine, and he regards it as a *political theory* that seeks a normative principle for a society consisting of differing comprehensive doctrines. This ended up attracting a severe rebuke to the tune that it was 'Rawls' downfall' from Tatsuo Inoue, who takes the position of comprehensive liberalism.

There are certain legitimate reasons for Rawls' change of course, however. One of these, naturally, was the existence of the situation whereby, out of all the various criticisms directed at *A Theory of Justice*, Rawls particularly took those from Harsanyi, Arrow and Hart seriously, and had to effect the necessary amendments. An even more important reason, though, is that the questions which he attempts to answer in the monograph called *Political Liberalism* have shifted to a different horizon from those in *A Theory of Justice*. Of course, the basic theme of establishing 'principles of justice' as 'fair conditions for free and equal citizens to carry out social cooperation' is coherent throughout, and there is no change on this count. The thing that has changed is the situational setting of 'the citizen' that appears in this theme. In the case of *Political Liberalism*, the premise that the citizens who take part in social cooperation differ not only in their qualities and circumstances, but also in terms of their comprehensive doctrines, is distinctly established. In short, cultural pluralism is made a presupposition.

A Theory of Justice was not clear on this point: at least it was not explicitly shown as the main subject. As I stated in the first section, social movements in the United States from the end of the 1960s through to the 1970s showed precipitous change from 'status-raising movements' to movements for the 'cultural citizenship' of a wide range of various minorities, including sexual or ethnic minorities, people with disabilities, and homosexuals. (This is called 'identity politics.') Such problem-situations are not reflected in *A Theory of Justice*, which was published in 1971. *A Theory of Justice* was obviously written with the intention of theorising the notion of 'legal, political, and social equality,' which was the objective of the 1960s civil rights movement, as well as the labour movements and the like that preceded it. The call for equality there is 'premised' upon a certain definite system of hierarchical values, and 'status-raising' for minorities meant their 'assimilation' into majority culture.

Rawls was aware that such a question-setting was inappropriate for a multicultural situation, with the severity of its problems clearly having come to light after 1970. In cases where people are presupposed to live different comprehensive doctrines, the device of rational choice by parties in the original position, especially, is of no use whatsoever for the purpose of gaining a certain consensus. People live divergent lifestyles and cultures under disparate comprehensive doctrines, and regard different things as valuable. Between someone who sees value in living as a devout religious person and someone who sees value in succeeding in business, what kind of rational choice could be considered to yield a common principle of justice?

In *Political Liberalism*, however, hardly any systematic explanation is presented as to how substantive justice principles are derived. This is due to Rawls' exclusion of an easily-understandable contractarian construct such as that in *A Theory of Justice*. Nevertheless, he still maintains the theoretical devices of the original position and veil of ignorance. Because of that, however, Rawls' claim about how the justice principles are derived has become extremely difficult to comprehend. As far as I can see, the most organised—and one might say almost the sole—explication in *Political Liberalism* regarding this point consists of the following passage. It is not in the text *per se*, but in a footnote. While it is a little lengthy, let me quote it here.

> We seek a *political conception of justice* for a democratic society viewed as a system of fair cooperation between free and equal citizens who, as politically autonomous…, willingly accept the publicly recognized principles of justice specifying the fair terms of cooperation. However, the society in question is one in which there is a diversity of comprehensive doctrines, all perfectly *reasonable*. This is the fact of reasonable pluralism, as opposed to the fact of pluralism as such…Now if all citizens are freely to endorse the political conception of justice, that conception must be able to gain the support of citizens who affirm different and opposing though reasonable comprehensive doctrines, in which case we have an *overlapping consensus of reasonable doctrines*. This suggests that we leave aside how people's comprehensive doctrines connect with the content of the political conception of justice and regard that content as arising from the various fundamental ideas drawn from the public political culture of a democratic society. We *model* this by putting together people's comprehensive doctrines behind the veil of ignorance. This enable[s] us to find a political conception of justice that can be the focus of an overlapping consensus and thereby serve as a *public basis of justification* in a society marked by the fact of a reasonable pluralism (1993, p. 24, n. 27; emphasis added)

In short, this means that people in a society live believing in various different comprehensive doctrines, from which they accept guidance and explanation about such issues as what is valuable, what kind of life constitutes a good life, what is correct, and the reasons why. In other words, comprehensive doctrines, in being 'comprehensive,' are things which, in their several ways, give an inclusive interpretation schema relating to the world surrounding each person. Accordingly, respective comprehensive doctrines will probably differ among themselves as to whether a certain political conception of justice will be worth accepting, and why it should be worth accepting. Here, Rawls thinks that in order for a particular normative principle to be a 'principle of justice,' it has to be one that is endorsed by all 'reasonable' comprehensive doctrines. On that occasion, however, the reason for 'why it is endorsed' is not asked. Whatever the rationale, it will suffice that a certain shared principle of justice—namely, a political conception—is approved. If that eventuates, then diverse comprehensive doctrines will be able to gather together in the one political society under that political conception. That is the solution to the problem of pluralism.

This solution does not at all mean eliminating pluralism and reducing it to a single comprehensive doctrine (culture). Each different comprehensive doctrine basically is left as it is, and people live according to their respective comprehensive doctrines (cultures). Still, people with disparate cultures find common value in a political conception, endorse it, and live under it. This Rawls calls 'overlapping consensus.'

As can be appreciated from the passage quoted above, a theoretical device such as the veil of ignorance only carries a figurative significance here, not a substantive one. People arrive at a consensus not because they have been in the original position covered by a veil of ignorance. Rawls describes the way of reaching a consensus through the aforementioned mechanism as being 'behind the veil of ignorance,' in the sense that the differences in rationale from the various comprehensive doctrines to support the consensus are not questioned, and are 'left aside.' This is what is expressed by the ambiguous term 'model.'

Political conceptions comprising reasonable people with public reason

Be that as it may, Rawls does not consider that overlapping consensus vis-à-vis a political conception of justice will be reached, irrespective of what kind of comprehensive doctrines might exist. That would be impossible. The political conception of justice that he has in mind would be feasible only in a society consisting of comprehensive doctrines, each of which satisfied certain specific conditions. These conditions Rawls describes by the quality of being 'reasonable.' This is the most important concept that plays a vital role in his latter-day theory, and is a kind of 'magic word' or 'spell' that has the strange magic power to enable his theory to triumph every time it confronts various difficulties. The instant something is described as 'reasonable,' every kind of obstacle to a political conception of justice vanishes there and then into thin air.

Rawls explains 'reasonable' as follows.

> [R]easonable persons will think it unreasonable to use political power, should they possess it, to repress comprehensive views that are not unreasonable, though different from their own...[When important political questions arise, certain persons] impose their beliefs because, they say, their beliefs are true and not because they are their beliefs. But this is a claim that all equally could make; it is also a claim that cannot be made good by anyone to citizens generally. So, when we make such claims others, who are themselves reasonable, must count us unreasonable. And indeed we are [unreasonable] (1993, pp. 60–61).

In other words, for comprehensive doctrines or beliefs to be 'reasonable' means that they also acknowledge that other comprehensive doctrines apart from themselves can be just as reasonable as their own; and they consider that it is unreasonable to repress the religious or ideological freedom of reasonable comprehensive doctrines other than theirs, or to subject them to political pressure. Of course, as they are comprehensive doctrines, they think that their own beliefs are true, while others are false. They do not impose that idea upon others through political force, however. The very kind of doctrine that sees taking such action as being 'unreasonable' will be 'reasonable.'

The difference between the theoretical construct in *Political Liberalism* such as the above, and that in *A Theory of Justice*, can be illustrated in a simplified form such as in Figure 7.1.

Political Liberalism is more clearly premised than *A Theory of Justice* upon the idea that people are already living by comprehensive doctrines, namely, cultures that include normative elements. Here, 'justice' is in a sense redefined as being a political principle for 'differing cultures' to constitute a common political society. That is

Figure 7.1: A Theory of Justice and Political Liberalism

a. The contractarian structure in *A Theory of Justice*

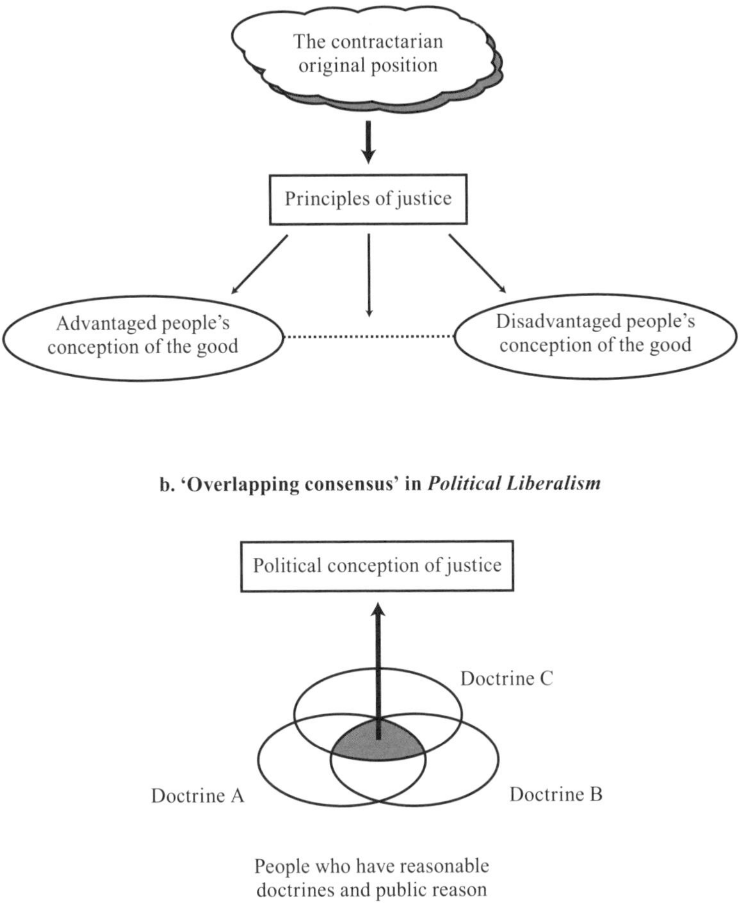

what is called a 'political conception of justice,' and is where public 'political values,' as overlapping consensus among comprehensive doctrines, integrate those various doctrines into one political community.

The individual here is *not an atomistic individual*, by any means. Rawls repeatedly emphasises that each individual is reasonable, and is a moral personality equipped with 'public reason.' 'Public reason' refers to the moral ability to consider what would constitute common public value for all people.

Furthermore, though Rawls has not stated it explicitly, the individual is subsumed by culture, and, according to his premise, culture is reasonable, and therefore the individual is also reasonable. A political conception of justice is regarded as legitimate from the perspective of each culture. Individuals, therefore, also rationalise political conceptions of justice from their respective points of view. A political conception of justice is something which is politically valuable for the individual, and she or he is committed to it. This kind of individual is a moral personality who is living a culture. If we ponder this in combination with the idea that the logic of the original position has ceased to be important, then, as I suggested in a foregoing section, Sandel's 'unencumbered self' will not equate to a criticism of *Political Liberalism*.

Not only that: people feel patriotic towards political communities established by this political conception of justice. The theory which Rawls presented in *Political Liberalism* is truly what Taylor calls patriotic liberalism.

Comprehensive liberalism and restricted liberalism

Strangely enough, the latter monograph has not been the target of such widespread and heated discussion as *A Theory of Justice*. There seems to be puzzlement and hesitation on the part of specialists as to how to attach meaning to it.

This is because the liberalism of the latter Rawls has the following kind of distinctive features. Reasonable pluralism is a pluralism consisting of comprehensive doctrines that recognise their mutual reasonableness, and is made up of comprehensive doctrines which accept that fact as a given. When that fact is made a precondition, under what principles is it possible to constitute a single political community? That was the question which the latter Rawls endeavoured to answer. Accordingly, for Rawls, his own liberalism remained a '*political conception*,' never a 'comprehensive doctrine,' because his theory in itself had to be something which could be accepted by all reasonable comprehensive doctrines. Thus, it had to be something that was always confined to a limited sphere of 'the political,' and it could never itself be a comprehensive doctrine. If it were the latter, then Rawls himself would end up repudiating pluralistic circumstances.

Here, there emerges an extremely serious point of contention as to what 'liberalism' means. In the second section of this chapter, I organised the characteristics of liberalism into five basic theses, but these were characterisations at an extremely general level, and there can be a diversity of concrete liberal theories according to how robust the content of those respective theses is, or which of the latter each theory emphasises. Even when upholding the same (B) The rights-based approach, for example, there are cases based on 'open freedom' as the content of those 'rights,' which assume basic liberties such as a quite general freedom of speech, freedom of religion, or political freedom (Rawls fits this definition); and there are cases based even more on freedom from constraint, which assume, for instance, the right to seek gender equality spanning all spheres of life, and the right to seek equal treatment, regardless of nationality. And these cases vastly differ, in spite of both being versions of liberalism.

As one example illustrating such diversity in liberalism, it is possible to set up the contrasting concepts of '*comprehensive liberalism*' and '*restricted liberalism*' along the lines of 'liberalism as a comprehensive doctrine' and 'liberalism as a political conception' from latter-day Rawls. From the same standpoint, Mikio Watanabe (2004) has contrasted 'liberal philosophy' with 'liberal life.' Liberal philosophy means liberalism as the sort of philosophy which eliminates other knowledge by upholding a demand for universal truth. Liberal life, on the other hand, is also rephrased as liberal 'political life,' and means the kind of liberalism that upholds its validity in the limited sphere of political life. As such a contrast between 'philosophy' and 'politics' is inconvenient, though, when thinking of latter Rawlsian theory as a single 'political philosophy,' I would prefer to differentiate by using terms such as 'comprehensive' or 'restricted.' (This contrast, also, is connected with Rorty's comparison of 'philosophy' and 'democracy,' which I mention in the concluding chapter.)

Comprehensive liberalism basically does not consider any comprehensive doctrines apart from itself (comprehensive beliefs as world-interpretations that underlie their respective religious and cultural lives) to be 'truths.' It regards them as mistaken convictions in terms of ways of understanding the world, and because they are mistaken, in cases where they are in conflict with 'liberalism' in various spheres of society, they have to strike a compromise with the assertions of liberalism, and subordinate themselves to these.

Conversely, 'restricted liberalism' does not consider itself to be something which embodies a 'comprehensive belief as a world-interpretation,' and it sees itself as a political theory that assumes an always limited role. In other words, having acknowledged the fact that a range of comprehensive doctrines (religions and cultures) do exist in society, it does not look down upon them as 'mistaken beliefs,' but sees its own task as being the theorisation of conceptions in which they could coexist as far as possible. As a political conception, this restricted liberalism ranks higher than comprehensive doctrines. On the level of political conceptions, comprehensive doctrines are seen as having to be subordinate to restricted liberalism. That, however, is not because they are wrong, but because in 'politics' as a restricted sphere within social life, there is a call for theory on a different dimension from that of divergent comprehensive doctrines. Rawls' *Political Liberalism* is thought to be a theory of restricted liberalism in such a sense.

There is a great difference between these two liberalisms in the way they respond to the issue of cultural pluralism. As a key to understanding this, let me describe how the culturally pluralistic world looks from the viewpoint of comprehensive liberalism. The first thing that can be said is that, from this perspective, the systems of religious or supra-empirical belief that belong to various cultural traditions in the world are fundamentally 'groundless,' 'products of imagination,' and are nothing more than ideas nurtured in ages when human knowledge was still unscientific, which have merely happened to develop or survive due to historical accident. As such, 'norms' and 'moral ideals' rooted solely in such beliefs or cultural traditions are baseless. The only thing that is ultimately applicable as a moral proposition is that which has been derived in line with the liberal way of thinking which alone has transcended the restrictions of cultural and historical tradition. If a moral assertion based on liberalism contradicts the teachings of another comprehensive doctrine, then the former must take precedence.

Secondly, seen from the viewpoint of liberalism, the most important thing for people's lives is not living according to groundless cultural traditions or being faithful to religious beliefs, but thinking autonomously without being constrained by such things, and making choices independently. Conversely speaking, for liberalism, it is the very life which each person has chosen upon mature deliberation that deserves respect. This does not always mean atomistic liberalism, but individuals remain the author of their own lives (freedom as autonomy), and the cultural traditions and communities in which they were born and raised are, in a manner of speaking, no more than an outer garment that they could throw off at any time.

Thirdly, from the two viewpoints above, liberalism is the sole correct theory that can discuss morality at the level of individual ways of life and social morality in a unified manner. In other words, maximally guaranteeing morality in terms of a liberal way of living on an individual level is the very thing that constitutes morality for society. Moreover, those people who live the religions and cultures that exist in conflict with each other can obtain the right form of solidarity from a liberal morality which is universally applicable to the human race. If they base themselves upon liberalism, the people who live in the world's disparate religions and cultures would have no need to oppose each other from the outset, and could be expected to be united into a single peaceful and fair order that transcended national boundaries and ethnic and religious differences. This is the world seen through the eyes of comprehensive liberalism, which considers that the problems of cultural pluralism will be overcome by those means.

By contrast, restricted liberalism firstly does not regard various religions and cultures as wrong—at least, it does not assert itself based on the idea that those things are mistaken interpretations of the world. Restricted liberalism only asserts its own validity in regard to questions limited to interrogating the kind of normative principles that politics in a plural society should follow.

Secondly, in relation to morality on the level of individual ways of life, apart from the regular moral norms commonly seen in most societies, restricted liberalism seeks 'a public reason fit to share the burdens of a plural society—in other words, a jointly-borne responsibility for toleration towards cultures, religions and ways of living that differ from one's own, and liberal politics.' It does not think, however, that it stands in opposition to the respective moralities which those religions and cultures prescribe. For individuals, it is ultimately their respective religious or cultural beliefs that lie at the core of life, and restricted liberalism demands merely that 'public reason in plural society' be additionally incorporated.

As such, thirdly, restricted liberalism does not consider that to guarantee a liberal way of life on an individual level to the maximum extent constitutes social morality. It takes the view that even in cases where the individual has chosen not a 'liberal' way of life, but one that is traditionally cultural or religious, if that way of life is 'reasonable,' then it must be respected.

In this way, comprehensive liberalism and restricted liberalism have extremely large differences in terms of their attitude to the various cultures present in a pluralistic society. For many people, though, liberal ideology probably tends to have the image of comprehensive liberalism. In the next chapter, I will examine whether liberalism truly presents an effective answer for pluralistic society. At that juncture, the liberalism that will be called into question is what is referred to here as comprehensive liberalism.

Chapter 8

Cultural Difference and Liberal Values

Multiculturalism

The Quebec issue

The series of political confrontations around the separation and independence of Canada's province of Quebec and the debate over its 'method of resolution' have been prime material whenever anyone has pondered the issue of cultural pluralism. Quebec, as is common knowledge, is a place where the majority of residents are of French ethnicity, and the language in daily use, in the main, is not English but French. (If one goes into a restaurant in Quebec City, one will be shown the menu only in French.) Though it originally was developed as a French colony by people who crossed from France, it was ceded to Britain due to France's defeat in the Seven Years' War over the colonies, which began in 1756. Then, after the United States of America became independent, the remaining British colonies in North America came together to form an autonomous territory; and when that later became independent and the Dominion of Canada was in the process of formation, Quebec became one of the provinces comprising the confederation. In the midst of the hegemony of the British cultural legacy in Canada as a whole, Quebec has long maintained and perpetuated its French cultural roots.

In Quebec, a movement centred upon its French-Canadian inhabitants calling for separation and independence from Canada became active from the mid-1960s. Of course, as far as the Canadian government was concerned, it was out of the question to recognise such independence. For a time, such fierce confrontation and tension arose that there were fears of radical action, such as armed conflict or a unilateral declaration of independence.

Subsequently, the Federal Government progressively promoted a policy of so-called 'multiculturalism,' and as the economic prosperity of Quebec and an improvement in the status of the French cultural sphere became obvious, the separation and independence movement lost the drive it had once had. Still, Quebec has yet to ratify the

Canada Act of 1982 which made substantial concessions to Quebec's standpoint, and the matter has not reached final settlement. For that reason, a strange political compromise is maintained in relation to the culture and language of Canadian society today (as of 2006), in which multicultural policy at a federal level coexists with a policy of prioritisation of French-Canadian language and culture in Quebec, in the following forms:

1. The official languages of Canada are designated as the two languages of English and French; and in Canada as a whole, all public announcements and signs in quasi-public places are to be written in both English and French.
2. The Province of Quebec maintains considerable autonomy vis-à-vis culture-related policy; and French is stipulated as the sole official language in Quebec.

Various theoretical problems are involved in regard to this kind of relationship in Canada between politics and culture, but when the main points of argument are teased out, they can be listed as follows:

1. What kind of minority culture can receive what sort of special treatment, and for what reason? At the federal level, French-Canadian culture in Canada basically has come to be treated equally to that of Anglo-Canadian culture. That means equality in regard to these two cultures. There are, however, many other minority cultures in Canada. In addition to various tribes of American Indians and Inuit, there are immigrants from countries other than Britain or France, such as people of Chinese or Korean ethnicity. In terms of Canadian society as a whole, their cultures have not received treatment equal to that of French-Canadians. (In Inuit and First-nation people's autonomous territories and the like, their specific languages are respected, however.) How could such discriminatory treatment be justified?
2. Can a group which has a minority culture impose that culture upon its members? As a general rule, it is mandatory for children in Quebec to be educated in French, and freedom of choice as the culture in which they receive their education is substantially restricted. How could such restriction of personal freedom be justified?
3. Even if the content of minority culture were judged to be 'illegitimate' when seen from a certain viewpoint, could its

continuation be allowed for the very reason that it was a minority culture?

This third point is not something which is explicitly apparent in the Quebec issue, but it is latently included and is manifest all over the world in various forms. There are numerous cultures in which types of discrimination due to sex are taken for granted, starting with the example touched upon in the previous chapter, about the *dohyō* (ring) in Japanese grand sumo. There are also many minority cultures which do not recognise freedom of thought and creed. Quebec, too, potentially could be viewed as 'illegitimate' for its lack of recognition of freedom of choice in education.

Generally, when there are minority groups with various different ethnic backgrounds and cultural traditions within a country, a policy or way of thinking that endeavours to respect those specific cultures as much as possible is called 'multiculturalism.' The word has been translated into Japanese as *tabunka-shugi*, but the term is easily confused with *bunka tagen-shugi*, which means 'cultural pluralism.' They are very different, as the latter simply refers to the fact that different cultures coexist, while the former signifies a normative assertion, namely, that those specific cultures 'must be respected.'

The conflict between Taylor and Kymlicka

The leading scholar to develop an argument for protecting French-Canadian culture—a minority culture in that nation—is Taylor, who is recognised as a communitarian. Taylor's assertion is spelt out in his essay of the same name in the edited volume, *Multiculturalism and the Politics of Recognition* (1994), in which he is top-listed author. Its logical construction is basically as follows.

The value to which Taylor gives most weight is self-identity for each respective individual and the feeling of 'authenticity' therein. A sense of genuineness, meaning that one's self is one's *real* self, constitutes the fundamental condition in order for a person to live as a moral personality among other people and in society. Individuals do not simply exist in isolation with desires relating to themselves alone: each lives as one member of society, or as one member of a world that transcends society.

The role of cultural communities in the formation of this kind of self-identity cannot be ignored. Moreover, the most important component of a cultural community is language. This is because language is not merely a means of communication and knowledge-accumulation, but is also the basis for interpreting the world, and thinking about the world and oneself within it; and, often, it is thought itself. Accordingly, when people live in a particular linguistic community, that linguistic community must be respected, and it is proper that politics operates in order to ensure its maintenance and continuation.

> [I]t is reasonable to suppose that cultures that have provided the horizon of meaning for large numbers of human beings, of diverse characters and temperaments, over a long period of time—that have, in other words, articulated their sense of the good, the holy, the admirable—are almost certain to have something that deserves our admiration and respect, even if it is accompanied by much that we have to abhor and reject (Taylor 1994, pp. 72–73).

In this way, Taylor argues that in cultures which have historically supported cooperation, there is a latent value which should be given political approval. This means that even if a culture were one that 'did not sufficiently qualify as right' in terms of the third point of discussion above, there would still be reason why it should receive a certain respect.

Taylor's fellow Canadian and political philosopher Kymlicka, while taking a stance partly shared by Taylor in regard to the Quebec issue, has thrown a harsh rebuttal at his fellow Canadian, basically from the standpoint of liberalism. His main point of criticism is that though Taylor appeals for the preservation of communities which have historically endured, he has not given sufficient consideration to personal choice and equality among individuals.

> [Speaking of historic communities, Taylor says that] there is some independent claim by the community itself to equal treatment. Now if this is meant literally, I find it incoherent. Groups have no moral claim to well-being independently of their members—groups just aren't the right sort of beings to have moral status. They don't feel pain or pleasure. It is individual, sentient beings whose lives go better or worse, who suffer or flourish, and so it is their welfare that is the subject-matter of morality (Kymlicka 1989, pp. 241–242).

A community itself is not a moral entity which can assert its rights. This proposition is in line with '(D) Serves individual welfare,' which is one of the basic tenets of liberalism.

Kymlicka is the scholar who has most energetically pursued theoretical consideration of what manner of situating minority cultures and cultural communities in a culturally-pluralistic society qualifies as just, and his theories are developed in detail in one of his works, *Multicultural Citizenship: A Liberal Theory of Minority Rights* (1995). Kymlicka says though it is not necessarily true that liberalism had no respect for minority rights, it hitherto has lacked sufficient theoretical structure relating to *how* to respect them, because fundamentally it has constructed its theory from the standpoint of individual freedom. In his work, he first presents the concept of 'societal culture.'

> [A] *societal* culture...[is] a culture which provides its members with meaningful ways of life across the full range of human activities, including social, educational, religious, recreational, and economic life, encompassing both public and private spheres. These cultures tend to be territorially concentrated, and based on a shared language (Kymlicka 1995, p. 76; emphasis in original).

As this illustrates, the ideas of Kymlicka diverge greatly from atomistic liberalism. His focus upon culture as something that 'provides its members with meaningful ways of life' parallels the assertions of Taylor and Sandel, who have been dubbed communitarians.

On the other hand, Kymlicka firmly maintains the basic thesis of liberalism in the following points: namely, he regards the ultimate basis of the normative principle for society as lying in rights of individuals being extensively respected; and he thinks that respect for minority culture is justified only in so far as it is given in light of the value it holds for each individual. To discuss this point, Kymlicka presents a set of several important concepts. One of these is 'external protections' and 'internal restrictions' of minority groups, which can also be restated as 'equality between minority groups and majority groups' and 'freedom within minority groups.' 'External protection' is 'to protect the group from the impact of *external decisions* (e.g. the economic or political decisions of the larger society),' while 'internal restrictions' mean 'to protect the group from the destabilizing impact of *internal dissent* (e.g. the attitude of individual members not to follow traditional practices or customs)' (Kymlicka 1995, p. 35). Kymlicka argues that the devising of external protections for a minority culture—in other words, its aiming for equality on a group level between minority and majority—is in itself something that echoes the principles of liberalism, and should be advanced. In regard to internal restrictions, he considers that even if their establishment were for the sake of external protections, they would be permissible only under the overarching principles of universal individual rights and respect for liberty.

Collective rights and group-differentiated rights

Another conceptual bifurcation related to this is 'collective rights (*shūgō-teki kenri*)' and 'group-differentiated rights (*shūdan-betsu kenri*).' In books translated into Japanese, the former is rendered as '*shūdan-teki kenri*,' so the two expressions could easily be confused. The difference between this pair of concepts is very important, not only for Kymlicka, but also in sociological terms. Yet Kymlicka's explanations cannot be said to be well-organised, so I will explain further below, blending in my own interpretations.

As may be understood by its use of the word 'collective,' collective rights are 'rights which a collective entity has as a collective entity.' It is not unusual for a clearly-defined, collective legal subject such as a company or nation to have rights. However, as something called minority culture or ethnicity cannot be an 'organisation' (Seiyama 1995), it cannot have 'rights' on the level of positive law. (In other words, it is never the subject in litigation or trials.) On a purely theoretical level, though, it is possible to conceive of 'the cultural rights of Inuit as a community,' or 'the cultural rights of Australian Aborigines as a community,' for example. Such rights as a community are not rights as individuals, but rights belonging to the community which transcends the individual. If, for instance, we assume that Inuit culture has collective rights worthy of protection, then that idea will be, in principle, independent from what all the individuals who belong to Inuit culture think as being their rights, and therefore will also be independent from the question of what rights each of those individuals has. Collective rights—if we presume their existence—will exist independently from each of the individuals who belong to the community in question, and without depending upon any of those individuals.

Yet Kymlicka denies the existence of 'collective rights' in such a sense. This is because a community does not exist as a substantive being: the only thing that actually exists is each individual; and 'the thing that becomes the subject of morality is the welfare situation of each individual.' To suppose that a collective thing had rights which transcended each individual would be counter to liberalism's individualistic principle of '(D) Service to individual welfare.'

Instead, Kymlicka recognises the existence of '*group-differentiated rights*,' as distinguished from '*collective rights*.' As can be appreciated from the fact that an alternative expression for 'group-differentiated rights' is 'group-differentiated citizenship,' such rights are one kind of civil rights that individuals possess. At the same time, however, ethnic and cultural differences are taken into consideration.

Group-differentiated rights are rights related to things on a group level, but, unlike collective rights, ultimately they are rights that are grounded in the major values of liberalism, namely individual equality, freedom and autonomy. In short, basically they are rights at an individual level. By instituting such a concept of group-differentiated rights, Kymlicka is attempting to situate within liberalism a theoretical framework that respects cultural distinctiveness and difference, which liberalism has hitherto ignored or downplayed.

Liberal values that predominate over minority culture

Kymlicka divides the problems relating to the conflict that can arise between minority culture and various principles of liberalism into the following two: (1) what sorts of minority claims are consistent with liberal principles; and (2) should liberals impose their views on minorities which do not accept some or all of these liberal principles? (1995, p. 164).

Kymlicka's response to the first question is that 'any form of group-differentiated rights that restricts the civil rights of group members is therefore inconsistent with liberal principles of freedom and equality' (1995, p. 165). In his view, 'a national minority which rules in an illiberal way acts unjustly' (1995, p. 168). In other words, in cases where group-differentiated rights generate friction with universal individual rights, he has no hesitation in thinking that the latter takes precedence.

The second question is a troublesome problem for liberalism, and Kymlicka has been unable to present an unambiguous answer. Liberalism, which respects freedom and autonomy, is not deft at constructing theories that would explicitly justify imposing something upon another. This especially holds true in relation to imposition of liberal norms in a forcible or violent manner. Accordingly, the only thing that Kymlicka clearly asserts vis-à-vis this question is that 'liberals have a right, and a responsibility, to speak out against injustice. Hence liberal reformers inside the culture should lend their [spiritual] support [and provide incentives] to any efforts the group makes to liberalize their culture' (1995, p. 168).

This aside, Kymlicka's ideas in respect to the first question are clear. Be as it may, any minority culture which opposes the various principles of liberalism is, in short, 'unjust.'

Incorporated with this are the claims that the normative principle called liberalism is something which is universally applicable, transcending divergent cultures and times; and that anything opposed to liberalism is, in other words, illegitimate, and warrants criticism.

The following kind of problem emerges here in consequence, namely the suspicion that though Kymlicka speaks of multiculturalism, in the end he is saying that most among the diversity of minority cultures are inferior to liberal ones, and ultimately ought to subordinate themselves to liberal culture. In other words, this means that as long as those various cultures do not counter liberal culture, it will be permissible for them to assert or enjoy their cultural uniqueness; and, in that sense, liberalism constrains each culture as a firm lateral restriction.

This issue has a deep connection with the question surrounding Rawls' later work as to whether liberalism is a political conception or a comprehensive doctrine—with the conflict mentioned in the foregoing chapter between 'restricted liberalism' and 'comprehensive liberalism.' As we have already seen, in regard to multicultural situations in which there coexisted diverse comprehensive doctrines containing a certain reasonableness, latter-day Rawls presented as political liberalism the conception of a political community integrated by principles of justice as overlapping consensus. Under his political conception of liberalism, even various illiberal cultures that opposed comprehensive liberalism would be tolerated if only they were 'reasonable.' The 'principles of justice' here are more moderate than the normative principles which comprehensive liberalism asserts. Here, the question of whether a particular culture is reasonable is a vital dividing line, and is a different matter from the issue of whether that culture is consistent with comprehensive liberalism.

On this point, one probably could say that Kymlicka is on the side of comprehensive liberalism. He criticises Rawls' argument as not being coherent in liberal terms, though it be a meaningful attempt to respond to multicultural circumstances.

> [F]or Rawls, people are communitarians in private life, and liberals in public life. But is this a coherent position? The problem is to explain why anyone would accept the ideal of autonomy in political contexts unless they also accepted it more generally (Kymlicka 1995, p. 160).

In Kymlicka's mind, if one accepts the liberal ideal of autonomy in the context of politics, which is a public sphere, then there will be a natural expectation that one will also accept that ideal in the in-group private sphere, and one *must accept it*. In order to discuss this point, he considers two court cases, one of which arose in a Canadian religious minority group called the Hutterites, the other being that of the Amish in America. In both cases, the point of contention referred to the right of persons who had been raised inside the group to leave it and live in the world outside. In the example of the Hutterite group, the issue was whether those persons who actually ended up leaving could take that portion of the colony's assets which could be considered their own share; while in the Amish case, the question was whether the group could curtail their children's schooling in order to prevent them from learning about the outside world (Kymlicka 1995, pp. 161, 162). Of course, those on the side of the respective groups argued from the perspective of their rights and culture as a group, with the former asserting that the persons in question could not take anything out, and the latter insisting that they could withdraw their children from school.

From these cases, Kymlicka points out that the illiberal people within the groups (the intra-group majority) had to 'explicit[ly] reject…Rawls' [liberal] "political conception of the person"' (1995, p. 162), and asserts that it is erroneous to assume, as Rawls did, that being a communitarian in private life could be compatible with being a liberal in public life. In the end, in Kymlicka's mind, the question of how liberalism will respond to multicultural circumstances can only be answered coherently by Kymlicka's concept of 'group-differentiated rights,' not by a strategy of restricted liberalism as a political conception, as Rawls asserts.

It is not clear how restricted liberalism such as Rawls' regards the two cases above. The clash here between Rawls and Kymlicka can, however, be reorganised as follows. Rawls hints at the possibility that even if the culture of a certain minority group is not sufficiently liberal, if it has a basic level of acceptance of the principles of justice and the political conception based upon it, then that minority culture will not be disavowed in the wider political community. By contrast, Kymlicka stresses that unless a group culture itself is not liberal, then that group will be unlikely to respect the liberal values which ought to be commonly applied in the wider political community. Rawls' argument opens the way for the 'cultural particularity' of respective groups and doctrines to be compatible with the liberal political conception. In response to that, Kymlicka emphasises that in a liberal political community, individual cultures should also be liberal.

In actual fact, the differences between the two are subtle ones. With Rawls' liberal political conception, as the principles of justice as overlapping consensus are things that should be applied to all groups and cultures, it differs not one jot from Kymlicka's assertion in the point that 'there exist liberal principles that should be applied commonly to all cultures.' Accordingly, Rawls, in turn, would probably take the same stance as Kymlicka in relation to the necessity for basic notions of freedom and equality to be carried through even in traditional minority groups.

An important difference, though, lies in the fact that, in contrast to Rawls' argument showing an intention to respect as far as possible the distinctiveness of each comprehensive doctrine and culture by means of a restricted conceptualisation of liberalism as a political conception rather than as a comprehensive doctrine, Kymlicka's argument substantially asserts that liberalism itself is a comprehensive culture, by insisting that 'ultimately, if a group lacks a liberal culture, then it will be impossible for it to gain proper membership of a liberal political community.'

Heretofore we have looked at the differences in the ideas of Taylor, Kymlicka and Rawls concerning minority culture. These three do not share atomistic liberalism's view that one needs to respect merely the rights of the individual: they agree in thinking that the culture of traditional minority groups must be respected in some way, but they diverge in relation to the extent and reasons for such respect. Taylor asserts that there exists such a culture of a group that should be given precedence, even if it meant that individual rights were restricted to a certain degree. He thinks, therefore, that it is permissible to restrict each person's freedom to choose the language in which they are educated and make schooling in French compulsory. By contrast, Kymlicka argues that respect for minority culture must be afforded only within its range of compatibility with the rights of the individual. Accordingly, (though this is not expressed explicitly), if one takes the freedom to be educated in whichever language one chooses to be an inviolable right, then that will mean that Quebec's cultural policy is illegitimate. Rawls, on the other hand, though not always speaking out about concrete issues, seems to disagree that the value of individual autonomy should extend its control to every nook and cranny of minority culture. His focus of questioning is upon the principles of justice that the social institutions in general in a political community should follow. He thus seems not to have had such court cases as those of the Hutterites or Amish in his sights. In relation to the Quebec problem, he would probably take the same position as Kymlicka in the aspect that he places importance on 'basic liberties being guaranteed equally for each person,' but the range of 'basic liberties' that Rawls posits is perhaps narrower than Kymlicka's.

Here, however, one should probably pay more attention to the points in which the difference between Kymlicka and Rawls is not too clear. On the level of labels, the difference is described as comprehensive liberalism versus restricted liberalism; or, more concretely, whether one puts priority on the liberal value of the 'autonomy and universal rights of the individual,' or emphasises a political value such as 'equal basic liberties.' Though these differ on the level of terminology, it is not clear whether they are divergent in terms of their respective content, or whether they are all the same in the end.

This point, in fact, is where the greatest problem in contemporary liberalism lies. I will consider that matter in the next chapter.

Feminist critiques of liberalism

It goes without saying that basically there are many aspects in which feminism shares the same assertions as today's liberalism. In regard to the importance of equality between the sexes, both ideologies are in the same camp.

Yet feminism is one of the most powerful opposing forces to have raised voices of criticism against liberalism. This, at first glance, might seem odd, but the problematical points in liberalism are thrown into ever sharper relief by way of criticism from the standpoint of feminism, which could almost be considered liberalism's ally.

Here, let us consider critiques of liberalism in relation to (1) the separation of the public and the private; and (2) the ethics of care.

Separation of public and private

The 'separation of the public and the private' signifies a kind of theoretical structure in which the family, which belongs to the private sphere, is differentiated from the external political or public sphere;

and liberal justice principles need not be applied to the family's internal matters. Feminism criticises liberalism for turning its back on problems of injustice and power-relations within the family, caused by its having established the family as a sanctuary into which public laws and regulation by means of norms cannot intrude.

Thanks to recent news reports of child-abuse, domestic or family violence and the like, we are well-informed as to the frequent presence of unjust discrimination and oppression within the family, and even occasional criminal acts, but what feminism questions is not so much such separate phenomena as the structural injustice that is thought to underpin it. The latter refers, in other words, to a social structure built upon a sexual binary of 'male' and 'female' which uniformly embeds unjust discriminatory treatment according to sex, regardless of whether it is inside or outside of the family. That structure is often discussed using the concept of 'patriarchy,' which means, for feminism, a structure of power-related gender discrimination and the political dominance structure rooted within it.

When one thinks in this way, it was a thoroughly inadmissible, grave error for liberalism to have removed the family in advance from the target zone of 'justice' in carrying out the construction of its theory, even if it did champion equality in the economic and political sphere. The feminist argument which directed the focus of its criticism upon liberalism's separation of public and private could be represented in the following excerpt from MacKinnon:

> The liberal ideal of the private holds that, so long as the public does not interfere, autonomous individuals interact freely and equally...It is personal, intimate, autonomous, particular, individual, the original source and final outpost of the self, gender neutral...To complain in public of inequality within the private contradicts the liberal definition of the private. In the liberal view, no act of the state contributes to shaping its internal alignments or distributing its internal forces, so no act of the state should participate in changing it. Its inviolability by the state, framed as an individual right, presupposes that the private is not already an arm of the state (MacKinnon 1989, p. 190).

After thus describing liberalism's separation of the public and the private, she makes the famous assertion below:

> For women the measure of the intimacy has been the measure of the oppression...This is why feminism has seen the personal as the political.

> The private is public for those for whom the personal is political. In this sense, for women there is no private, either normatively or empirically (MacKinnon 1989, p. 191).

This slogan, 'the personal is political,' permeated feminism all over the world as if it were indeed the basic thesis of the 'Feminist Manifesto'; it gave clear direction to the theory, and inspired the movement. This slogan appeared to have had the inherent power to establish feminist theory not as an epigone or an offshoot of liberalism or Marxism, but as an independent social theory that differed from either of these.[1]

Strictly speaking, not all liberal theoreticians have extolled or made the separation of the public and the private a prerequisite. In her critique of liberalism, MacKinnon did not definitely indicate specific theoreticians (including Rawls) or particular arguments, either. That being said, MacKinnon by no means wilfully invented liberalism's separation of public and private. There is fixed evidence for liberalism's separation of public and private. Particularly as Susan Okin's *Justice, Gender and the Family* (1989) points out, there are ample grounds for casting doubt upon Rawls.

When Rawls describes the original position, for example, he writes that the parties could be regarded as the 'heads of their families.' One must be forewarned that this description appears in a part which explains that the establishment of the original position also works well for the question of fairness between generations. In this part Rawls suggests that, just as the head of a family would take the welfare of all members of the family into consideration when making decisions, the parties in the original position would similarly take the welfare of people of future generations into consideration when selecting the various principles of justice. He is certainly not arguing, for example, that the citizens' representatives whom he calls the parties are limited to male heads of families, not female; nor that the interests of all citizens are represented solely by males. Still, Rawls assumes that the head of the family (whether male or female) is the person able to represent the welfare of family members in everyday social life, and so one should not doubt that in the construction of his justice theory, he has excluded from his field of vision any conflicts of interest or inequalities among members within the family.

Let me cite another example of what appears to be evidential. Towards the end of *A Theory of Justice*, Rawls writes as follows, stating that the handing-down of people's morality between generations constitutes one of the conditions for a just society.

> Now I shall assume that the basic structure of a well-ordered society includes the family in some form, and therefore that children are at first subject to the legitimate authority of their parents. Of course, in a broader inquiry the institution of the family might be questioned, and other arrangements might indeed prove to be preferable...
>
> The parents, we may suppose, love the child and in time the child comes to love and to trust its parents...[The child's] love of the parents is a new desire brought about by his recognizing their evident love of him and his benefiting from the actions in which their love is expressed (Rawls 1971, pp. 462–463).

The family image drawn here, though accompanied by the warning that it 'might be questioned,' is a community of love, and at the same time is the source of authority. In this way, having assumed the family to be a basic institution supporting a liberal society, Rawls has conceived his principles for a fair society outside the family. He has not, therefore, directed his eye towards injustices that may have taken root in the very family that feminism has problematised.

It is not correct, however, to regard liberalism as always incorporating an insistence on the separation of public and private. Contemporary liberalism, in particular, which has evolved post-Rawls, has taken on a form far more individualistic than Rawls. Nussbaum (1999), for instance, has endeavoured to construct a feminist theory that eliminates the separation of public and private while still being based upon liberalism. Okin, mentioned above, also thinks that though the present condition of the family is unjust, it is possible to conceive of the family as a just institution by considering it after the application of Rawls' original position setup to marriage and the family. In other words, this means that the kind of system should be established in which principles of justice chosen within the family or else by the original-position model penetrate throughout.

In actuality, the issue of the separation of public and private has the same composition as the problem of minority culture which was seen in the foregoing section. When thinking of the family as a minority group, so to speak, it is a question of to what extent liberal values should be respected within it. Liberal feminism thinks that it is also possible for the family to be internally ordered by liberal values, and it assents to such action. MacKinnon, by contrast, regards marriage (let alone the family) as something inherently illiberal and unjust. By extension, there even emerges the assertion, as in Young, that the unjust institution, family, should vanish altogether (Young 1997).

Whichever the case, the issue will probably boil down to one of how to locate the institution of the family. If we were take the standpoint of focusing upon a society composed only of adults who have little interest in the handing-down of the institutions of that particular society between generations, and who are presently already independent, there would be no reason whatsoever for giving the family special treatment when examining 'justice.' This is because everything should be reduced to the presently-existing individuals for such a standpoint. Accordingly, it would mean that such actions as forcing couples to take the same surname, for instance, or denying legal recognition to same-sex marriage, would be injustices that robbed individuals of their freedom. If, on the contrary, one were to look towards the particular properties of children—in other words, beings that in actuality need protection, education and love—then there would probably be considered to be some logic in setting up some kind of special social space separated from the outside by a fixed barrier. I do not intend to enter into this issue in the present volume, however.

The ethics of care

In 1982, when the American psychologist Carol Gilligan wrote her book, *In a Different Voice*, surely she herself never envisioned that her own work would become 'a different voice' stating objections to liberalism. The target at which her work directed its spearhead of criticism was the moral development theory of moral psychologist Lawrence Kohlberg, in which there was not even the letter 'l' of liberalism. Still, this book of Gilligan's seized the limelight as something that criticised the androcentric moral view in liberalism, and championed the 'ethics of care' which emphasise each person's contribution to consideration and help towards the weak.

Kohlberg's theory, based on his own empirical research with reference to prior studies including Freud, Piaget and others, is one which says that the moral development of the child consists of six stages. Its final, highest stage is the 'morality of justice (fairness, rights and the golden rule),' and the fifth stage is 'autonomy,' as summarised in Kohlberg's 1984 work, *The Psychology of Moral Development: Essays on Moral Development.* What Gilligan could not overlook was Kohlberg's stating that females were inferior to males, and that females could advance to a higher stage like males by participating in historically male spheres of activity.

From Gilligan's perspective, Kohlberg has merely fabricated an androcentric theory through data collected by means of male subjects, and fails to achieve a correct understanding of the following sort of moral development in females:

> In this conception, the moral problem arises from conflicting responsibilities rather than from competing rights and requires for its resolution a mode of thinking that is contextual and narrative rather than formal and abstract. This conception of morality as concerned with an activity of care centers moral development around the understanding of responsibility and relationships, just as the conception of morality as fairness ties moral development to the understanding of rights and rules (Gilligan 1982, p. 19).

In this way, Gilligan strikes a contrast between the 'ethics of care' for females as a mature morality that would correspond to the 'ethics of rights' for males.

Candidly speaking, Gilligan's argument is something which emphasises the difference between females and males, and in this aspect, it greatly differs from that of many other feminists.

> My research suggests that men and women may speak different languages that they assume are the same, using similar words to encode disparate experiences of self and social relationships (Gilligan 1982, p. 173).

This has unsurprisingly attracted a critical response from people such as the aforementioned MacKinnon, arguing that something like the ethics of care is simply giving additional acknowledgement to something which females have generated within a power relationship with males. From a feminist perspective, this is certainly close to heresy. Be that as it may, the 'ethics of care' that Gilligan discovered was seen by many scholars as forming a criticism or counterargument to liberalism. The ethics of care thus was regarded as expressing something important that liberalism had overlooked.

In his recent volume in Japanese, *Economy and Ethics: Philosophy of the Welfare State* (2002), one such scholar, Yūichi Shionoya, having regarded that the 'dispute over "equality and disparity" has given birth, on the level of moral philosophy, to an ethics of "care" differing from the ethics of "justice"' (p. 298), rates the ethics of care as having constituted a 'virtue' that is indispensible for the ethics of social welfare, and as something that opens up a dynamic vision of intergenerational justice that is not necessarily included in principles of justice (p. 301).

Such a mode of positioning in respect to the ethics of care can be understood as the ethics of care having reminded people of something major that they faintly sensed was missing from liberalism. The ethics of care is something that asserts the morality of people's each having close relationships with and responsibility for the weak that are present in their vicinity, such as children, the elderly and the disabled; but it was understood as having posed the question of how *morality on a personal level* is positioned for a society qualified as just from a liberal viewpoint.

Though the 'ethics of rights' counterposed by Gilligan to the 'ethics of care' is seen by many scholars as being an ethics of liberalism, this in fact is ridiculous. As the 'ethics of rights' which was positioned in the highest stage in Kohlberg's theory of moral development is an ethics in which each individual respects the rights of others and the rules of society, it is an ethics on a personal level. Yet as I stated in a previous chapter, liberalism—taking as a typical example its most extreme form, atomistic liberalism, but in general, too—does not have a central focus upon presupposing or demanding some kind of moral capability on each individual's part as a primary condition for a society to qualify as just. There is no assertion of an ethics of liberalism there. Certainly, there are also arguments such as the assumption of a public person in latter-day Rawls, or Dworkin's 'liberal community,' which say that individuals who respect people's rights also will support the justice of a community that respects rights, but these were aired after the publication of Gilligan's book. Liberalism's main theme, above all, is 'the morality of society,' and it does not have a focus on people's acting morally on a concrete behavioural level. An 'ethics of liberalism' has never been presented by liberal scholars.

This can better be interpreted as follows: liberalism has merely talked about what sort of circumstances are 'just,' and remained ambiguous concerning the subject for putting that 'justice' into practice, but many people unconsciously have assumed something to the tune of that if liberalism were a moral theory at all, then it would be likely to contain some kind of theory of personal morality, and they have thought that an ethics of rights would indeed answer to that.

This could also be expressed in the following manner, namely that the 'ethics of care,' by way of emphasising the morality of responsibility and relationships among people, has reminded us that liberalism lacks such an ethics of 'responsibility' and 'commitment,' and has identified liberalism—as a condition deficient in the ethics of care—as an ethics of rights, constituting a counter-argument to the ethics of care.

Whatever the case, in one sense, this issue of the ethics of care also expresses the conflict between particularistic culture or ethics among people who are intimately connected—typified by the family—and universalistic liberal values. It is tantamount to claiming that even though 'rights' might be important values in the public sphere, different values, such as 'care,' are essential in the private sphere.[2]

The issue of cultural neutrality

The universal viewpoint

What lies at the starting-point of liberalism is a hope for making as universal as possible the position of the viewpoint upon which the theory stands, in its search for normative principles that constitute a desirable society. Of course, other theories besides liberalism, such as social contract theory, social evolutionism, Marxism, and so on, have also in their respective ways attempted to take a universal point of view, or have imagined that they do take one. Yet liberalism, in its own opinion, differs decisively from the others in the following aspect: namely that liberalism has not taken on the kind of theoretical strategy adopted by those other theories whose foundations are premised upon extremely strong (but completely unlikely) hypotheses to do with society. These are, for example, the primordial natural state, the irreversible mechanisms of social evolution, or historical materialism as historical truth. These are not empirical things, but impinge upon the realm of belief. When any such hypothesis loses its credibility, its very theory collapses simultaneously.

Liberalism could be said to be the one that kept on pursuing a universal point of view on the premise that it would not stand upon such a fictional hypothesis. This is well exhibited in the constitution of Mill's 'harm principle.' Originally, utilitarianism was representative of liberalism in this sense. The social theory that clearly set forth the standpoint of individualism, which thought of a desirable society only on the basis of the conception of the good of individuals, was utilitarianism. There, the universality of its viewpoint is planned in that it treats the conception of the good of all individuals equally.

From Rawls' perspective, however, this still is restricted to a non-universal viewpoint. This is because people's conception of the good as pleasure and utility is limited by the abilities and resources bestowed upon people by chance.

Rawls' concept of 'justice' was something that tried to express a new universal viewpoint in a form which transcended utilitarianism; and the model devised for it was the establishment of the original position. What is important for the universal viewpoint to do is to detach itself from individual points of view, and to transcend these. That is why the just takes precedence over the good. And *Political Liberalism* further apprehends as 'individual viewpoints' not only people's personal interests, but also the comprehensive doctrines that subsume people's lives and form their basis; and it endeavours to formulate a 'political conception of justice' as something that exceeds those viewpoints.

For liberalism, which takes such a methodological strategy, cultural neutrality was thought to be a natural thesis. This is because otherwise it would be considered to degenerate into a case of particular culture that liberalism itself ought to overcome.

The meaning of freedom of religion

The thesis of liberalism's 'cultural neutrality' resembles so-called 'separation of religion and politics' and 'freedom of religion' in some ways, but it is by no means the same. It is extremely important to pay heed to the difference.

Originally, the ideology of religious tolerance, related to the Catholic and Protestant factions that had hitherto repeatedly engaged in fierce life-and-death struggles through the early seventeenth-century religious wars, the Puritan Revolution and the like, was one that pointed out the error of political authority backed by one of the sides persecuting the other side. Locke's *Four Letters on Toleration* is a representative example. The idea of 'separation of religion and politics' is not contained in it, however. As evidence of that, even in Britain ever since the 1688 Glorious Revolution, which received Locke's ideological support, the Church of England has continued to be the state religion to the present day.

The idea of the 'separation of church and state' (adopting terminology more suitable to the American Constitution) hails back to

Thomas Jefferson, a thinker and politician at the time of American Independence. As can be understood from the fact that the word 'church' is employed, rather than 'religion,' it is something that prohibits the state from having a special connection with any specific denomination in Christianity, especially in relation to the different Protestant denominations. This was the means whereby America prohibited the 'establishment of a state religion' in the First Amendment to the United States Constitution in 1791, and came definitively to stipulate 'freedom of religion.'

After that, the majority of modern nations and codified constitutions came to uphold 'freedom of religion,' but there are not many that have 'separation of religion and politics.' There are several different levels of this separation, which can usually be divided into the next four types:

1. Prohibition of state compulsion of belief in a specific religion
2. Prohibition of establishment of a state religion
3. Prohibition of state favouritism to a specific religion
4. Prohibition of religious activity by the state itself

There is a large discrepancy even among those states which usually are called democracies vis-à-vis what type of separation of religion and politics they have adopted. The element which is common to all 'democratic states' is (1) 'prohibition of compulsion.' But, as is understood from the example of Britain, which has a state religion, (2), (3) and (4) differ depending upon the country. The elements explicitly raised in the United States Constitution are (1) and (2). France is one place that extols complete separation of church and state, including (4), and in the second provision of its constitution, it declares that: 'France is a non-religious state.' As Japan, too, extols (4), it is similar to France, but as is widely known, there is serious conflict of opinion in Japan over what corresponds to 'state religious activity.'

It is no mistake to say that liberalism's so-called 'neutrality' includes the above (1) to (3). In regard to (4), if the state's religious activity were equal in respect to all religions, then it probably would not go against the neutrality thesis.

The idea of separation of religion and politics may appear to be one example of the application of the neutrality thesis. Most politico-religious separation that has been actually carried out, however, is more moderate than that which the neutrality thesis advocates. Not only Britain's, but also Germany's Basic Law is premised on the existence of 'God,' and it is well-known that American Presidents often say the words, 'God bless,' during their official speeches.

(Recently, though, there has been a move even in America to dilute the religious flavour, with the President not saying 'Merry Christmas!' on public occasions.) Would liberal theorists look at such a society and judge it 'just,' I wonder?

Strangely enough, liberal theorists seldom ever mention or examine any such connection between politics and religion that actually exists. When they do refer to concrete examples, these are only cases where neutrality has already been established as social consensus, or else where it is considered it would be better to be neutral in the eyes of people with a standpoint generally seen as liberal.

One example is a favourite topic of Dworkin's: 'discrimination against homosexuals' or 'discrimination due to sexual preference.' He says that such discrimination is judged to be unjust by liberalism's neutrality thesis. It is clear, however, that this not an appropriate line of argument. The logical sequence of 'if A, then B,' 'B is true,' 'therefore, A is true' does not hold. This will be understandable if 'all politicians are male' is substituted for A, and 'the present prime minister is male' for B, for example. Many Japanese and liberal Americans accept as natural that it is unjust to penalise or discriminate against people because of homosexuality or sexual preference in terms of hiring or qualifications. (I do not know, though, whether they would go so far as to think that same-sex 'marriage' also should be treated equally to that between opposite sexes.) The judgement that such discrimination is unjust is compatible with the liberal thesis of neutrality, and can be logically drawn out from the latter. Nevertheless, this does not mean that the correctness of the neutrality thesis conversely is proven by this instance.

Returning to the topic of religion, the toleration of different creeds and the prohibition of political persecution based upon religion are great achievements of classical liberalism. This fact can never be overemphasised. Contemporary liberalism advocates the neutrality thesis just as if it were a developmental form of the above. However, between classical liberalism, which preaches religious freedom, and 'cultural neutrality' lies a qualitative difference that is not merely a question of degree. This is related to the fundamental character of 'religion' and 'culture.'

The word 'religion' originally only indicated Christianity in the main, or then at the very most Judaism and Islam (and sometimes Buddhism). The first three, barring Buddhism, had identical beginnings; and they share the same text in the Bible's Old Testament, and 'God.' That is what 'religion' originally signified for European society. For that reason, when the concept called 'religion' was introduced into Japan, there arose the problem of whether such things as Japanese Shintoism and folk beliefs counted as 'religions.' If only the four major religions of the world were signified by the word 'religion,' then issues of the separation of religion and politics, and of the neutrality thesis relating to religion, would probably have become clear-cut. There is obviously no reason, though, to limit religions to those four.

Can politics be separated from culture?

Taken in its broadest sense, religion comes to include all manner of 'beliefs' and the behaviour and phenomena based upon them. The concept of 'belief' itself is extremely broad. It could even be said that the very ideology called liberalism, for example, is one belief, the reason being that such concepts as 'freedom' and 'equality,' or 'justice' and 'fairness' are 'notional ideas' that we have created in thought, and certainly do not have concrete existence. Furthermore, if we take 'belief' in the sense of 'what is believed,' then even our 'scientific knowledge' becomes a 'belief.' If that were the case, then the knowledge that 'the earth rotates' and the knowledge that 'the sun rotates' would both be 'beliefs,' and so, in terms of the neutrality thesis, they would have to be treated equally. (This means that it would be unjust only to teach Copernican theory at school.) Of course, some people will probably try to distinguish between science and belief. Though there is no room for a full discussion on this matter in this volume, it is necessary to note that in modern scientific philosophy there is no small number of arguments saying that it is not possible to make a precise distinction between the two.

In either case, what is clear is that a great deal of our knowledge constitutes 'belief,' and for that reason a great many social phenomena are 'religious' ones, and so the boundary between what is religion and what is not is not definitive. (Actually, in court cases to do with Japanese politico-religious separation, the question as to whether Shinto prayer ceremonies such as the *jichinsai* (ground-breaking ceremony) qualify as 'religious' becomes an issue. If one thinks of them as 'things that include belief,' these will splendidly constitute religious activities, but by the same token, the payment of subsidies for school education and cultural activities will also become a state's religious activities. Thus far, however, the Supreme Court seems to have endeavoured to interpret 'religious activities' as being limited to those explicitly relating to legally-defined 'religious organisations.')

The concept of 'culture' has been inclusive from the start, unlike 'religion,' of course. Science, religion and folkways are all 'culture.' It is difficult even to imagine such a situation of politics being neutral vis-à-vis 'culture in which everything is included.' This is because both democratic government and the parliamentary system, and even the defining territories for political space, all comprise 'culture' themselves.

The same thing can basically be said in respect to the individual conception of a good life. The 'conception of a good life,' too, is an extremely comprehensive one. A conception of life such as 'I want to play an active role internationally, using my bilingual ability' is one conception of a good life. Likewise, so is: 'I want to be a good farmer like my father.' On such occasions, it is impossible for political authorities to remain neutral towards people's conception of a good life. For example, a policy which promoted language-teaching would mean prioritising the former conception of life, while a policy for promotion of agriculture would give priority to the latter conception.

We live in a world whose every nook and cranny is imbued with culture, and various cultures coexist in their respective ways. Yet this does not mean that all cultures are being lived with identical rights and weights. Assuming that is the case, what on earth was liberalism's project? I shall ponder that issue again in the next chapter.

What does the neutrality thesis bring about?

The neutrality thesis in liberalism is often criticised by the following kind of communitarian argument, namely the criticism that 'we our actual selves inhabit individual cultures and communities, and find meaning in our lives only among these. Whatever we do, we cannot be neutral.' But liberalism will not sustain any damage from this alone, because such criticisms merely assert 'empirical' facts. Liberalism, by contrast, talks about 'normative principles' which precede and transcend such empirical facts. No matter what kinds of facts are accumulated, these will not constitute a critique of normative principles.

Pure atomistic liberalism, incidentally, makes no demands whatsoever upon the morality of citizens. It matters not if they are the sort of people who care nothing about others or about society as a whole. It is atomistic liberalism that attempts to think of the kind of structural institution that would make a 'desirable society,' even if the society were one consisting of people such as the above. Market fundamentalism, which anticipates that desirable outcomes can be obtained by the market mechanism, also is included in this category. This basically holds true for libertarianism, too.

This kind of atomistic liberalism is precisely the one that could be the most readily compatible with the neutrality thesis. Based on some sort of 'rights' and 'free domains' that are regarded as neutral, this philosophy requires merely that the work of government be limited to ensure that these issues are maintained. Naturally, there is still some ambiguity as to what 'neutral rights' might be, but there is no doubt that they closely approximate neutrality.

In regard to atomistic liberalism, this book has already pointed out the problem of what Taylor terms 'viability' and the question of the idea of compartmentalisation. In the first place, it is impossible to establish something like 'objectively universal rights' or a 'sphere of discretion' independently from cultural norms.

Furthermore, even assuming that such a thing could be established by any chance, there would still be the following two problems: firstly, since the establishment of spheres of discretion to a larger extent would substantially reduce the range of social cooperation, a large proportion of the values expected to accrue from social cooperation would probably be lost. For example, if a clash of people's interests occurred in a sphere that breached the bounds of the sphere of discretion, atomistic liberalism would be highly likely to wash its hands of the matter, saying that it had nothing to do with it, because it contains no guidelines as to how to arbitrate in a conflict of interest. If it were too much trouble, then it would suffice to make the parties live on isolated islands and do away with mutual interaction. But in any case it is clear that people's benefits and values would greatly decrease. We ought to be able to build a better society by cooperating with each other in the same society.

Secondly, if, for argument's sake, 'neutrality' actually came into force, it would probably mean substantial inequality and discrimination among other cultures. If, for example, the policy of affording preferential treatment to the French language were abolished in Quebec on the basis of the neutrality thesis, the number of children studying French would keep decreasing, and, in the long term, there is a strong possibility that it would bring about the disappearance of francophone culture. This would be all the more likely in even less robust minority cultures. In other words, if 'neutrality' means 'non-interference by government,' then this would result in 'strong' cultures winning the fight to survive, while 'weak' cultures atrophied and disappeared through the competitive mechanism of a kind of cultural market. This means that the criticisms Marx once (rightly) levelled against the injustices arising in the shadow of the superficial 'freedom' in capitalism's laissez-faire market can be applied here as well. A tendency can be seen among liberal scholars to assume tacitly, as Dworkin does, that 'the market' is a fundamentally fair thing, but competition under fair conditions will not necessarily bring about a desirable fair outcome.

In this way, atomistic liberalism is the one that best coincides with the neutrality thesis, but it is firstly an impossible conception, and if by the remote chance it *were* possible, the resulting society would be far from a desirable one.

Liberalism which cannot be neutral

Next, in cases of the kind of liberalism that Taylor calls 'patriotic liberalism,' or, more precisely speaking, the sort that has citizens' possession of a certain moral or personal quality as a constitutive element of its theory, this itself stands in opposition to a thesis of neutrality. This is because a liberalism supported by such a morality, as is Mill's, ends up not only endorsing society's morally educating citizens, but also actively incorporates it into its theory. Morality means the culture that ordains the way people live, and is the thing that prescribes what kind of life is a good life for each person. A liberalism supported by such a morality relating each person to others or to society probably can no longer be culturally neutral, in a genuine sense.

As we saw in the foregoing chapter, Rawls' later theory has deviated from cultural neutrality in a strict sense. The pluralistic society which he presupposes is something which consists of various 'reasonable' comprehensive doctrines. Unreasonable culture and individuals have been purged from it beforehand. Moreover, its citizens are moral persons equipped with ample public reason. How could such a scenario be possible? In a liberal society, how do unreasonable doctrines come to disappear, and how do people come to be equipped with public reason? Clearly, one would expect there to have been a tacit assumption of action by political power to ignore or remove any unreasonable doctrines, and to lead people to cultivate public reason.

Furthermore, when it comes to comprehensive liberalism, this more clearly conflicts with the neutrality thesis. Comprehensive liberalism has the view that the principles of liberalism should permeate into every corner of society, and it requires that every individual person adopt a way of life aligned with the liberal ethos. This could by no means be called 'neutral,' at least from the perspective of other beliefs or doctrines.

In the case of feminisms, too, whether aligned with liberalism or anti-liberal, they will include assertions that are fundamentally incompatible with the neutrality thesis. This is because most feminisms have presented not 'neutral' but 'critical' theories vis-à-vis phenomena that are rooted in the extremely traditional culture of 'family and sexuality.' The thesis that 'the personal is political' is one that renounces 'neutrality' from the start. According to this thesis, it is impossible—as restricted liberalism considers—to 'separate out' only 'political conceptions' from the comprehensive doctrines which prescribe individual lives, and therefore it is unjust. Criticism towards the 'separation of public and private' is a criticism that says, in essence, that there can be no such thing as a position that claims to be 'politically neutral towards culture.'

Even Gilligan's 'ethics of care' can be understood as completely disregarding the sort of 'neutrality' that liberalism assumes, from the fact that it insists upon an ethics that should exist for the individual.

In contrast to these, in the case of restricted liberalism, perhaps it could be called comparatively 'neutral,' since it does not intervene in comprehensive doctrines more than to call for 'reasonableness.' But even so, simply being 'neutral' would probably make it a theory with almost no effectiveness vis-à-vis the problems of pluralism that we face in actuality.

In contemporary society, for example, there exist numerous doctrines that are fundamentalist and intolerant of others, including not only religious ones such as Islamic fundamentalism or Christian fundamentalism, but also philosophical ones such as market fundamentalism, fundamentalist liberalism or libertarianism. When we ponder the problem of how to cope with this reality, even liberal political authority probably will have to act towards intolerant fundamentalist doctrines in a somewhat non-neutral (unfavourable) manner (even if it stops short of prohibiting them).

Furthermore, we have been afforded few guidelines from restricted liberalism about how we should make judgements in relation to the various concrete questions revolving around what constitutes 'public.' For example, Rawls' later theories have not presented anything resembling a clue to finding some kind of clear-cut 'solution' to the issues beset by serious confrontation in America, with abortion topping a list that includes pornography, prostitution, organ transplantation, reproductive technology, and so on. Certainly, there is slight reference to the abortion issue in a footnote in *Political Liberalism*. But, it merely states: 'now I believe any reasonable balance of these three values will give a woman a duly qualified right to decide whether or not to end her pregnancy during the first trimester' (Rawls 1993, p. 243, n. 32). Here, both the fundamentalist pro-choice and fundamentalist pro-life factions are removed in advance from the scope of debate.

Dworkin sees this kind of serious conflict situation concerning abortion as a 'religious war,' and that probably is correct in a certain sense. In this regard, in his 1993 book, *Life's Dominion: An Argument about Abortion, Euthanasia, and Individual Freedom*, from the position that such conflict is a 'religious confrontation,' Dworkin draws out the principles of 'separation of church and state' and 'freedom of religion,' and concludes that their various beliefs must be respected together. This indeed appears to be a coherent judgement in line with his 'neutrality thesis.'

This ruling, however, seems very similar to saying in relation to the problem of organ transplantation after brain death that 'it is a question of each person's belief, so it should be left up to each person's free choice.' If governments and courts act on the basis of this kind of rationale, and stop at merely prohibiting third parties' aggressive intervention in certain people's carrying out of abortions or organ transplants, even then the seriousness of conflict would be unlikely to lessen.

In fact, there have been increasing numbers of voices questioning the neutrality thesis emerging from among recent liberal debates, also. Dworkin does not say so directly, but he is clearly deviating from the neutrality thesis in discussions about 'liberal communities' and 'the authenticity of personality.' Ackerman (1990), too, has majorly amended its argument. Furthermore, the liberal advocate Brian Barry (1990) says that it would be better for liberalism itself for the superiority of liberal values to be asserted, rather than the neutrality thesis.

'Neutrality' originally was an idea for actualising a 'universal perspective.' At least on the superficial level of the word itself, it appears to be a valid notion. As with 'equality,' however, when it comes to applying it to the actual world, its idealistic or illusionary character is revealed in plain view.

Chapter 9

Liberalism's Miscalculations

The empire of the universal

Universal values

The classical liberalism of Locke and Mill originally had a strong slant towards ideas of freedom and tolerance, which placed high value on accepting cultures and ways of life divergent from one's own. Mill's harm principle, too, was not a principle aimed at advocating atomistic liberalism, but rather a principle for toleration towards things that were different. Yet contemporary liberalism since the late 1970s has intensified the 'justice ideology' aspect. Right at the same time, the United States—having lost the Vietnam War and lost its military prestige—promoted 'human rights diplomacy' as its diplomatic strategy in international politics in the period from the time of the Carter administration into that of Reagan (though it is true that glaringly obvious human rights violations, such as that of the Vietnamese Boat People and the genocide in Cambodia, did occur.) Though we will have to wait for international political historians to analyse how America's strategy and its manoeuvres were connected, in the 1980s, at any rate, the major theme of international forums and international organisations, led by the United Nations, was 'human rights.'

It was contemporary liberalism that played a central role in supporting such international movements and politics. The conception of 'human rights' was positioned at the core of terminology that expressed universal normative principles. It embodies the idea that there are rights common to all humankind that all people deem worthy of respect, and which transcend locality, culture and religion, not to mention sex, age and social stratum.

As long as one is thinking at an abstract level, there is no problem whatsoever with this idea. The assumption that there are common values applicable to any person in the world is an unmistakeably better assumption than relativism and scepticism, which take the view that such things do not exist at all. The basic standpoint of this volume regards the quest for such universal values to be a noble one.

It is necessary, however, to be aware that hidden pitfalls lurk here. To 'assume that universal normative principles exist' does not guarantee the actual existence of such principles, nor would it enable us by any means to give a direct answer to the question: 'what constitutes a universal normative principle?' A separate quest must be undertaken to find out how one could specify universalisms in concrete terms, and whatever kind of principle would be truly universal. Accordingly, even if it could be considered correct from a universal point of view to uphold the notion of 'human rights,' this would not necessarily mean that a precise answer to the question of what constitutes human rights could immediately be obtained.

Sadly, the conception of 'human rights' has been promoted from the beginning by people who are convinced that they themselves 'know what universal values are.' At the time of the French Revolution, when a 'Declaration of Human Rights' was proclaimed as something that 'set forth…the natural, unalienable and sacred rights of man,' the people who adopted it believed that 'they themselves knew what constituted sacred natural rights.'

Of course, the content is lofty in tone, but (with the attachment of some slight proviso) it is something that would be acceptable more or less in its original form even today. That does not signify, though, that 'natural rights' are 'set forth' in it. In one sense, we today have merely inherited the greater part of the conception of society that the enlightened intellectuals of that time had imagined.

Now, to return to the present, the theses of contemporary liberalism, including the 'rights-based approach' and 'the priority of the right over the good,' lead to the assertion that fundamental human rights which should apply universally to all the people of the world ought to be protected, yet we have already seen that this tends to clash with the issue of pluralism in its relationship with minority culture. Then again, the points of contention with feminism can, in one sense, be seen as problems to do with the culture that comprises the family. Various normative relationships of the family or between the sexes have developed and continued to exist as diverse cultural traditions in all parts of the world. As those respective societies have modernised, many traditional customs and conventional practices have vanished, but it has been those institutions connected with the family that have retained the tone of specific cultures more strongly than political institutions or economic systems. The family, especially, will not become established solely upon the liberal presupposition of a 'society composed of independent adults,' because it is the place where dependent children are raised. For that reason, it is a sphere where the direct application of liberal universalism is difficult. As we have already seen, Rawls did not think of his principles of justice being applied within the family directly, but this point attracted the criticism from one feminist camp that liberalism was not sufficiently universalistic, preserving the separation of the public and the private. On the other hand, from another branch of feminism the criticism was raised that liberalism had insufficient respect for the culture of the family and intimate relationships, and the ethics of care was emphasised.

Here, along with the confrontation between the particularities of individual cultures and the notion of 'universal' that liberalism has presented, there is a question of on what grounds could anything that liberalism considers to be 'universal' be truly 'universal.'

The rivalry between the universal and culture

While it is only natural, liberalism's universalism is often criticised for being imperialist or colonialist. From the viewpoint of Islamic fundamentalism, liberalism's preaching of freedom of belief, gender equality and political democracy is something which plays a part in Christian religious hegemony and American imperialism. Even if one does not think to such extremes, one cannot deny that universalistic liberalism contains an aspect that does threaten traditional individual cultures that exist in every part of the world. This has recently even prompted doubts to be raised towards 'justice.'

Of course, liberalism's universalism, even if 'imperialistic,' still has no lack of aspects to which one can intuitively give approval. Among customs relating to the family and sexuality, for example, those which are often cited from feminist or liberal perspectives by Western scholars as being 'counter to human rights' are the sort of practices that are so cruel in anyone's opinion as to make one want to avert one's eyes, such as the (once-prevalent) *sati* (the burning to death of widows) in India, and female genital mutilation (still being practised) in African countries. It would be natural for these to be criticised in the name of 'universal human rights.' This, too, might constitute imperialism, but even if it did, most of us would probably support the imperialist position.

Not all problems can be so easily decided, however. To cite a Japanese example, is the custom of females being barred from the sand ring (*dohyō*) in grand sumo and from tunnel-construction sites really one that must be denounced as unjust? Alternatively, there seems to be no simple answer to the question of whether Japan's denial of legal recognition for separate surnames for married couples or for same-sex marriage should be seen as a bad system that suppresses individual freedom. The issue of how, and to what extent, the various liberal principles can be applied vis-à-vis customs and institutions that are deeply rooted in culture is not a simple question.

Let us consider, for example, the question of why only men are allowed to be priests in the Roman Catholic Church. From the liberal viewpoint of sexual equality and freedom of choice of occupation, the exclusion of women from the priesthood is unlikely to be anything other than unjust discrimination. In actual fact, harsh criticism has been directed at this institution from the angle of feminist theology.

In response, basically the following kind of argument has been tendered from the orthodox standpoint: 'the job of a priest is to represent Jesus Christ, to conduct mass, and serve God; Christ himself was male, and the Twelve Apostles were also male. In that, there must had been some deep consideration on the part of God and Christ that surpassed human understanding; and in this point, the culture of gender roles is certainly not one that signifies inequality. Nowadays, in public-opinion polls and the like, results show that there are many people who agree with women being in paid employment, but who also say that the Church is 'a place for seeking "truth"—in other words, God's teachings—and not a place that adheres to public opinion.'

In this argument, it is understood that everything ultimately is ascribed to the grace of Christ and God. For a non-Catholic, such an argument might have no power of persuasion whatsoever. Conversely, though, for people within the Catholic faith, this is probably a sufficiently meaningful argument. If one takes the Bible as one's premise, it is a fact that Christ and the Twelve Apostles were male, and it is also a fact that the Catholic priesthood historically has been limited to males. It is difficult to refute the presumption that some kind of deep deliberation is likely to have been involved.

Here, one might conceive of an idea to utilise the legal system of secular society to mount an unconstitutionality suit, claiming that 'the Catholic Church's prohibition of female priests is opposed to equality of the sexes.' What would the court rule then, I wonder?

At this point, liberalism probably would divide into two camps. One camp would consider that, regardless of whether their adversary is the Catholic Church or any other traditional culture, liberal normative principles still have to pervade every sphere of society, as a general rule. The Catholic Church's exclusion of females from the priesthood would therefore probably be judged 'unconstitutional.'

On the other hand, there would probably be a moderate liberal camp, as well. Here, they would consider autonomy to be admissible in the respective groups or cultures within certain parameters, with no necessity to have fundamentalist equality or individual freedom forced upon them. Of course, there would be limits to their autonomy. Not only would usual crimes like homicide and larceny be prohibited, naturally, but so would cruelty and markedly unjust discrimination and oppression. Yet, excluding such clear contraventions of 'trans-cultural norms,' that camp would consider that each respective cultural tradition ought to be 'respected' in the secular politico-legal system, along with their faith and doctrines.

The latter is the standpoint of restricted liberalism. As I stated in Chapter Seven, restricted liberalism tolerates the coexistence of the sort of comprehensive doctrines that do not serve solely liberal values in political society. Apart from the various faiths—Catholicism, the various Protestant denominations, Islam, Judaism, and so on—nationalism, cosmopolitanism, Marxism, feminism, and the like, are such doctrines. Political liberalism or restricted liberalism would endeavour to posit justice principles as normative principles applying commonly to these doctrines, on the condition that the latter were 'reasonable.' Nevertheless, the substance of these justice principles would probably be quite moderate.

Comprehensive liberalism, by contrast, sees itself as the sole 'true' comprehensive doctrine, and considers that all other doctrines should be subordinate to it. Accordingly, it requires that the other various doctrines also ultimately respect liberal values. Within comprehensive liberalism, though, there are also some advocates who do not go so far as to demand that liberal values always be completely actualised. Kymlicka, for instance, who strives to recognise the significance of socially-constructed culture, would probably allow minority culture to deviate to a certain extent from liberal values (though it is unclear how he regards the exclusion of women from joining the priesthood). On the other hand, many scholars who take the perspective of comprehensive liberalism would probably think that, Catholic or not, all groups and cultures have to comply with liberal values; and it is liberal values that ultimately govern political society. One can call this kind of comprehensive liberalism, which holds the view that 'in every time and in every case, liberal values must be carried through' can be called '*fundamentalist liberalism*.'

What constitutes the universal?

Whether fundamentalist or moderate, both kinds of liberalism agree on the point that liberal values should be respected in political society. The difference between the two lies in what they concretely consider ought to be achieved in all cases. This reflects the disparity in their attitude to the question of 'what should universally apply.'

Now, in the case of the Catholic priest issue, whatever should we really think? Should we, as advocates of fundamentalist liberalism, consider that even in a traditional religious culture such as Catholicism, the liberal value of equality of the sexes must be respected? Or else, even if we ourselves are not Catholics, should we think that as the Catholic faith considers that women ought not to become priests, then that faith has to be respected, and should be judged in that manner even in public politics and the judicature?

The answer to these questions is divided even within liberalism, but the point of contention ultimately depends on whether one considers that 'every kind of liberal value should be universally and absolutely applicable, anytime and anywhere.' If one thinks that unconditional sexual equality is such a universally and absolutely-applicable value, then it will mean that the Catholic Church is carrying out an injustice. If, on the contrary, while maintaining that political freedom and freedom of religion are absolute values, one does not think that 'unconditional' sexual equality is always absolute, then the Catholic Church's practice will be tolerated by reason of freedom of religion.

So, in the end, whatever *does* constitute a 'universally-applicable value?' Certainly, we consider that prohibiting *sati* and female genital mutilation accords with universal values. In this manner, as long as we think something is 'universally right,' we will consider that to require it of somebody other than ourselves, even if it smacks of imperialism, will qualify as just. Perhaps, though, this might be nothing more than our simply saying 'we think it is universally right.' Are there in fact any objectively correct judgements or criteria on earth pertaining to the question of what universal values are, other than merely those which we subjectively suppose to be such?

Actually, contemporary liberalism has been founded on the presupposition that such 'objectively correct criteria are likely to exist.' It considers that 'there exist correct values and criteria that are indubitable in anyone's eyes, and we are assuredly able to discover them, and deduce universally-applicable normative principles based upon them.' We call such a way of thinking 'foundationalism,' and contemporary liberalism is, in its fundamental aspects, a project of foundationalism. It is extremely doubtful, however, that this project will succeed.

The foundationalism of justifiability

The problem of justification

Liberalism aims to establish universally-applicable normative principles, and to order political society by those means. At this time, liberalism considers that universally-applicable normative principles are expected to be 'justifiable.' Rawls, for example, in an essay published after he had ceased using the logic of the original position, emphasises that the conception of justice 'can be justified to all citizens,' 'by citing what are publicly recognized as sufficient reasons' (Rawls 1980, p. 517). For him, this constitutes the basis of the reason why the conception of justice might be universally applicable. Rawls thinks it possible to establish the validity of a certain conception of justice or normative principle by showing that it is 'justifiable.' A certain norm's being 'justifiable' is seen to warrant the objective correctness of that norm. That is not a pattern of thought only seen in contemporary liberalism, but the notion of 'justifiability' has fulfilled an extremely important role in the arguments of contemporary liberalism, in particular. It is inseparable from contemporary liberalism's foundationalism.

As I will also explain in the next section, contemporary liberalism strives to formulate the principles of justice as the supreme normative principles for a society that is a *tabula rasa*, so to speak. These principles cannot be derived from some kind of other pre-existing (that is, culturally-constrained and historically-formed) norms. Nevertheless, they need grounding. There was the expectation that the contractarian logic of the original position in *A Theory of Justice* would provide such grounds. That logic was regarded as constituting a basis for the justification of the two principles of justice. And, even after abandonment of the logic of the original position, their justification is still necessary. Rawls considered that their being 'justifiable to all citizens' would constitute the rationale for authorising the principles of justice.

Here, let us pay attention to the fact that a double meaning is embedded in the word 'justifiable.' Its first meaning is that the thing in question can be seen and accepted as 'something legitimate' by actually-existing, particular people. In this case, 'legitimacy' always appertains to the judgement of the people who see and accept the thing as 'legitimate'—it is a subjective judgment on the people's part, so to speak. In short, it means nothing other than 'they think it is legitimate.'

The other meaning is that 'it can be established that it is legitimate from an objective viewpoint' which transcends people's judgment. This bears no relation to whether people think that the thing is legitimate. Even if it cannot be justified in the former sense, it might be legitimate in the latter, and the converse also might be true.

The former case can be called '*empirical justifiability*,' and the latter '*notional justifiability*.' It is actually possible to verify whether something is empirically justifiable, or has been empirically justified. For example, most Japanese see the current Japanese political system as basically legitimate, and also accept as legitimate such norms as 'one must not steal,' 'one must not kill,' and so on. Many of the presently-existing institutions and norms are 'regarded as legitimate' by many people. It would be a different matter, though, if they were asked whether they could justify them in an objective sense. I have discussed this issue of normative discourse in an earlier paper (Seiyama 2001).

How, then, is it possible to verify whether something is objectively justifiable, or has been justified? We cannot avoid coming to a standstill here. Regardless of whatever empirical fact we bring to bear, we cannot verify whether a certain thing is objectively justified. This would be the case even assuming it could be 'empirically' justified to all citizens. There is a categorical difference between these two questions.

On this point, Rawls' expression, 'justifiable to all citizens' is ambiguous. If it meant 'empirically justifiable to all actually-existing citizens,' then there would probably be a necessity actually to demonstrate it. But, even assuming that the attempt were successful, it would simply mean that 'it was agreed by all the people then present that it is legitimate,' but would never mean that it was objectively justified as legitimate. While 'agreement' constitutes an important component of normative social theory, as I will later discuss, it tends to be undervalued as being 'mere agreement' from the usual standpoint of contemporary liberalism. This is because people's agreement is often incorrect, as nationalistic fervour once was. Contemporary liberalism holds that it would not be appropriate to make such an untrustworthy thing its theoretical foundation.

Considering that Rawls has given no hint of any sort of intention actually to question citizens as to the legitimacy of the conception of justice that he himself presented, one should probably understand the phrase 'justifiable to all citizens' as meaning notional objective justification, after all. If that were the case, though, it would make it impossible in the end to verify the matter, because there is no way of verifying something to be objectively justified. For liberalism, justice principles are things that must be 'objectively justifiable,' but their justification will be eternally impossible.

The English expression 'justifiable' or 'can be justified' approaches the word 'justice,' though these differ in Japanese, the latter two being '*seitōka dekiru*' and '*seigi*,' respectively. The English word that equates to the Japanese '*seitōsei*' (which could equally be translated as 'justifiability' or 'legitimacy') is 'justice' itself. In other words, in English contexts, 'justice (*seigi*)' is something which has 'justifiability (*seitōsei*),' and therefore is something that is 'justifiable (*seitōka dekiru*).' However, it would not be permissible to depend upon something's being 'justifiable' as a way of establishing the grounds for it being 'just,' because it is not at all clear how something would become 'justified.'

There have been various other attempts to establish the meaning of 'justifiability' using different terminology, however. A typical example is the 'contractualism' of Rawls' disciple, the philosopher T.M. Scanlon. He aims to construct justice in a more direct, contractarian manner, without depending upon a fiction like the original position. But here, what plays a core role is the thesis that a person's act is justified if it is required or tolerated by 'principles which no one could reasonably reject' (Scanlon 1982, p. 111). This constitutes a theory that explains the substance of something being 'justifiable.' On close examination, though, it will be seen that the issue is simply being postponed. This is because the very idea of something that 'no one could reasonably reject' is also a notional concept, and is by no means something that could be empirically verified. In fact, anyone, really, could think up and present some kind of 'reason' for rejecting any sort of demand for rights. Of course, Scanlon's theory would probably say that if it were not 'reasonable,' then it would not be a 'true reason.' Even if this were acknowledged, who on earth could verify 'what was a reasonable reason,' and by what method?

Foundationalism

The project to seek a theory to justify some kind of normative proposition is not one that began with liberalism. Most modern social theories since Hobbes—apart from sceptics like Hume—have been involved in this project. At the forefront in their minds was the success of mathematics and the natural sciences. The time- and culture-transcendent 'truths' which were presented with irrefutable persuasion for all were the very things that moral philosophers also unendingly sought. If normative propositions were correct, then—just as it was possible to justify scientific 'truth'—those propositions, too, were likely to be justifiable. Philosophers, starting with Kant, have continued a single-minded quest for a theory to satisfy justifiability, and a 'universally-applicable normative proposition' that would be obtained as a result. By upholding 'justice' as the goal of its quest, liberalism has merely hastened that tendency.

Here, what must not be overlooked is the fundamental misunderstanding about the success of the natural sciences. This misapprehension is that correct propositions in natural sciences are things that have been deduced 'logically' from 'laws' that are supposed to be true, and facts that have been observed to be true. This is the 'axiomatic' understanding of natural sciences, but this is backed by mistaken interpretations relating to the spectacular success of Newtonian mechanics, and, furthermore, to Euclidean geometry as a model for correct intellectual inquiry (which still retains its attractiveness even today).

I must omit any detailed explanation, but the natural sciences' axiomatic image may be depicted in a schema such as Figure 9.1. If we, and scientific explorers, precisely observe the world, discover correct laws, and, combining these, reason accurately and logically, then we can be expected to arrive at correct propositions. Out of these, 'discovering true laws' is considered the most important task in the inquiry. They, as represented by the three laws of motion in Newtonian mechanics, are the objectively true, fundamental principles that control the natural world.

This schema is wrong, but modern thinkers since Spinoza and Hobbes have been of the opinion that there is also likely to be some kind of 'objectively true fundamental principle' for normative order in society. It is well-known that Kant assumed the existence of 'moral laws' as such principles. Both the aforementioned Bentham's utilitarian principle, that says that the only thing that exists is the individual, and

Figure 9.1: The (mistaken) axiomatic image relating to the natural world

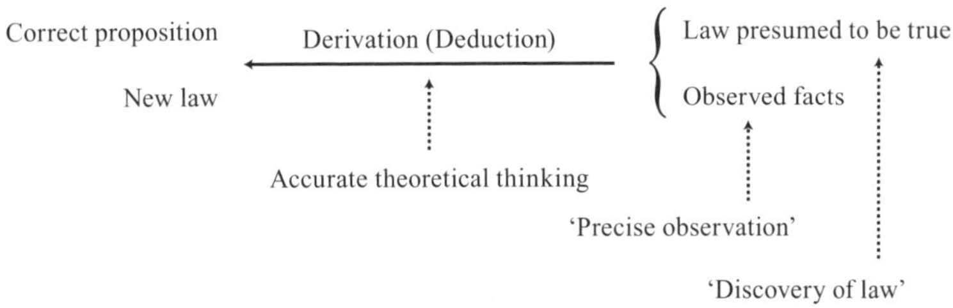

what solely should be counted in terms of social desirability is people's pleasure and happiness, and Mill's 'harm principle,' too, were things that were thought up corresponding to such 'fundamental principle.'

Contemporary liberalism continues this tradition faithfully, or even more robustly than hitherto. The basic theses that I discussed in Chapter Seven: (A) neutrality towards cultures and the conceptions of good; (B) the rights-based approach; (C) the priority of the right (justice) over the good; and (D) a society which serves individual welfare, are ones that in themselves constitute such fundamental principles, or else form their foundations. Thesis (E), compartmentalisation, represents a parallelism with a strategy of theoretical construction in the success of atomistically-created natural sciences. It goes without saying that the model of the 'original position' in Rawls' *A Theory of Justice* was one set up to be a 'fair basis' for deducing 'correct norms.' At the very least, that is how it was apprehended. Moreover, this contractarian schema was the very thing that attracted people's enormous interest, and brought about the flourishing of contemporary liberalism.

What is especially important is the following kind of special property or meaning of the 'normative principles' that are being sought here, namely that contemporary liberalism aims to establish higher-order normative principles which transcend the individual cultures and comprehensive doctrines that comprise today's cultural pluralism. This means that the normative principles which should be established are things that are independent of any kind of individual traditional culture or moral ideology, and must not be deduced from, or reduced to, a proportion of these. Those normative principles must therefore be established completely afresh on a so-called *tabula rasa*, without relying upon any pre-existing culturally bound moral theory. To that end, it would not be strange even if the method of foundationalistic justification were thought to be the most fitting, and actually this is what has happened. If it is possible to discover laws that hold true for any perspective when seeking normative principles independent from any type of individual interests or cultures, then, on that basis, it will be considered feasible to deduce a system of universally-applicable normative principles and a normative order. That is something that would be 'justifiable.' Things truly universal were thought to be notionally just, as a matter of course.

This is the reason for contemporary liberalism's emphasis upon the foundationalistic notion of 'justifiability.' The thing that best represents this schema is the 'neutrality thesis,' as the idea of 'neutrality' itself should incorporate a universal quality. Again, the 'responsibility/circumstance' binary in luck-egalitarianism is also something that has been used as grounds for justifying equality because it was seen as something that stood on a universal foundation.

'Justifiability' was an illusion, however. The 'neutrality thesis,' which was intended to induce an establishment of normative institutions that would be 'neutral' in situations where different cultures and conceptions of the good coexisted, cannot, in concrete terms, actually state what kind of law would need to be set up, and what sort of policy adopted. No laws or policies can ever avoid inviting outcomes advantageous to one or other culture or conception of the good, and disadvantageous to others. Even assuming that the government took a position of non-intervention (like a libertarian), this would merely result in differential advantages and disadvantages due to market competition. The political theories of feminism and postmodernism are correct, at least on the point that they claim 'everything is political,' and 'everything is culturally-bound.' In addition, if one were to try to resolve conflict by compartmentalising different cultures or conceptions of the good in order to circumvent such annoyance, it would only materially dismantle social cooperation or society itself.

The 'responsibility/circumstance' binary, also, seems at first glance to be something that tries to forge a basis out of indubitably objective 'responsibility,' but the notion of 'responsibility' is by no means objective: rather, it is culturally-bound.

In the case both of 'neutrality' and 'responsibility/circumstance,' each appears to be universal on the level of words. As long as it is considered only on the level of words, such a thesis might justifiably be called universal. Here, though, the persons who accept it as 'justifiable' will be only those advocates of contemporary liberalism who have taken its conceptual scheme and terminology for granted. Being 'justifiable' for them does not guarantee that it is 'genuinely' justifiable. If one minutely examines theses that have been considered 'justifiable,' unjustifiable aspects will become variously clear. This means, at least, that they are 'empirically unjustified.' While this does not signify immediately that they cannot be notionally and objectively justified, their 'justifiability' still will not be established.

Justice as transcendent and its impossibility

Justice's lack of substance

Contemporary liberalism has endeavoured to establish the thesis that 'justice' is an indubitable truth. Tatsuo Inoue's 1999 book, *Tasha e no jiyū* (Freedom towards others), could be cited as a typical example.

In Inoue's eyes, 'justice' is 'a value applicable as a common constraint upon diverse conceptions of a good life' (1999, p. 102), and a fundamental normative principle for political society. He calls this the 'fundamentality of justice.' This notion, he says, is composed of the following three propositions:

1. Justice is a constitutive principle of political society, and one which, while regulating the exercise of public and private power in political society, can be forcibly practised by means of public power. (The publicness (*kōkyōsei*) of justice)
2. Justice principles must be justifiable without depending upon the particular conception of 'a good life.' (The independence of justice)
3. When the particular conception of 'a good life' clashes with the demand for justice, the latter will take priority. (The restrictiveness of justice) (Inoue 1999, p. 98)

As a concise formularisation of the principles of justice by way of Inoue's unique method, these are exceptionally worthy of attention. They have the following characteristics: firstly, the assertion that justice is a principle which 'regulates the exercise of public and private power' is one that says that regardless of whether in the public or private sphere, the use of power must obey the normative principle called justice. Here, Inoue includes the private sphere, bearing in mind the critique of the separation of public and private. As 'private power' is something that relates to all manner of social interaction (Seiyama 2000a), this means that Inoue is asserting that justice consequently is a principle that controls all areas of the political world.

Secondly, in terms of political power in society, the claim is made that it exists in order to usurp justice, and to carry out justice. Justice is not only fundamental, but also ubiquitous. I beg your attention to the fact that this implies a staggeringly severe assertion that 'unless it qualifies as just, political power must not be exercised.'

Thirdly, the 'independence of justice' in 2, above, while based on Dworkin's and Ackerman's 'neutrality,' comprises a more refined assertion than theirs. Justice does not need to be neutral towards diverse conceptions of a good life, but must be something independent of these.

Fourthly, as another important point in 2, one can understand that 'the justifiability of justice' seen in the previous section is advocated, namely, that 'justice must be justifiable.'

Fifthly, and finally, considering the above in combination, the assertion is implied that 'in order for political power and its exercise to meet the criteria for justice, it must be justified independently from any sort of conception of the good.' Naturally, this means 'political independence from culture,' or, alternatively, 'political impartiality (not necessarily neutrality) towards culture.'

Inoue's liberalism conceptualises justice in a very strong sense, and, at the same time, by so doing, effectively imposes very forceful conditions upon politics. It goes without saying that such a strong conceptualisation reflects an intention to establish liberalism as the supreme normative principle for the task of politically ordering a society that is fragmented by pluralistic values. The way being advocated by liberalism for a political society is one that should be universally applicable, transcending times and cultures, and 'justice,' which is its core value concept, must be equipped with such a capacity. Such an intention has thus brought about a strong conceptualisation.

There is, however, a serious matter to which I draw your attention here, namely that the all-important 'concrete substance of justice principles' has not been presented by Inoue. This is still the case, even in his later works. This is odd, but it is not an incomprehensible situation. It means that because Inoue has imposed such strong conditions upon justice, the sort of substantive justice principles such as would fulfil those terms may possibly be non-existent. And even if they did exist, it seems that it would be impossible for anyone to discover some substantive justice principles which would conform with the terms perfectly.

Such a tendency for the 'content' to be missing is, in fact, not confined to Inoue: it is common currency in all theories in contemporary liberalism, bar Rawls, who concretely presented the two principles of justice. But Rawls' two principles of justice, too, remain fairly abstract when it comes to content. In these cases, it is akin to simply intoning a mantra. Let us look back at Dworkin's resource-egalitarian argument. While basing it upon luck-egalitarianism, he was advocating fundamental equality of resources by making use of theoretical mechanisms such as the initial equal allocation of resources, the auction, and the hypothetical insurance market. In concrete terms, however, he has not said anything about what kind of resources should be equalised, and in what way. The same holds for Sen. As I have already touched upon in Chapter Five, his egalitarian theory of 'capability' has not stated what sort of capabilities should be substantively equalised. Those who champion the 'rights-based approach,' also, never concretely discuss what kind of rights ought to be universally acknowledged. On this point, Kymlicka, who refutes collective rights and advocates the prioritisation of individual rights, is the same as the rest.

The reason why they are unable to present the content of justice or equalisation in a concrete manner is that the scholars themselves do not know what it is in the first place, but a psychological mechanism is also at work to inhibit them from directing their efforts towards finding out. They know that if they produced substantive content, then they would not fail to be the target of complaints from some other scholars or groups that were fervent about political pronouncements. Alternatively, at best, they would simply be completely ignored. The same applies even in the case of concrete 'universal rights.' Even in response to Western arguments criticising the practice of female genital mutilation, counter-criticisms that such claims are too Eurocentric are presented by liberal specialists in the societies concerned. Still more, if they said anything like 'abortion is a woman's right,' then objections would flood in from pro-child groups all over the United States.

In other words, any substantive content of justice that liberalism were to produce, considering it 'justifiable,' would become the target of bitter criticism the instant it was presented—indeed not the kind of situation that one would call 'justifiable.' Many scholars are well aware of this.

Of course, this is not to say that there is actually nobody presenting concrete 'justice' or 'universal rights' from a liberal standpoint; and there are some scholars who gain many people's approval. In regard to heated points of contention in which quite different cultures or beliefs sharply conflict, however, liberal assertions generally end up simply being seen solely as 'something from a unilateral camp.' On an empirical level, this is far distant from being 'justifiable.' Not only that: there is even a tendency to intensify controversy, and to split people into factions. This is the case with the issues of abortion and marriage in America, and with the Yasukuni Shrine and 'gender-free' matters in Japan. The headscarf incidents in France, also, can be seen as religious conflicts that liberalism incited in the name of 'separation of religion and politics.'

Here, an extremely ironic situation has arisen. Contemporary liberalism was aiming to establish normative principles such as would transcend antagonistic, divergent cultures and have universal application. In actual practice, though, the concrete presentation of the substance of such normative principles is avoided; or else, such presentation having been done, it then has the opposite effect of fuelling the conflict. Many scholars desire liberalism to be a comprehensive doctrine that surpasses existing cultures, but in reality, liberalism is nothing more than one among all of today's opposing doctrines.

Herein reposes contemporary liberalism's miscalculation.

Justice as transcendent

'Justice' is the value which contemporary liberalism places in supreme position. It signifies a universal normative principle that ought to transcend different cultures and struggles among religious deities, and to bring order to society (not merely one national society, but the whole world). Its validity applies 'absolutely,' transcending individual cultures and circumstances. The value called 'justice' is assumed to be such a thing.

Here, it will probably be appreciated that 'justice' is actually established in the same hypostasis as a type of 'transcendental being.' In contemporary liberalism, 'justice' is a transcendental being to which all cultures and religions and people's conception of the good should submit. It could be termed 'God'—but, of course, liberalism does not call it so. Contemporary liberalism is none other than a doctrine that reverentially accepts such 'justice as transcendental' as its ideal.

It is not that the word 'justice' had such a transcendental sense from the beginning, however. As I also briefly mentioned in Chapter Two, this is something that was developed in contemporary liberalism from Rawls onwards.

There is little worth in asking what 'justice' essentially means. It is necessary, though, to know precisely what is being discussed or sought in using that term, when people employ the word 'justice' to pursue something or assign value to something.

It was only recently that 'justice' came to be seen as a central value in the fields of moral philosophy and ethics, but this does not mean that it was completely ignored even prior to that. Traditionally, for the concept of 'justice,' the method of classification that Aristotle indicated in *Nicomachean Ethics* is invoked as standard practice. There, justice is roughly divided into three categories. The first is 'distributive justice,' which stipulates the correct way of allocating among people the burdens necessary for the group and the benefit produced by the group. The second is 'corrective justice,' which expresses the norm saying that if B sustains injury because of A, then A must make reparation for that injury. The third is 'commutative justice,' which expresses the fairness of terms of exchange in transactions.

Each of these three types of justice is one that sets out how social collective decisions should be normatively correct in relation to the kind of interests and burdens it ascribes to whom within the potential conflicts of interest that beset social relationships in everyday life. The one which stipulates the normatively correct manner of dividing the benefit generated by group effort is distributive justice; that which stipulates the normatively correct manner of righting injury that has arisen from illegal acts is corrective justice; and that which stipulates what kind of terms of exchange are normatively correct is commutative justice.

In everyday life, 'justice' is talked about in various other settings than these, but here let us confine ourselves to 'justice' as an academic term. If we centre our thinking around Aristotle's three types, the 'justice' in question could be understood as one of the qualities of social judgements or social decisions, and as a concept signifying, in their case, the quality of being 'normatively correct.'

On the other hand, in the field of jurisprudence, it is often said that 'the objective of law is justice.' In other words, the value that law ultimately serves could be said to be 'justice.' Though its content is also ambiguous, it is possible to list several of its characteristics. Firstly, in legal terms, justice is not necessarily the same as general morality. For example, it may be morally acceptable to protect a person to whom one is beholden by giving false evidence in court, but it is not legally correct. Secondly, even if the objective of law is justice, we are well aware that not all actual laws meet justice criteria. Seeing that there are occasions when the law fails to implement justice, justice is assumed to be in a position that surpasses law. Thirdly, nevertheless, justice is a value whose manifestation by, or within, the law is the target of aspiration.

Aristotle's three types of justice are each the sort of justice that could become the objective of law. In relation to distributive justice, there are laws pertaining to income tax, various social policies or social security; as for corrective justice, there are criminal and tort laws; and there is commercial law relating to commutative justice.

Seen in this manner, the expression 'the objective of law is justice' could be considered one that has deftly conveyed the intimate connection between law and 'justice.' And it follows that the meaning of 'justice' on this occasion is strongly drawn towards 'law.' This also can be argued from the fact that the English and French word 'justice' derives from the Latin *jus*, whose meanings include 'law' and 'right.' The naming of the United States' Department of Justice, too, expresses the notion that the law aims to serve justice.

The above sums up the way that 'justice' was used before it was endowed with a transcendental meaning by contemporary liberalism. It could be said to signify 'the supreme normative principle to which the law should adhere,' so to speak. Firstly, what is important here is that 'justice' in this case is not necessarily the one that stands in a superior position vis-à-vis numerous other values. It is not considered, for example, that the whole of individuals' personal morality will be reduced to what is stipulated by law. Personal morality can be opposed to 'legal justice,' and this does not mean that legal justice ought to take precedence over morality at such times. Alternatively, the value of 'tolerance,' also, is independent of 'legal justice.' The term 'right,' when used in discourse comparing 'right' and 'good' in terms of individual morality, incorporates obeying not legal justice, but primarily moral obligations; this meaning of 'right' is not necessarily the same thing as 'justice' in law.

Secondly, before contemporary liberalism appeared, there existed a general principle relating to 'legal justice,' namely the fair and equal application of the law. But a theme such as 'the establishment of justice principles' was scarcely pursued. Even when thinking that distributional justice should be brought about by law, nobody asked the question: 'What is true equality?' There had been virtually no attempt to seek a principle that could generally regulate distributional justice: in sum, though the question: 'What constitutes justice?' was sometimes asked in relation to concrete points at issue, the task of inquiry as to 'what should be meant generally by "justice"' had not yet been thematised.

Thirdly, it may also be noted that 'justice' has been frequently discussed even in the past in a more radical sense that surpassed 'legal justice,' as in 'even should the world perish, justice should be done.' In such cases, 'justice' signified some sort of 'ruling' from a transcendental perspective. Usually its content was not specified, but it was something that symbolised a kind of 'moral rightness as a society,' which was ultimate and surpassed human understanding, one might say. The substance of such 'justice' could be freely assumed (according to one's respective creed), but there was never any attempt to establish the validity of its content by means of mundane theoretical work.

Contemporary liberalism since Rawls did, however, set up 'justice,' imbued with a totally new meaning, as the central theme of investigation in legal philosophy and moral philosophy. From the moment that Rawls gave 'justice' the meaning of 'the first virtue of social institutions,' it came to express, on the level of secular theory, the supreme moral value by which society should abide. Contemporary liberalism flourished for the very reason that it established such a subject of study, but it was almost inevitably one that oriented that liberalism towards a foundationalistic pursuit. 'Justice' is a fundamental normative principle that society should establish in the first place, at its point of departure, and it is something that has to be inscribed upon society in a *tabula rasa* condition, without reliance upon various pre-existent beliefs. Its 'universal validity' must be grounded by logic of a certain universal perspective. Moreover, for many scholars it had to be independent of any kind of pre-existing culture or individual interest, as in the case of 'God,' so to speak, though in a secular sense.

Such a pursuit of 'transcendental justice,' precisely as I have already repeatedly emphasised, is set against a background of the diverse issues that have arisen in pluralistic modern society since the 1970s, and is aimed at presenting a 'moral compass for their resolution.' This quest is by no means a simple theoretical game. It is led by moral concerns towards various problems of real world.

But, any project intended to establish universally-valid justice principles on a *tabula rasa* inevitably has to be foundationalistic, and foundationalism will never succeed. Any strategy that tried to overcome pluralism was itself destined to be buried within pluralism.

Conclusion

Normative Principles as a Hypothesis

Justice as a construct

It was a magnificent achievement of liberalism to have broken a long standstill that had endured until 1970, when it set up an inquiry which took the morality of society as its direct theme, blowing new breath into moral philosophy and normative theory, and opening up new pathways. We can see there a sumptuous intellectual feast that continues even now. Its primary task was to establish a normative principle for political society whose validity would transcend different cultures in its application to the culturally-pluralistic circumstances of today's society. Contemporary liberalism named this normative principle 'justice.' Justice was represented as a value which ought to be valid in every political society, irrespective of temporal and cultural boundaries. This representation in itself is exceptionally persuasive and difficult to deny, yet it is precisely in 'justice' as represented in this way that the difficulty of contemporary liberalism is located.

The 'justice' which today's liberalism endeavours to establish must reign transcendentally over all cultures and religions. This kind of transcendent 'justice' must therefore be posited without dependence upon any particular culture or religion. But, simply speaking, this means trying to make something normative appear on the surface of a *tabula rasa* upon which nothing normative has been presupposed. How on earth could such a trick of conjuring something from nothing be possible? Most people have not realised how difficult a task this is.

Its discussants could not avoid tacitly adopting a strategy of foundationalism. In other words, the aim was to start from axiomatic propositions that were both undeniable and independent of any religion or culture; or else to establish such axiomatic propositions.

The 'neutrality thesis,' for example, was proposed in this way. While it is indeed independent from any culture or conception of the good, one will immediately see that this thesis signifies 'the impossibility of politics.' There can be no such thing as a politics that is neutral towards all cultures. Hence, the 'neutrality thesis' is an impossible thesis. It is, in a manner of speaking, something akin to a 'tautological axiom' that can derive nothing. Alternatively, there is the 'rights-based approach.' If we assume that there indeed are 'universally-applicable rights,' then these will form a common foundation transcending divergent cultures and religions. As long as we remain at a level of mere supposition of such things, we will be able to maintain a transcendent viewpoint. Once we attempt to specify such rights in concrete terms, however, we will inevitably become involved in a struggle between gods in the real world.

The other theses characterising contemporary liberalism—'the priority of the right over the good,' 'a society serving individual welfare' and 'compartmentalisation'—are intended to be transcendent 'axioms.' Advocates of 'compartmentalisation,' in particular, are convinced that it is possible to overcome conflict among conceptions of a good life at an individual level by means of the compartmentalisation of social space into a discretionary sphere for each individual.

In any case, though, 'transcendent justice' and the theoretical strategy of foundationalism aimed at deducing it are simply impossible. The fundamental reason for this is that we live in a world which is culturally signified. The theoretical strategy which endeavours to establish universal justice based on the setting-up of universally-valid individual rights, for example, presupposes that such 'universal rights' do exist. Yet a 'right' is something that is culturally and historically constructed, as is the 'luck' (in other words, 'responsibility') in 'Luck-egalitarianism.' Every day, the issue of what constitutes a right is examined afresh and new rights incorporated, while certain others are abolished. The 'right to privacy,' for example, is one that has been newly adopted; meanwhile, the 'right to sunshine' that was introduced at one point into the Japanese legal system through court judgements has since ceased to receive serious consideration.

In judicial thinking, a certain legal basis must be presupposed in order for a decision to be handed down in each case. At its very core is posited the idea of 'rights.' Many rights have been enacted in positive law, but some others have been created through a judicial process without resort to legislation, such as the right to privacy and the right to sunshine. In either case, they are something *supposed* as the logical basis for justifying a judicial decision. Though some such suppositions are further justified by such means as a codified constitution or uncodified 'natural rights,' those suppositions will not have been fully justified. There can be various interpretations of constitutions and natural rights, and so, in making their judgement, judges are merely constructing a logic that they consider the most appropriate at that point in time, on their own responsibility. The construction of that logic is usually based upon both the legal culture of the legal community of the jurist group to which the judges in question belong, and the broader social culture to which all jurists belong.

The concept of 'universal human rights' is something akin to this. The concept and its contents are constrained by the culture to which the person who postulates them belongs. In fashionable parlance, they are 'social constructs.' This also holds for 'responsibility,' or for Sen's 'basic capabilities.'

Legal judgment and positive law, which stipulate what constitutes a right, are presented logically as if they were universally valid, though in actual fact they are culturally constrained. Law is represented as something serving the values which transcend the various contingencies of the society and age in question; and, in this way, the universal value called 'justice' is established as providing the ultimate basis for law. Existing law is sometimes criticised as going against 'justice,' but even then—or, rather, all the more if that be the case—the authority of 'justice' as the ultimate basis for law will be elevated. By such means, conversely, there is an attempt to justify the assertion of concrete rights on a level that transcends positive law by appeal to the notion of 'justice.'

In this way, 'justice' has been represented in judicial thinking as the idea of a universal value that provides the basis for proper legal judgement, transcending the respective positive law or the power structure and cultural constraints of the various societies connected with it.

When contemporary liberalism established 'justice' as the fundamental normative principle for ordering society, this composition in legal thinking came to be expansively applied to the whole of society beyond the bounds of the legal world. In regard to the problem of culturally pluralistic circumstances, such a conception of 'justice' was just the thing to signify a universal normative principle which transcended individual cultures.

The words of deconstructivist philosopher Jacques Derrida are suggestive on this point: in his *Force of Law*, Derrida contrasts 'justice' and 'law,' saying that law is 'essentially deconstructible,' but that '[j]ustice is not deconstructible' (1992, pp. 14–15). Here, Derrida himself is exposing the fact that he is striving to believe in the notion of 'justice' as the universal and transcendental basic norm—this illustrating the very breadth and seriousness of faith in the transcendental 'justice' that contemporary liberalism has constructed. The important thing here, however, is that this belief of Derrida's is supported by his keeping the substance of justice not concretely specified. In other words, justice can be an 'ultimate basis' only as long as its advocates evade the job of actually establishing the concrete foundations of justice.

The project of contemporary liberalism greatly differs from deconstruction, however: it took on the challenge of concretely presenting the substantive content of justice. To that end, it had to discover universally-applicable principles in a concrete manner. The result of those efforts was such theses of liberalism as 'cultural neutrality' and the 'rights-based approach,' which were regarded as principles that could transcend cultural constraints. Their 'universality' is only superficial, however. If we are going to get down to discussing the substance of justice in concrete terms, we will have to face up to the fact that we are deeply culturally circumscribed.

Rorty's liberal utopia

One of the theorists to have developed an argument similar to that in this volume, which criticises the foundationalism in contemporary liberalism, is Richard Rorty, an American philosopher who advocates pragmatism. Rorty is a theorist who has developed an argument which, on the one hand, invokes French deconstructivist philosophers such as Derrida as it expounds the deconstruction of philosophy, while criticising the foundationalism in contemporary liberalism and defending the 'liberal community' (in a different sense from Dworkin's) that emerged as a historical contingency, on the other. Rorty has developed his own pragmatic liberalism in a form stripped of the foundationalistic elements of liberalism. For him, just as 'truth' is a concept that is both unjustifiable and dispensable, 'justice,' too, is unjustifiable; and contemporary liberalism, which attempts to establish a basis for justice in some form, is a metaphysical undertaking, and is destined for failure—as has been many a philosophical quest in modern times. Though I myself do not think that 'truth' is dispensable, I do agree with Rorty's criticism directed at 'justice.' In his 1999 book, *Philosophy and Social Hope*, Rorty gives the name 'liberal utopia' to his own conception which does not uphold 'justice,' but I question its suitability for overcoming contemporary liberalism.

What first deserves special mention in reference to Rorty is the fact that, at an extremely early stage, he displayed a totally heterodoxical reading of Rawls' *A Theory of Justice* (the same as that presented in this volume): namely, reading it not as something presenting a foundationalistic contractarian theory, but as something which set out a political theory whose central value was 'toleration,' as would later come to light with *Political Liberalism*. In specific terms, this was presented in a conference paper entitled 'The Priority of Democracy to Philosophy,' written in 1984 and first published in 1988 (Rorty 1991, pp. 175–196). Here, Rorty interprets Rawls' *A Theory of Justice* as being 'historicist and antiuniversalist' (1991, p. 180), '[not] as "rights-based" [and]...closer to Walzer than Dworkin' (1991, p. 181)—the former being a typical communitarian theoretician. At first, Rorty, too, had misunderstood Rawls' *A Theory of Justice* to be 'a continuation of the Enlightenment attempt to ground our moral intuitions on a conception of human nature,' but he claims that Rawls' subsequent writings 'helped us realize that we were misinterpreting his book' (1991, pp. 184–185). Of Rawls' subsequent writings, Rorty especially mentions the 1980 article, 'Kantian Constructivism in Moral Theory,' which discusses several fundamental ideas that later bore fruit in *Political Liberalism*.

Shortly before that, in a brief paper entitled 'Postmodernist Bourgeois Liberalism' (1991, pp. 197–202), Rorty had published an argument that defended 'liberalism' in a Hegelian or Walzerian manner by comparing Kant with Hegel on the one hand, and Dworkin with Walzer on the other. There, already, the outline of his 'liberal utopia' theory had been spelled out. The central assertion there is a denial of the existence of a transcendent 'basis' for moral convictions. As a corollary of this view, it is assumed that 'the moral justification of the institutions and practices of one's group...is mostly a matter of historical narratives...rather than of philosophical metanarratives' (Rorty 1991, p. 200). In other words, institutions and practices are not things that can be justified theoretically by philosophical argument; they can be justified only by a self-consciousness of the collective identity embedded in the history of a certain group or community. If this were the case, however, then fears and suspicions of a descent into 'relativism' might arise. Of course, relativism is 'self-refutative.' Recognising that, Rorty defends the practice of conforming to the history of the community to which one belongs, as 'there is a difference between saying that every community is as good as every other and saying that we have to work out from the networks we are, from the communities with which we presently identify (1991, p. 202).

In yet another essay, Rorty formulates this as follows:

> [John Dewey, Michael Oakeshott, and John Rawls]...would happily argue that a circular justification of our practices, a justification which makes one feature of our culture look good by citing still another, or comparing our culture invidiously with others by reference to our own standards, is the only sort of justification we are going to get (1989, p. 57).

This, in other words, is a way to improve institutions and customs while continuing to belong to one's own culture, by extracting its better features and developing them. Rorty rejects Enlightenment rationalism which induces foundationalism, but champions 'Enlightenment liberalism.' He considers that the social conception of liberal democracy which emerged in late-eighteenth- or nineteenth-century Western Europe points to the social hope of a liberal utopia for present-day America. This, in his eyes, is also the liberal democratism envisioned by John Dewey, a representative pragmatist philosopher from the early twentieth-century. As such, the liberalism that Rorty has in mind consists in speaking about hopes for progress that, while based on such cultural and historical traditions, is more open, and abounds in imagination and curiosity.

This liberalism of Rorty's is often criticised for being 'ethnocentric,' but even if that were so, it is exceedingly appealing, and has many angles that merit close attention. Nevertheless, one big problem has been left—to put it bluntly, the fact that Rorty has not attempted to answer the question: 'So, what should people from non-Western cultures do?' From Rorty's viewpoint, the response might be: 'Think for yourself!'

His indifference to this question conceals problems that go beyond a joke, however. Firstly, Rorty's liberalism has changed little in substantive terms from classical liberalism, which centres upon 'open freedom' and 'toleration.' While his ideas undoubtedly deserve respect, what we need now ought to be something a little more advanced. In short, that means—and this is the second issue—that there is not the slightest indication of a signpost pointing towards anything resembling a solution to the plethora of difficult questions that culturally-pluralistic circumstances have posed—the kind that cannot be dealt with simply by preaching tolerance.

Certainly, as Rorty says, we do not set off from an absolute *tabula rasa*, but have no option but to start from the culture which we currently accept—one formed by historical contingency, and which could by no means be called universal. But even if that were true, such fundamental questions as: 'What range should the "we" that are supposed to be setting off together encompass?' and 'What is meant by that culture?' would still remain unanswered. The wider we expand the boundaries of 'we,' the more diverse will be the culture we accept, and the more internally conflict-ridden it will become. Rorty does not seem to be able to address this well.

In evidence here is an opinion shared by many communitarians that 'we' and 'community' are self-explanatory. It is a fact that people, including theoreticians, adhere to that idea of self-evidence, and this is not something that can be completely eradicated; but without at least including it in a reflective cycle, we will not have aimed towards a theory that would respond to today's culturally-pluralistic circumstances.

Is there nothing but the *modus vivendi*? Gray's minimum liberalism

In a different direction from Rorty, one scholar who has endeavoured to reconstruct liberalism without depending on anything such as 'justice as transcendent' is the British political philosopher, John Gray. He insists that political society's only possible response to culturally pluralistic circumstances is by the *modus vivendi*—the 'way of living together' (Gray 2000). The *modus vivendi* is a way of order such that, while sustaining the inevitable coexistence of various comprehensive doctrines with others by means of political compromise, it strives to segregate them. The one-time international order consisting of sovereign nations in the second half of the nineteenth through to the first half of the twentieth century could be considered a typical example. There, each nation, while harbouring its respective hegemonic ambitions, somehow strove for coexistence through a fragile balance of power. (Of course, one could also say that the failure of this *modus vivendi* system was demonstrated by World Wars I and II, as is common knowledge.)

The most prominent feature of the *modus vivendi* is its establishment of 'coexistence' as the sole value that is mutually applicable for different comprehensive doctrines.

Regardless of how fierce their conflict might be in other aspects, the various comprehensive doctrines temporarily endorse their mutual coexistence and agree on a minimum political compromise for that purpose. Freedom of religion and freedom of speech can be seen as manifestations of such a compromise. The respective parties do not interfere in any other matters except those subject to such minimum consensus. Both cultures and minority groups which, considered from a liberal perspective, might be carrying out extreme sexism, and lifestyles which might appear outrageously laissez-faire from the angle of traditional culture, would be tolerated as things that are living those respective comprehensive doctrines.

Gray thinks that a very *modus vivendi* such as this is the only possible way for liberalism to be. It is something that is fearsomely different from the liberalism we have examined thus far. While contemporary liberalism leans more towards comprehensive liberalism, Gray's could be called an extremely minimal kind of liberalism, even within restricted liberalism.

The mode of order called the *modus vivendi* would be exceedingly unstable, however. The present relationship between Quebec and the Canadian Federation, for example, can be seen as such a *modus vivendi*. Still without having endorsed the 1982 federal constitution, Quebec has adopted its own policy of prioritising French culture, and the latent movement for separation and independence has not weakened one iota. The Federation does not approve of Quebec's way of doing things, nor does Quebec recognise that of the Federation's, but they somehow have managed to evade decisive opposition.

In such cases, though realistically the *modus vivendi* is an inevitable system, it cannot be called a desirable state of affairs. If a normative social theory were to assert that the *modus vivendi* was the sole mode of order among mutually-opposing comprehensive doctrines, then that would probably mean that it was not fulfilling its role as a normative social theory. This is because the task of a normative social theory is to seek a normative principle for ordering society in a better way, and the *modus vivendi* could by no means be said to have ordered society 'better.'

Seeking common values

So, if we are satisfied neither with today's comprehensive liberalism which endeavours to frame a transcendent 'justice,' nor with an ethnocentric liberal utopia such as Rorty's, nor with minimum liberalism which takes the *modus vivendi* to be an inevitable choice, then whatever sort of a normative social theory could we have? Could we expect something constituting a normative social theory to be possible in the first place?

What I wish to confirm first of all at this point is that the quest for a normative principle to regulate the structure of a fair political order such as would be mutually acceptable to different cultures and beliefs under culturally-pluralistic social circumstances is indeed an important task, and we can on no account deny the achievement of contemporary liberalism which has explicitly raised this theme.

This search for a normative principle is supported by our 'belief' or 'conviction' that such a thing as a 'mutually-valid universal normative principle' is *likely to exist*. Its existence has not been verified, nor is it self-evident, but just as the quest for empirical scientific knowledge has been sustained by a belief in the existence of 'truth,' or as the discovery of the ruins of ancient Troy was bolstered by Schliemann's convictions, it is the very belief in the existence of the thing to be discovered that makes investigation possible. Regrettably the importance of counting on a 'belief in the existence of a universally-applicable normative principle' is something missing from both Gray's *modus vivendi* and Rorty's liberal utopia.

On the other hand, one of contemporary liberalism's strategic errors lies in its having immediately regarded as self-evident the existence of something that would be universally valid as such a normative principle, out of mere a belief in its presence: it considers that it is necessary, and actually possible, to present something that is indeed such a principle. Yet that would be an impossible mission, as we cannot prove what really is universally valid, however hard we may try. (This misapprehension is similar to that of scientism, which regarded current scientific knowledge alone as absolute truth, and despised other types of knowledge as irrational or metaphysical.) In order to avoid this error, we should think of any normative principle that we can present as being nothing but a '*hypothesis*.' Whatever were counted as a universally valid normative principle is only a temporal conclusion which its advocate would consider the most reasonable at the time. It is basically open to criticism, and we must regard it as something that can be proven wrong, or replaced with a different hypothesis.

Because any normative principle that is presented is a hypothesis, it is certainly not something that is unconditionally 'justifiable.' At the very most, it could only survive rigorous critical examination at that particular point in time.

To see something as a 'hypothesis' is to acknowledge that it might be wrong, and that there might be a more correct way of thinking. This is closer to restricted liberalism than to comprehensive liberalism, and signifies greater tolerance towards cultures, values and doctrines which differ from the thinker's own.

Yet another mistake of contemporary liberalism is its having made light of, or ignored, the role of politics. This point has been criticised by political theorists including Habermas and Mouffe,[1] but let me add a few more observations. Foundationalism, after all, is the reason why politics has not been given serious consideration. A universal normative principle (that one would expect to be) deduced in a foundationalistic manner is: 1) supposed to be 'justified' theoretically, certainly not by 'mere' political deliberation or accommodation of interests; and 2), moreover, unlikely to become the target of criticism in later political debates, or—still more—to be modified, once established. In other words, the universal normative principle (justice) is something which relies solely upon the theoretical fact that it is 'justifiable,' and in both its derivation and its maintenance, there is no likelihood of it depending upon the uncertain and imperfect process of politics. Contemporary liberalism sees it that way. Though it would not be untoward to think thus if foundationalism were a correct method, it is *not* correct. Any normative principle that we could actually develop would be nothing but a hypothesis. If that were the case, then politics would have to become involved in it.

Politics is a process for making a *collective determination* which people with differing interests, opinions and beliefs can provisionally accept together, through having them engage in debate in a given space for discussion. There is no guarantee for any collective determination actually obtained to be a decision that is correct 'from an ideal viewpoint,' but, after all, no other method of actually obtaining a collective determination exists. (Theory might sometimes exert an influence upon collective determination, but cannot supplant it.) Various interests, prejudices and the like—which, from a theoretical standpoint, are considered to be nothing but noise—interfere in politics, but as long as it is impossible to obtain an effective collective determination solely on a theoretical level, that interference will have to be endured to a certain extent.

It is also true, however, that dangers lurk in this kind of politics. A major reason for the frequent favouring of foundationalistic theory is that actual politics is always imperfect, and is prone to error. Theorists insist on esteeming purity. That aside, undoubtedly the fallacies of politics must be kept at the barest minimum possible. The device which already exists for that purpose is the system called constitutional government. This is a means of constraining politics by a constitution, which is law in which are inscribed a certain set of normative principles that can be seen to apply universally. A constitution itself, though, is also something which should constantly be modified into something better (though I shall not delve further into that matter now). Normative theory, as a matter of course, needs also to discuss the normative principles and institutions that should control politics.

Understandably, even theories that stress politics, such as represented by Habermas, there is a tendency to try to guarantee 'correct decision-making' by purifying politics itself. In recent years, prolific discussion of this has been developed with such names as deliberative democracy and radical democracy. But here, too, a foundationalistic hue is often seen, and I might add that we must be wary on that point.

There is one more reason why politics is important, namely that it can actually generate provisional agreement among people with divergent interests, opinions and beliefs. The significance of this has been shockingly ignored in contemporary liberalism. This is because, for many advocates of contemporary liberalism, the ideal image of the process in which a collective determination is derived is that of 'judicial process.' As I have already stated, the idea that society would be better-ordered if only we imagined a notion of transcendental justice and could establish it takes its model from judicial process, which hands down concrete judgements via a logical procedure from conceptual legal norms. Court judgements are one type of collective determination, and they constrain people in a peremptory manner. Someone like Dworkin, a legal scholar with a career history of engagement in legal practice, can be said to best represent such a way of thinking. In the *judicial process model*, however, there is one more problem apart from the issue of foundationalism, namely the question relating to the *process of creation of law* which the political philosopher, Jeremy Waldron, raises in his 1999 publication, *The Dignity of Legislation*.

In the United States, the judicature is allowed extensive authority to create new laws, and, not infrequently, the federal Supreme Court creates a new legal norm by a fairly free interpretation of the constitution, and hands down a judgement accordingly. But as neither citizens nor the politicians who are their representatives participate in that law-creation process, there is no small potential for social consensus vis-à-vis the legal norms in question not to be achieved. In actual fact, the greatest factor in the serious controversy over abortion in America could be said to be the decision in the Roe versus Wade case which the US Supreme Court handed down in 1973. By deciding that state laws banning abortion were unconstitutional, it drew tremendous applause from the liberal camp. From the standpoint of the pro-child faction, however, it was seen as nothing other than a decision that a few liberal jurists handed down at their own discretion without democratic political debate. It would be hard for that faction to feel that they had to respect this decision.

On this point, the way whereby the brain-death issue in Japan was agreed upon by the legislature after almost a decade of discussion in the concrete form of the Organ Transplant Law—however imperfect and provisional it may be—can be considered a far superior example of a method for obtaining a collective determination.

As will be clear from this point, 'agreement' procured in a political arena is not something that ought simply to be an object of contempt as something imperfect and biased, as contemporary liberalism considers it to be. Agreement is nothing more than something provisional, both in conceptual and empirical terms, but the undeniable fact will remain that people with many different interests, opinions and beliefs have agreed—at least at that point in time. It has been empirically 'justified.' Obviously, the various normative theories of different theorists could also be expected to have had a hand in it. From the viewpoint of individual theorists, the agreement might only be something all too incomplete, but, as I repeatedly emphasise, on an objective level, there is no guarantee that any one theory is right, and that an agreement is wrong. An agreement ought to create a new, common point of reference in society, as a historical and social fact, and constitute a shared starting-point for a quest for something even better.

The above is nothing more than an exceedingly rough sketch of the way to seek a normative principle in a different manner from the strategy adopted by contemporary liberalism. The normative principle envisaged here diverges from Rorty's liberal utopia and Gray's *modus vivendi* mainly in the following aspect. That is, unlike these two, the anticipated normative principle here is not one signified only from the perspective of 'our' culture, but one whose objective is the *common interest* of many people and cultures, such as does not stop at mere coexistence among different cultures. It is an endeavour that assumes the existence of some kind of common interest, and searches for a normative principle that would bring it about. If the word 'interest' sounds calculating, we could equally say 'common value.' In other words, it aims to present as a normative principle a value that people with divergent interests and cultures could commonly accept with reverence.

Something which is presented as such a normative principle is a 'hypothesis' not only in the sense that it can be amended or discarded through discussion. It is also a 'hypothesis' in that it is accepted at a particular point in time by many cultures as something they mutually could live under, but could later prove false, or could be replaced by something else.

Nevertheless, we may presume that this kind of normative principle is one that constitutes a fair condition for free and equal citizens to participate spontaneously in social cooperation, as Rawls has formulated. Under this normative principle, social cooperation will (as a general rule) become something of value to all citizens—in other words, to people with various interests and cultures. Moreover, in light of his notion of 'reflective equilibrium,' Rawls, in turn, surely intended to present his own theory as one 'hypothesis.' Such a search for normative principles as a hypothesis which was opened up by Rawls is undoubtedly a challenge for social theory to tackle, surmounting contemporary liberalism.

If this point is to be appreciated, then it does not matter whether one calls this normative principle 'justice.' Nevertheless, the word 'justice,' while signifying a conceptual value expressing the objective of law, has simultaneously been inflated to mean something that expresses a kind of supreme social value that transcends cultural pluralism. The quest for 'justice' inevitably strives to construct social principles on a legal model. If one seeks to avoid this, then it might be better not to call this normative principle 'justice' after all. Japanese has the word '*kōkyōsei* (meaning something like "publicness")' as a candidate for a substitute term. If that be the case, then, given that the limitations of contemporary liberalism have been confirmed, it will probably be necessary to establish a new normative social theory that investigates *kōkyōsei*. That topic is one I wish to address in a separate work.

Afterword

This volume is not just a simple exposition of the theoretical structure of contemporary 'liberalism,' but is one aimed at presenting my own brand of analysis and commentary. As I stated in the Preface, liberalism is the one idea among the diverse currents in contemporary social theory and public philosophy that has been the most prolifically discussed. In addition, in debates around actual social problems and policies, considerations and assertions that are in alignment with liberalism—or in a form that approximates it—are frequently voiced, either explicitly or implicitly. If one is going to try to think about society from a normative perspective even a little, then an accurate grasp of the theory of liberalism will be seen to be a task that cannot be circumvented.

This is the reason why I, one who specialises in sociology, have endeavoured to write a book called *Liberalism: Its Achievements and Failures*, a title which might be construed as being somewhat removed from my domain.

It was quite late in my career that I became acquainted with Rawls' name. I have the feeling that while I was tackling such issues as social order, social dilemmas and rational choice theory from around the mid-1980s, I came to the knowledge that Rawls' book, *A Theory of Justice*, had apparently derived 'justice principles' by means of a 'contractarian-like' logic, namely the 'veil of ignorance' in the 'original position.' It made me recall how once, in my days as a postgraduate student, I had learned of the existence of Arrow's impossibility theorem, and had excitedly worked my way through Arrow's small original article together with a friend, Bunshirō Andō, now at Kwansei Gakuin University. At some stage, the thought germinated in my mind that if such logic about society were in existence, then I absolutely had to understand it correctly.

The first time I actually read *A Theory of Justice* was when I dealt with it as a text for a graduate-school seminar as 1990 was approaching, and I struggled to get through a badly-bound paperback version with my graduate students at the time. I say 'struggled' because, frankly, the format of *A Theory of Justice* was exceedingly hard to comprehend. This was due to my having strong preconceived notions and expectations that *A Theory of Justice* would be a book put together in axiomatic fashion. If one tries to read it on that premise, its lack of logicality is all too conspicuous. One cannot proceed as in the case of Arrow's volume, by coming to understanding through solving the mathematical theorem oneself. These misgivings did not dissipate for a long time.

Several years later, this time I decided to read *Political Liberalism* with a new generation of postgraduates. In addition to the usual seminar, I held a summer residential session at Norikura (a highland area in Japan's central Honshu), and tackled that book intensively. In the latter work, though, such characteristic theoretical mechanisms as the 'original position' or the 'veil of ignorance' hardly make a showing. Instead, in one respect, it can only be read as merely consisting of the repeated appearance of quite vague expressions such as 'reasonable' so-and-so, or 'public' something. I feel apologetic towards the postgraduates who attended, because even as I read through the book with them, I myself could not sense that I had 'understood' it after all. It was some consolation that (though the weather was not the best) we were still able to enjoy the refreshing atmosphere of the summer highlands, and soaking in the open-air bath.

In spite of harbouring a few such reservations, I had previously made the issues of social order and social stratifications my topics of expertise, in my own way, so for me, the various theories in egalitarianism to which liberalism and the 'difference principle' are centric were things I could not evade. While working on the 1995 SSM survey research (a longitudinal nation-wide survey on social stratification and mobility carried out by sociologists in Japan), I had various opportunities to proceed with exploration of Dworkin's resource-egalitarianism, Sen's arguments, and so on. Naturally, that was not done simply from a sense of obligation: the act of reading their discourses, which were at least supported by an orientation towards a certain type of logicality, was in itself enjoyable.

In the meantime, I reached the stage where I could begin to think I 'got' Rawls, triggered by two things. The first, I should say more of a 'light-at-the-end-of-the-tunnel' moment rather than a trigger, was that in the process of pondering and exploring the meaning of the 'difference principle,' I gradually became aware that the existing readings which focused on a maximin-type interpretation were mistaken. In other words, when focusing attention on the person who can enjoy only the least benefit in each social condition, and on that person's benefit, the difference principle does not mean that the social condition which would maximise the latter should be chosen. This signified that Rawls' *A Theory of Justice* was not something which would fit into the scheme in the quest for 'social optimality,' as in social choice theory and modern welfare economics that take Arrow as their starting point. Not only that, more importantly, it made me realise also that it was highly likely that the interpretations of Rawls which already had wide currency were wrong in various ways.

The second trigger was my taking up *Political Liberalism* once more, this time when I was in charge of a graduate school tutorial in 2001, in my position as a part-time staff member at Waseda University. There was a mere handful of postgraduates, perhaps meaning conversely that I had to be all the more vigorous in my preparation, but this time, the logical structure of the book lucidly entered my head. Of course, that was after I had discarded my preconception of it being 'contractarian.' (I am very grateful to the students who patiently stuck by me at that time.) If, conversely, one completely banishes such perspectives as social choice and social contract theory, and rereads *A Theory of Justice* with the theoretical structure of *Political Liberalism* as a guide, then an image about Rawls quite different from the one in current public circulation clearly emerges. This conviction became unshakeable within me. At the same time, it became obvious overall under what sort of research strategy the respective theories in contemporary liberalism led by Rawls were put forward, what was seen as self-evident, and what things, under what kind of premises, they were trying to clarify.

The basic conception of this book emerged in 2002, and the initial rough draft was penned fairly soon, but after that, while simultaneously compiling textbooks on statistics and social survey methods, I revised the manuscript several times, tinkering with the composition and the placing of focal points by trial-and-error. Around the final chapter, in particular, after having ascertained the limitations of contemporary liberalism, I continued to be perplexed and hesitant about how far I could hammer out my own conception of normative social theory, but now I have decided to bring it to an end in a form that asserts the very minimum I can say with certainty for the time being.

In bringing the book to completion in such a form as this, I have been helped by a great number of people. The first of those I wish to thank are the then postgraduate and undergraduate students who bore with my research interests in diverse ways. I was blessed with enthusiastic students, especially in graduate school, where, in spite of the fact that the classes were called 'sociology seminars,' I dealt with nothing but articles and books on public philosophy or ethics, or, sometimes, mathematical economics, yet the participants responded frankly and with incisive sensibility to the questions I threw at them, and all this was of immeasurable encouragement to me. Akira Inoue, in particular, who attended my undergraduate and postgraduate seminars over several years from the end of the 1990s, always generously enlightened me (though I was not even his supervisor) with information on broad-ranging research trends and academic literature relating to public philosophy. I cannot thank him enough.

Apart from teaching classes, for several years I had been carrying on with a research project entitled: 'A comprehensive sociological study relating to publicness and cooperativity in an ageing society,' funded by a Grant-in-aid for Scientific Research: Basic Research (A) Title no. 14201020. The fellow researchers participating in it were Shūichirō Ike, Gaku Doba, Chiyo Yonemura, Ken'ichi Itō, Naoki Sudō, Hideki Tarumoto, Manabu Akagawa and Isamu Sugino, as well as the then postgraduate students Hideki Kamiyama, Jun Tsunematsu, Yūsuke Iijima, Hiroki Takikawa, Kōjirō Seta, Jun Naitō, Takeshi Mitani, Sumika Yamane, Takahiro Akedo and Yasunori Saitō; and we were able to examine in detail, from a variety of angles, broad-ranging issues revolving around contemporary public philosophy and normative social theory. The discussions involved were of immense value to me in writing this book. Please also note that I republished part of the Japanese version of this volume's Chapter Nine and Conclusion (with some alteration to the wording) in the final report for this project, which ended in March 2006.

Furthermore, it was extremely beneficial to my research for this book to have been able to take part in a study group based at the National Institute of Population and Social Security Research, led by three scholars representing Japan's research into public philosophy, pivoting around welfare economics: Yūichi Shionoya, Kōtaro Suzumura and Reiko Gotō. At this study group, members such as Naoshi Yamawaki, Itaru Shimazu, Susumu Morimura, Mikio Watanabe, Takatoshi Imada and Masaya Kobayashi always engaged in outspoken discussion and gave enormous stimulus to my thinking.

Apart from this, though it was for a short period only, I was blessed with the opportunity to address a Suntory cultural foundation research group which has 'the state and ethics' as its theme, presenting my ideas on the condition of normative social theory, and exchanging views in dense discussion. My deep gratitude is owed to the late Takao Sakamoto, who invited me to join this study group.

In addition to those I have mentioned, there have been innumerable teachers, mentors and friends who have given me enormous intellectual stimulation and warm encouragement through research exchange in various forms. Though I do not name them individually here, I extend to them my heartfelt thanks.

In compiling the Japanese version of this manuscript, I had enormous help from Kyōko Matsumoto from keyboard input to proofreading, and making comments on the manuscript as the first reader. I thank her very much.

Finally, the writing of this book was something which I undertook on the enthusiastic urging of Shin'ichirō Tokuda of the publishing house, Keisōshobō, and I received valuable advice from him all the while regarding such matters as format and turns of phrase; while Michiko Doi, his successor in charge of my project, waited patiently for the completion of my manuscript. My sincere gratitude goes to both of them for helping me to launch this book into the world in its Japanese version.

Moreover, this English version owes its existence to the kindness of Yoshio Sugimoto of Trans Pacific Press in Melbourne, Australia. I express my deep gratitude for his encouragement towards this publication. I also extend my thanks to Leonie Stickland for her professional skill as translator and editor, without which this volume could not be published in such a wonderful style.

Postscript

After the publication of the Japanese version, I received various comments and criticisms from many scholars, including those who are referred to in this volume. Of course, these were generally quite stimulating, but I found that they did not harm my basic assertions, so I left this English version intact except for some minor refinements of expression.

Kazuo Seiyama
2009

Notes

Preface

1 The main commentaries and introductory volumes published since 2000 include the following: Satō 2000; Ariga et al. 2000; Koizumi 2002; Tsuchiya 2002; Gotō 2002; Se 2003; Yasushi Yamaguchi et al (eds) 2003; Abiko and Tanimoto (eds) 2004; Ariga et al. (eds) 2004; Hirai (ed.) 2004; Yamawaki 2004; Shionoya, Gotō and Suzumura (eds) 2004; and Katsuragi 2005. In addition, a series entitled *Kōkyō tetsugaku* (Public philosophy) has been published since 2001 by University of Tokyo Press.

2 John Gray has published one more volume, with the extremely confusing title of *Liberalisms: Essays in Political Philosophy* (1989), and this has been translated into Japanese and published by Minerva Shobō as *Jiyū-shugi ron* (On liberalism). Unlike Gray's previous book, this is a collection of papers, and is not something whose goal is to discuss liberalism in a systematic manner. It does contain a chapter which discusses the contractarian aspect of Rawlsian theory, but overall it centres on debate concerning Mill, Popper, Hayek, Berlin and the like, and therefore cannot be said to deal with contemporary liberalism as such.

3 Recent publications include Saeki 2001; Yamaguchi 2002; Nakamasa 2003; Kobayashi 2004; and Saeki 2005.

Chapter 1

1 This law was amended in 2009 in a way that brain death was recognised as 'death,' but the account here refers to the situation before this amendment.

2 There is a wealth of material dealing with the issue of brain death, but on this controversy, see Umehara (ed.) 2000; and for an overview of the problem, see Katō 1999.

3 The very issue of whether empirical and normative questions can and should be differentiated, and why, is an enormous point of contention in philosophy and scientific methodology, and there is no small number of theorists who repudiate such a distinction. Quite a large amount of thorough discussion is necessary to give a precise answer to this, but there is not enough space here to develop it, unfortunately. (Strictly speaking, however, the situation differs between the natural sciences and the social sciences.) Fundamentally, though, this distinction can be considered justified because it is essential for the establishment of 'knowledge such as constitutes "truth" in regard to the empirical world.'

4 For a detailed treatment of issues concerning the multicultural situation in France, such as the headscarf incident, see Miura (ed.) 2001.

Chapter 2

1 Precisely speaking, even prior to Arrow's theorem which is discussed below, there had been G.E. Moore's indication of the 'naturalistic fallacy' in his 1903 *Principia Ethica*, and economist Lionel C. Robbins' argument that 'interpersonal comparison of utility is impossible.' Shimizu's aforementioned book, *Rinrigaku nōto* (Notes on ethics) (1972), gives details.
2 For a detailed treatment of Arrow's impossibility theorem, see Sen 1970; and Suzumura and Gotō 2001.
3 This point is not noted in works introducing the diverse meanings of 'justice,' including Hirano et al. 2002; Hasegawa and Tsunoda (eds) 2004; or Hirai (ed.) 2004.

Chapter 3

1 Though I will not encroach on this area in this volume, I have my doubts as to whether it does coincide with utilitarianism. See Mitani 2006.

Chapter 5

1 For a detailed introduction of libertarianism in Japanese, see Morimura 2001.
2 Nozick's book was published in 1974, and it can be surmised that Rawls, as Nozick's colleague in the same Department of Philosophy at Harvard University, was well-acquainted with the latter's libertarian argument.
3 On contemporary egalitarian theory, see, for example, Takeuchi 1999; 2001.
4 See Suzumura and Gotoh 2001 for a detailed introduction of Sen's theory in Japanese. Wakamatsu 2003 is also a useful reference.
5 Among the work of Japanese scholars Takikawa 2003 and Kitada 2003 can be seen several attempts to reconstruct responsibility theory with a concept of 'response-based responsibility' which borrows theory from the philosopher Levinas, author of such works as *Totalité et infini* (Totality and infinity) (1961), though it is not considered valid to use such extremely theological theory as Levinas as grounds for an objectivistic concept of 'responsibility.'
6 Luck-egalitarianism has a variety of points of contention apart from those discussed here. Examples include Inoue 2002, one which provides a somewhat favourable examination; and Takikawa 2006, which severely attacks its defects.

Chapter 6

1 See Ogino 2001.
2 On the arguments around bioethics, see such introductory volumes as Katō 1999, 2002; Katō and Kamo 1998; Okamoto 2002; and Singer 1993.
3 On the cloning issue, see, for example, Nussbaum and Sunstein 1998; Kato 1999; Okamoto 2002; and Uemura 2003.
4 On the meaning of freedom in Kantian moral philosophy, see Kant 1785, 1797.

Chapter 7

1 Other critiques of liberalism from communitarianism include MacIntyre 1981, who criticises the fact that individual virtue is ignored theoretically; Bellah 1985; 1991, who problematises the atrophy of republican solidarity in actual US society; Etzioni 1988; 1995; 1996, who advocates the revitalisation of the community; Selznick 1992, who expounds a moral community based on justice; and Walzer 1993; 1997, who conceives of a republican civil society supported by a spirit of cooperation.

Chapter 8

1 Though the phenomenon of male dominance exists in various forms in actuality, feminist theory which claims that a consistent patriarchal and inter-gender authority structure should exist is probably incorrect in the same way as Marxism, which tried to read a consistent control of capital into the background behind actual hierarchical inequality. See Hara and Seiyama 1999; Seiyama 2000a, 2000b.

2 Between feminism and liberalism there are diverse other points of controversy: see, for example, Ehara (ed.) 1996, 2001; Nagata 1997; Nozaki 2003; Yamane 2004.

Conclusion

1 In a 1995 paper, Habermas comments upon Rawls' *Political Liberalism*, criticising the point that Rawls has not given theoretical positioning to the process of deliberation of public opinion, which is an arena for the 'public use of reason.' Chantal Mouffe, also, takes Rawlsian theory as being 'political philosophy without politics' (1993, p. 41).

Bibliography

Abiko, Kazuyoshi and Mitsuo Tanimoto (eds), 2004, *Kōkyōsei no tetsugaku o manabu hito no tame ni* (For people who study the philosophy of publicness), Kyoto: Sekaishisōsha.

Ackerman, Bruce A., 1980, *Social Justice in the Liberal State*, New Haven: Yale University Press.

———, 1990, 'Neutralities,' in R. Bruce Douglass, Gerald M. Mara, and Henry S. Richardson (eds), *Liberalism and the Good*, New York: Routledge, pp. 29–43.

Anderson, E.S., 1999, 'What is the Point of Equality?' *Ethics*, 109 (2), pp. 287–337.

Ariga, Makoto, Yasuhiko Itō, and Satoshi Matsui (eds), 2000, *Posuto-riberarizumu: shakaiteki kihan riron e no shōtai* (Post-liberalism: an invitation to social normative theory), Kyoto: Nakanishiya shuppan.

———, 2004, *Gendai kihan riron nyūmon: posuto-riberarizumu no shintenkai* (Introduction to modern normative theory: new developments in post-liberalism), Kyoto: Nakanishiya shuppan.

Arneson, Richard, 1989, 'Equality and Equal Opportunity for Welfare,' *Philosophical Studies*, 56 (1), pp. 77–93.

———, 1990, 'Liberalism, Distributive Subjectivism, and Equal Opportunity for Welfare,' *Philosophy and Public Affairs*, 19 (2), pp. 159–194.

———, 2000, 'Luck Egalitarianism and Prioritarianism,' *Ethics*, 110 (2), pp. 339–349.

Arrow, Kenneth J., [1951] 1963, *Social Choice and Individual Values*, 2nd edition, New Haven: Yale University Press.

———, 1973, 'Some Ordinalist–Utilitarian Notes on Rawls's Theory of Justice,' *Journal of Philosophy*, 70 (9), pp. 245–263.

Barry, Brian, 1990, 'How Not to Defend Liberal Institutions,' in R. Bruce Douglass, Gerald M. Mara, and Henry S. Richardson (eds), *Liberalism and the Good*, New York: Routledge, pp. 44–58.

———, 2001, *Culture and Equality: an Egalitarian Critique of Multiculturalism*, Cambridge, Massachusetts: Polity Press.

Bellah, Robert N., Richard Madsen, William M. Sullivan, Ann Swidler, and Steven M. Tipton, 1985, *Habits of Hearts: Individualism and Commitment in American Life*, Berkeley: University of California Press.

Bellah, Robert N. et al., 1991, *The Good Society*, New York: Knopf.

Bentham, Jeremy, [1789] 1970, *An Introduction to the Principles of Morals and Legislation*, J.H. Burns and H.L.A. Hart (eds), London: Athlone Press.

Berlin, Isaiah, 1969, *Four Essays on Liberty*, London; New York: Oxford University Press.

Cohen, G.A., 1989, 'On the Currency of Egalitarian Justice,' *Ethics*, 99 (4), pp. 906–944.

———, 1992, 'Incentives, Inequality, and Community,' in *The Tanner Lectures on Human Values 13*, Salt Lake City: University of Utah Press, pp. 261–329.
———, 1995, *Self-Ownership, Freedom, and Equality*, Cambridge; New York: Cambridge University Press.
Coleman, James S., 1974, 'Inequality, Sociology, and Moral Philosophy,' *American Journal of Sociology*, 80, pp. 739–764.
———, 1990, *Foundations of Social Theory*, Cambridge, Massachusetts: The Belknap Press of Harvard University Press.
Dahl, Robert A., 1956, *A Preface to Democratic Theory*, Chicago: University of Chicago Press.
Derrida, Jacques, 1992, 'Force of Law: the Mystical Foundation of Authority,' in Drucilla Cornell and Michael Rosenfeld (eds), *Deconstruction and the Possibility of Justice*, New York: Routledge, pp. 3–67.
Dewey, John, 1916, *Democracy and Education: An Introduction of the Philosophy of Education*, New York: The Macmillan Company.
Dworkin, Ronald, 1977, *Taking Rights Seriously*, Cambridge, Massachusetts: Harvard University Press.
———, 1978, 'Liberalism,' in S. Hampshire (ed.), *Public and Private Morality*, Cambridge: Cambridge University Press, pp. 114–134. Also in Dworkin, 1985, *A Matter of Principle*, pp. 181–204.
———, 1981, 'What is Equality? Part 1: Equality of Welfare,' *Philosophy and Public Affairs*, 10 (3), pp. 185–246; 'What is Equality? Part 2: Equality of Resources,' *Philosophy and Public Affairs*, 10 (4), pp. 283–345.
———, 1985, *A Matter of Principle*, Cambridge, Massachusetts: Harvard University Press.
———, 1993, *Life's Dominion: An Argument about Abortion, Euthanasia, and Individual Freedom*, New York: Knopf.
———, 1996, *Freedom's Law: The Moral Reading of the American Constitution*, Cambridge, Massachusetts: Harvard University Press.
———, 2000, *Sovereign Virtue: The Theory and Practice of Equality*, Cambridge, Massachusetts: Harvard University Press.
Ehara, Yumiko (ed.), 1996, *Seishoku gijutsu to jendā: feminizumu no shuchō 3* (Reproductive technology and gender: feminism's assertions 3), Tokyo: Keisō shobō.
———, 2001, *Feminizumu to riberarizumu: feminizumu no shuchō 5* (Feminism and liberalism: feminism's assertions 5), Tokyo: Keisō shobō.
Elster, Jon., 1985, *Making Sense of Marx*, Cambridge, UK: Cambridge University Press.
Etzioni, Amitai, 1988, *The Moral Dimension: Toward a New Economics*, New York: The Free Press.
———, 1995, *New Communitarian Thinking: Persons, Virtues, Institutions, and Communities*, Charlottesville: University Press of Virginia.
———, 1996, *The New Golden Rule: Community and Morality in a Democratic Society*, New York: Basic Books.
———, 2001, *Next: The Road to the Good Society*, New York: Basic Books.
Gilligan, C., 1982, *In a Different Voice: Psychological Theory and Women's Development*, Cambridge, Massachusetts: Harvard University Press.
Goodin, Robert E., 1988, *Reasons for Welfare: The Political Theory of the Welfare State*, Princeton: Princeton University Press.

———, 1995, *Utilitarianism as a Public Philosophy*, Cambridge University Press.
Gotō, Reiko, 2002, *Seigi no keizai tetsugaku: Rōruzu to Sen* (The economic philosophy of justice: Rawls and Sen), Tokyo: Tōyōkeizai shinpōsha.
Gray, John, 1986, *Liberalism*, Milton Keynes: Open University Press.
———, 1989, *Liberalisms: Essays in Political Philosophy*, London; New York: Routledge.
———, 1995, *Enlightenment's Wake: Politics and Culture at the Close of the Modern Age*, London; New York: Routledge.
———, 2000, *Two Faces of Liberalism*, Cambridge, UK: Polity Press.
Habermas, Jürgen, 1995, 'Reconciliation through the Public Use of Reason: Rawls's Political Liberalism,' *Journal of Philosophy*, 92 (3), pp. 109–131.
Hara, Junsuke and Kazuo Seiyama, 2005, *Inequality amid Affluence: Social Stratification in Japan*, trans. by Brad Williams, Melbourne: Trans Pacific Press. (Originally published in 1999 as *Shakai kaisō: yutakasa no naka no fubyōdō* (Social stratification: inequality amid affluence), Tokyo: Tōkyō daigaku shuppan kai).
Hare, R.M., 1981, *Moral Thinking: Its Level, Method, and Point*, Oxford University Press.
Harsanyi, John C., 1975, 'Can the Maximin Principle Serve as a Basis for Morality?: A Critique of John Rawls's Theory,' *American Political Science Review*, 69 (2), pp. 594–606. Also in John C. Harsanyi, 1976, *Essays on Ethics, Social Behavior, and Scientific Explanation*, Dordrecht, Holland: D. Reidel Publishing Company, pp. 37–63.
Hart, H.L.A., 1975, 'Rawls on Liberty and its Priority,' in Norman Daniels (ed.), *Reading Rawls: Critical Studies on Rawls' A Theory of Justice*, New York: Basic Books, pp. 230–252.
Hasegawa, Akira and Takeshi Tsunoda (eds), 2004, *Burijjibukku hōtetsugaku* (Bridging book [series]: legal philosophy), Tokyo: Shinzansha.
Hayek, Friedrich A. von, 1944, *The Road to Serfdom*, London: Routledge.
———, 1960, *The Constitution of Liberty*, London: Routledge.
Hegel, G.W. Friedrich, 1821, *Grundlinien der Philosophie des Rechts* (The philosophy of right). (1952, *The Philosophy of Right; The Philosophy of History*, trans. by T.M. Knox and J. Sibree, Chicago: Encyclopædia Britannica.)
Hirai, Ryōsuke (ed.), 2004, *Seigi: gendai shakai no kōkyō tetsugaku o motomete* (Justice: seeking a public philosophy for contemporary society), Kyōto: Sagano shoin.
Hirano, Hitohiko, Hiroshi Kamemoto and Takahiro Hattori, 2002, *Hōtetsugaku* (Legal philosophy), Tokyo: Yūhikaku.
Hobbes, Thomas, [1651] 1965, *Leviathan*, Clarendon Press.
Hume, David, [1739–40] 1984, *A Treatise of Human Nature*, London: Penguin Books.
Hurley, S. L., 2003, *Justice, Luck, and Knowledge*, Cambridge, Massachusetts: Harvard University Press.
Inaba, Shin'ichirō, 1999, *Riberarizumu no sonzai shōmei* (Liberalism's proof of existence), Tokyo: Kinokuniya shoten.
Inoue, Akira, 2002, 'Byōdō-shugi to sekinin (Egalitarianism and responsibility),' in Keishi Saeki and Ryūichirō Matsubara (eds), *'Atarashii shijō shakai' no kōsō* (The conception of a 'new market society'), Shinseisha, pp. 275–333.

Inoue, Tatsuo, 1986, *Kyōsei no sahō: kaiwa toshite no seigi* (The etiquette of coexistence: justice as conversation), Tokyo: Sōbunsha.

———, 1999, *Tasha e no jiyū: kōkyōsei no tetsugaku toshite no riberarizumu* (Freedom towards others: liberalism as a philosophy of publicness), Tokyo: Sōbunsha.

———, 2004, 'Riberarizumu no saiteigi (A redefinition of liberalism), *Shisō* (Thought), 965, pp. 8–28.

Ishiyama, Fumihiko, 2004, 'Tabunka-shugi to riberarizumu: sono deai to shōtotsu wa nani o motarasu no ka (Multiculturalism and liberalism: what do their encounter and collision bring about?), *Shisō* (Thought), 965, pp. 176–194.

Itoh, Yasuhiko, 2002, *Tagen-teki sekai no seiji tetsugaku* (A political philosophy of the pluralistic world), Tokyo: Yūhikaku.

Kant, Immanuel, [1785] 1993, *Grounding for the Metaphysics of Morals* (*Grundlegung zur Metaphysik der Sitten*), trans. by James W. Ellington, 3rd edition, Indianapolis, Indiana: Hackett.

———, 1797, *Metaphysik der Sitten*. (1964, *Groundwork of the metaphysic of morals*, trans. and analysed by H.J. Paton, New York: Harper & Row.)

Katō, Hisatake, 1999, *Nōshi, kurōn, idenshi chiryō: baioeshikkusu no renshū mondai* (Brain death, cloning, genetic treatment: practice exercises in bioethics), Kyoto: PHP shinsho.

———, 2002, *Gōi keisei to rūru no rinrigaku: ōyō rinrigaku no susume* (Consent formation and the ethics of rules: an encouragement of applied ethics), Tokyo: Maruzen raiburarī.

Katō, Hisatake and Naoki Kamo (eds), 1998, *Seimei rinrigaku o manabu hito no tame ni* (For people studying bioethics), Kyoto: Sekaishisōsha.

Katsuragi, Takao, 2005, *Kōkyō tetsugaku to wa nan darō: minshu-shugi to shijō no atarashii mikata* (What might 'public philosophy' be?: a new way of looking at democracy and the market), Tokyo: Keisō shobō.

Kawamoto, Takashi, 1995, *Gendai rinrigaku no bōken: shakai riron no nettowākingu e* (The adventure of contemporary ethics: towards networking in social theory), Tokyo: Sōbunsha.

———, 1997, *Rawls: seigi no genri* (Rawls: principles of justice), Tokyo: Kōdansha.

Kitada, Akihiro, 2003, *Sekinin to seigi: riberarizumu no ibasho* (Responsibility and justice: the place where liberalism belongs), Tokyo: Keisō shobō.

Kobayashi, Kazuyuki, 2004, *'Orokamono' no seigiron* (Justice theory for 'dummies'), Tokyo: Chikuma shinsho.

Kohlberg, L., 1984, *The Psychology of Moral Development: Essays on Moral Development*, Vol. 2, San Francisco: Harper & Row.

Koizumi, Yoshiyuki, 2002, *Riberaru na kyōdōtai: Dwōkin no seiji–dōtoku riron* ([A] liberal community: Dworkin's political and moral theory), Tokyo: Keisō shobō.

Komatsu, Yoshihiko, 2004, *Nōshi: zōki ishoku no hontō no hanashi* (Brain death: the real story of organ transplantation), Kyoto: PHP shinsho.

Kuhn, Thomas, 1962, *The Structure of Scientific Revolutions*, Chicago: University of Chicago Press.

Kymlicka, Will, 1989, *Liberalism, Community and Culture*, Oxford, UK: Clarendon Press.

———, 1990, *Contemporary Political Philosophy: An Introduction*, Oxford, UK: Oxford University Press.

———, 1995, *Multicultural Citizenship: A Liberal Theory of Minority Rights*, Oxford, UK: Clarendon Press.

———, 2001, *Politics in the Vernacular: Nationalism, Multiculturalism, and Citizenship*, Oxford, UK; New York: Oxford University Press.

Kymlicka, Will, and Alan Patten (ed.), 2003, *Language Rights and Political Theory*, Oxford, UK; New York: Oxford University Press.

Locke, John, 1689, *A Letter concerning Toleration*. (1955, *A Letter concerning Toleration*: with an introduction by Patrick Romanell, 2nd edition, New York: Bobbs-Merrill.)

———, [1690] 1972, *Two Treatises of Government*, London: [s.n.].

Luther, Martin, 1520, 'Von der Freiheit eines Christenmenschen (Concerning Christian Liberty,' *The Harvard Classics, 1904–14*, in http://www.barleby.com/36/6/2.html).

MacIntyre, Alasdair, 1981, *After Virtue: A Study in Moral Theory*, Notre Dame, Indiana: University of Notre Dame Press.

MacIver, Robert M., [1917] 1924, *Community: A Sociological Study: Being an Attempt to Set out the Nature and Fundamental Laws of Social Life*, 3rd edition, Oxford: Frank Cass/Macmillan.

MacKinnon, C.A., 1989, *Toward a Feminist Theory of the State*, Cambridge, Massachusetts: Harvard University Press.

Malinowsky, Bronislaw, 1922, *Argonauts of the Western Pacific*: *an Account of Native Enterprise and Adventure in the Archipelagoes of Melanesian New Guinea*, New York: E. P. Dutton.

———, 1944, *The Scientific Theory of Culture and Other Essays*. Chapel Hill: The University of North Carolina Press.

Marshall, T.H., and Tom Bottomore, 1992, *Citizenship and Social Class*, London: Pluto Press.

Mill, John Stuart, 1849, *On Liberty*, (In *The Utilitarians*, Anchor Books edition, 1973, New York: Anchor Books, pp. 473–600).

———, 1863, *Utilitarianism*. (In *The Utilitarians*, Anchor Books edition, 1973, New York: Anchor Books, pp. 399–470.)

———, 1869, *The Subjection of Women*. (1924, *The subjection of women* by John Stuart Mill; edited, with introductory analysis by Stanton Coit. London: Longmans.)

Mitani, Takeshi, 2006, '"Kōyō" no rinri: Hāsani-gata kōyō sōwa-shugi no shippai (The ethics of "utility": the failures of Harsanyi-type outcome utilitarianism),' in Gaku Doba and Kazuo Seiyama (eds), *Seigi no ronri: kōkyōteki kachi no kihan-teki shakai riron* (The logic of justice: normative social theories of public values), Tokyo: Keisō shobō, pp. 59–78.

Miura, Nobutaka (ed.) 2001, *Fuhensei ka sai ka: kyōwa-shugi no rinkai, Furansu* (Universality or difference?: France, the critical edge of republicanism), Tokyo: Fujiwara shoten.

Moore, G.E., 1903, *Principia Ethica*. Cambridge: The University Press.

Morimura, Susumu, 2001, *Jiyū wa doko made kanō ka: ribatarianizumu nyūmon* (How far is liberty possible?: introductory libertarianism), Tokyo: Kōdansha gendai shinsho.

Morimura, Susumu 2005, *Ribatarianizumu dokuhon* (Libertarian reader), Tokyo: Keisō shobō.
Morishima, Michio, 1973, *Marx's Economics: a Dual Theory of Value and Growth*, Cambridge: Cambridge University Press.
Mouffe, Chantal, 1993, *The Return of the Political*, London: Verso.
Nagao, Ryūichi and Rin'itsu Kawakami, 1994, *Hirakareta shakai no tetsugaku: Kāru Poppā to gendai* (The philosophy of an open society: Karl Popper and the modern age), Tokyo: Miraisha.
Nagata, Eriko, 1997, *Dōtokuha feminisuto sengen* (A moralist feminist manifesto), Tokyo: Keisō shobō.
Nagel, Thomas, 1979, *Moral Questions*, Cambridge, UK: Cambridge University Press.
———, 1991, *Equality and Partiality*, Oxford: Oxford University Press.
Nakamasa, Masaki *'Fujiyū'-ron: 'nandemo jiko kettei' no genkai* (On 'non-liberty': the limitations of 'self-determination in everything'), Tokyo: Chikuma shinsho.
Narita, Kazunobu, 2004, *Sekinin to jiyū* (Responsibility and freedom), Tokyo: Keisō shobō.
Nozaki, Ayako, 2003, *Seigi, kazoku, hō no kōzō henkan* (Structural changes in justice, the family, and law), Tokyo: Keisō shobō.
Nozick, Robert, 1974, *Anarchy, State, and Utopia*, New York: Basic Books.
Nussbaum, Martha C., and Cass R. Sunstein (eds), 1998, *Clones and Clones: Facts and Fantasies about Human Cloning*, London: W.W. Norton & Company.
Nussbaum, Martha C., 1999, *Sex and Social Justice*, Oxford: Oxford University Press.
Odaka, Tomoo, [1936] 1968, *Kokka kōzō ron* (Theory of state structure), Tokyo: Iwanami shoten.
Ogino, Miho, 2001, *Chūzetsu ronsō to Amerika shakai: karada o meguru sensō* (The abortion debate: a war over the body), Tokyo: Iwanami shoten.
Okamoto, Yūichirō, 2002, *Igi ari! Seimei, kankyō rinrigaku* (Objection! Bio-environmental ethics), Kyoto: Nakanishiya shuppan.
Okin, Susan Moller, 1989, *Justice, Gender, and the Family*, New York: Basic Books.
Parsons, Talcott, 1937, *The Structure of Social Action*, New York: Free Press.
Popper, K.R., 1945, *The Open Society and its Enemies*, Princeton: Princeton University Press.
———, 1994, *In Search of a Better World: Lectures and Essays from Thirty Years*, trans. by Laura J. Bennett, London: Routledge.
Rakowski, Eric, 1991, *Equal Justice*, Oxford: Clarendon Press.
Rawls, John, 1958, 'Justice as Fairness,' *Philosophical Review*, 67 (2), pp. 164–194.
———, 1963, 'Constitutional Liberty and the Concept of Justice,' in C. J. Friedrich and John Chapman (eds), *Nomos 6: Justice*, New York: Atherton Press, pp. 98–125.
———, 1971, *A Theory of Justice*, Oxford: Clarendon Press.
———, 1975, 'A Kantian Concept of Equality,' *Cambridge Review*, February, pp. 94–99.
———, 1980, 'Kantian Constructivism in Moral Theory,' *Journal of Philosophy*, 77 (9), pp. 515–572.

———, 1993, *Political Liberalism*, New York: Columbia University Press.
———, 1995, 'Reply to Habermas,' *Journal of Philosophy*, 92 (3), pp. 132–180.
———, 1999a, *A Theory of Justice, Revised Edition,* Cambridge, Massachusetts: Harvard University Press.
———, 1999b, *Collected Papers*, Samuel Freedman (ed.), Cambridge, Massachusetts: Harvard University Press.
———, 2000, *Lectures on the History of Moral Philosophy*, Barbara Herman (ed.), Cambridge, Massachusetts: Harvard University Press.
———, 2001, *Justice as Fairness: A Restatement*, Erin Kelly (ed.), Cambridge, Massachusetts: Harvard University Press.
Raz, Joseph, 1986, *The Morality of Freedom*, Oxford: Clarendon Press.
Robbins, Lionel, 1938, 'Inter-personal Comparisons of Utility,' *Economic Journal*, 48, pp. 635–641.
Roemer, John E., 1982, *A General Theory of Exploitation and Class*, Cambridge, Massachusetts: Harvard University Press.
———, 1996, *Theories of Distributive Justice*, Cambridge, Massachusetts: Harvard University Press.
———, 1998, *Equality of Opportunity*, Cambridge, Massachusetts: Harvard University Press.
Rorty, Richard, 1982, *Consequences of Pragmatism*, Minneapolis: The University of Minnesota.
———, 1989, *Contingency, Irony, and Solidarity*, Cambridge, UK: Cambridge University Press.
———, 1991, *Objectivity, Relativism, and Truth*, Cambridge, UK: Cambridge University Press.
———, 1999, *Philosophy and Social Hope*, London: Penguin Books.
Rousseau, Jean-Jacques, 1755, *Le Discours sur l'origine et les fondements de l'inégalité parmi les hommes* (Discourse on the origin and basis of inequality among men).
———, 1762, *Du Contrat Social* (1947, 'The Social Contract,' in *Social Contract: Essays by Locke, Hume and Rousseau*, with an introduction by Sir Ernest Barker, London: Oxford University Press, pp. 237–440.)
Sacks, David O. and Peter A. Thiel, 1998, *The Diversity Myth: Multiculturalism and Political Intolerance on Campus*, Oakland: The Independent Institute.
Saeki, Keishi, 1999, *'Shimin' to wa nani ka: sengo minshu-shugi o toinaosu* (What is a 'citizen?': redefining post-war democracy), Kyoto: PHP Shinsho.
———, 2001, *Kokka ni tsuite no kōsatsu* (Considerations on the state), Tokyo: Asuka shinsha.
———, 2005, *Rinri to shite no nashonarizumu: gurōbarizumu no kyomu o koete* (Nationalism as ethics: transcending the emptiness of globalism), Tokyo: NTT Shuppan.
Saeki, Yutaka, 1980, *'Kimekata' no ronri: shakaiteki kettei riron e no shōtai* (The logic of 'decision-making': an invitation to social decision theory), Tokyo: Tōkyō daigaku shuppan kai.
Saitō, Jun'ichi, 2000, *Kōkyōsei* (Publicness), Tokyo: Iwanami shoten.
———, 2005, *Jiyū* (Liberty), Tokyo: Iwanami shoten.
Sandel, Michael J., 1982, *Liberalism and the Limits of Justice*, Cambridge University Press.

———, 1996, *Democracy's Discontent: America in Search of a Public Philosophy*, Cambridge, Massachusetts: Harvard University Press.

Scanlon, T.M., 1982, 'Contractualism and Utilitarianism,' in Amartya Sen and Bernard Williams (eds), *Utilitarianism and Beyond*, Cambridge, UK: Cambridge University Press, pp. 103–128.

———, 2003, 'Rawls on Justification,' in Samuel Freeman (ed.), *The Cambridge Companion to Rawls*, Cambridge: Cambridge University Press, pp. 130–167.

Se, Teruhisa, 2003, *Riberarizumu no saisei: kabyū-shugi ni yoru seiji riron* (The rebirth of liberalism: political theory according to fallibilism), Tokyo: Keiō gijuku daigaku shuppan kai.

Seiyama, Kazuo, 1995, *Seidoron no kōzu* (The theoretical structure of institution), Tokyo: Sōbunsha.

———, 2000a, *Kenryoku* (Power), Tokyo: Tōkyō daigaku shuppan kai.

———, 2000b, 'Jendā to kaisō no rekishi to ronri (The history and logic of gender and social stratification,' in Kazuo Seiyama (ed.), *Nihon no kaisō shisutemu 4: jendā, shijō, kazoku* (The Japanese social stratification system 4: gender, the market, and the family),' Tokyo: Tōkyō daigaku shuppan kai, pp. 3–26.

———, 2001, 'Kihan wa ika ni katarareuru ka: jimei sekai no kiretsu to gakuchi (How can norms be discussed?: cracks in the self-evident world and academic knowledge,' *AΣTEION*, 56, pp. 43–64.

———, 2004, 'Fukushi ni totte no byōdō riron: sekinin-byōdō-shugi hihan (Equality theory for welfare: a critique of Luck-egalitarianism),' in Yūichi Shionoya, Kōtarō Suzumura and Reiko Gotō (eds), *Fukushi no kōkyō tetsugaku* (The public philosophy of welfare), Tokyo: Tōkyō daigaku shuppan kai, pp. 179–193.

Selznick, Philip, 1992, *The Moral Commonwealth: Social Theory and the Problem of Community*, Berkeley: University of California Press.

Sen, Amartya, 1970, *Collective Choice and Social Welfare*, San Francisco: Holden-Day.

———, 1976, 'Liberty, Unanimity and Rights,' *Economica*, 43, pp. 217–245.

———, [1980] 1985, 'Equality of What?' in Sterling M. McMurrin (ed.), *Liberty, Equality, and Law: Selected Tanner Lectures on Moral Philosophy*, Salt Lake City, Utah: University of Utah Press, pp. 137–162.

———, 1982, *Choice, Welfare and Measurement*, Oxford: Basil Blackwell.

Shimizu, Ikutarō, 1972, *Rinrigaku nōto* (Notes on ethics), Tokyo: Iwanami shoten.

Shionoya, Yūichi, 2002, *Keizai to rinri: fukushi kokka no tetsugaku* (Economics and ethics: the philosophy of the welfare state), Tokyo: Tōkyō daigaku shuppan kai.

Shionoya, Yūichi, Reiko Gotō and Kōtarō Suzumura (eds), 2004, *Fukushi no kōkyō tetsugaku* (The public philosophy of welfare), Tokyo: Tōkyō daigaku shuppan kai.

Singer, Peter, 1993, *Practical Ethics*, 2nd edition, Cambridge, UK: Cambridge University Press.

Smith, Adam, 1759, *The Theory of Moral Sentiments*.

Suzumura, Kōtarō and Reiko Gotō, 2001, *Amarutia Sen: keizaigaku to rinrigaku* (Amartya Sen: economics and ethics), Tokyo: Jikkyō shuppan.

Takamasu, Akira and Satoshi Matsui (eds), 1999, *Anaritikaru Marukishizumu* (Analytical Marxism), Kyoto: Nakanishiya shuppan.

Takeuchi, Akirō, 1999, *Gendai byōdōron gaido* (A guide to contemporary equality theory), Tokyo: Aoki shoten.

———, 2001, *Byōdōron tetsugaku e no michinori* (The way to egalitarian philosophy), Tokyo: Aoki shoten.

Takikawa, Hirohide, 2003, *Sekinin no imi to seido: futan kara ōtō e* (The meaning and system of responsibility: from burden to response), Tokyo: Keisō shobō.

Takikawa, Hiroki, 2006, '"Byōdō" no rinri: riberarizumu to no kankei o jiku ni shite (The ethics of "equality": pivoting round its connection with liberalism),' in Gaku Doba and Kazuo Seiyama (eds), *Seigi no ronri: kōkyō kachi no kihan-teki shakai riron* (The logic of justice: normative social theories of public values), Tokyo: Keisō shobō, pp. 79–100.

Tateiwa, Shin'ya, 2004, *Jiyū no byōdō: kantan de betsu na sugata no sekai* (The equality of freedom: a world of a simple and different shape), Tokyo: Iwanami shoten.

Taylor, Charles, 1992, *The Ethics of Authenticity*, Cambridge, Massachusetts: Harvard University Press.

———, 1995, *Philosophical Arguments*, Cambridge, Massachusetts: Harvard University Press.

Taylor, Charles et. al., 1994, *Multiculturalism: Examining the Politics of Recognition*, Princeton: Princeton University Press.

Tsuchiya, Keiichirō, 2002, *Seigiron/jiyūron: kan'yō no jidai e* (On justice/on liberty: towards an age of toleration), Tokyo: Iwanami gendai bunko.

Uemura, Yoshirō, 2003, *Kurōn ningen no rinri* (The ethics of cloned humans), Tokyo: Misuzu shobō.

Umehara, Takeshi, 2000, *'Nōshi' to zōki ishoku* ('Brain death' and organ transplantation), Tokyo: Asahi bunko.

Wakamatsu, Yoshiki, 2003, *Sen no seigiron: kōyō to kenri no aida de* (Sen's theory of justice: between utility and rights), Tokyo: Keisō shobō.

Waldron, Jeremy, 1999, *The Dignity of Legislation*, Cambridge, UK: Cambridge University Press.

Walzer, Michael, 1993, *Spheres of Justice: A Defence of Pluralism and Equality*, New York: Basic Books.

Walzer, Michael (ed.), 1997, *Toward a Global Civil Society*, Oxford: Berghahn Books.

Watanabe, Mikio, 1999, *Richādo Rōti: posutomodan no majutsushi* (Richard Rorty: the postmodern wizard), Tokyo: Shunjūsha.

———, 2000, *Rōruzu seigiron no yukue (zōho shinsō ban)* (Whither Rawls' theory of justice?) (enlarged and remodelled edition), Tokyo: Shunjūsha.

———, 2004, 'Riberaru na tetsugaku ni taisuru riberaru na sei no yūi (The primacy of liberal life vis-à-vis liberal philosophy), *Shisō* (Thought), 965, pp. 47–64.

Weber, Max, 2007, *Max Weber's Complete Writings on Academic and Political Vocations*, ed. and with an introduction by John Dreijmanis, trans. by Gordon C. Wells, New York: Algora Publishing.

Yamaguchi, Okitomo, 2002, *Seigi o utagae!* (Distrust justice!), Tokyo: Chikuma shinsho.

Yamaguchi, Yasushi, Harukichi Satō, Shigeki Nakajima and Masafumi Ozeki (eds), 2003, *Atarashii kōkyōsei: sono furontia* (The new publicness: its frontiers), Tokyo: Yūhikaku.

Yamane, Sumika, 2004, *Umu umanai wa onna no kenri ka?: feminizumu to riberarizumu* (Is to give birth or not woman's right?: feminism and liberalism), Tokyo: Keisō shobō.

Yamawaki, Naoshi, 1999, *Shin shakai tetsugaku sengen* (A new social philosophy manifesto), Tokyo: Sōbunsha.

———, 2004, *Kōkyō tetsugaku to wa nani ka* (What public philosophy is), Tokyo: Chikuma shinsho.

Young, Iris M., 1997, *Intersecting Voices: Dilemmas of Gender, Political Philosophy, and Policy*, Princeton: Princeton University Press.

Name Index

Subject Index